AF825201

IMAGES
of America

CLARKSTON

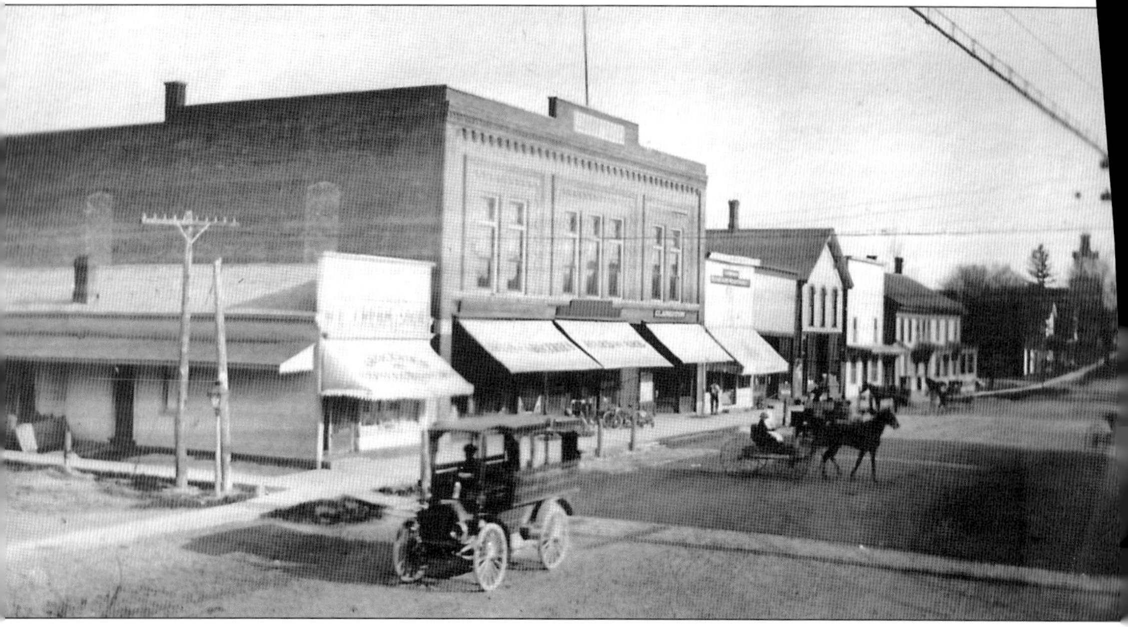

Main Street, c. 1914. This photograph captures a moment in time when cars and carriages shared Main Street in Clarkston, Michigan. (Clarkston Heritage Museum.)

On the Cover: In 1922, Clarkston came together to attend the Masonic Order of the Eastern Star carnival and parade to raise money to repair the fire-gutted Masonic temple and celebrate the recent paving of Main Street. A photographer captured the village in a panorama. To see the entire image, go to pages 98–99. (Clarkston Heritage Museum.)

IMAGES
of America

CLARKSTON

Cara Catallo for the
Clarkston Community Historical Society

ARCADIA
PUBLISHING

Copyright © 2015 by Cara Catallo
ISBN 978-1-4671-1415-8

Published by Arcadia Publishing
Charleston, South Carolina

Printed in the United States of America

Library of Congress Control Number: 2014958681

For all general information, please contact Arcadia Publishing:
Telephone 843-853-2070
Fax 843-853-0044
E-mail sales@arcadiapublishing.com
For customer service and orders:
Toll-Free 1-888-313-2665

Visit us on the Internet at www.arcadiapublishing.com

For Bird, with high hopes that someday she will carry a torch for her own community, wherever she chooses to nest, or for whatever her passion may be.

Contents

Acknowledgments

The first crucial steps toward recording history—long before recounting history—require engaged individuals stepping forward to recognize the need to knock on doors, sift through paperwork, and begin the important process of gathering telltale artifacts.

For Clarkston, such a concerted effort began in the early 1970s when a small band of concerned citizens gathered in Elizabeth Lambert's living room to discuss the need to document Clarkston's history. With still time to speak with some whose families experienced it firsthand, and the forethought that otherwise information may be lost forever, these residents, including Lambert, Ruth Basinger, Betsy Travis, Ginny Schultz, Bill Martin, and John Bisha, realized Clarkston needed an organized effort and established the Clarkston Community Historical Society. This group started the mission to purposefully safeguard Clarkston heritage and the village itself by gathering the necessary information that culminated in the Village of Clarkston being listed in the National Register of Historic Places.

Three others made particularly notable contributions to sharing Clarkston's history.

Constance Lektzian's columns for the *Clarkston News* in the late 1960s help to connect the dots for many who followed. Though she passed away in 2006, Lektzian serves the community still with the words she left behind.

Jennifer Radcliff's steadfast efforts in the realm of local, county, and state preservation are incomparable. Her book *Heritage: A Pictorial History of Independence Township and the Village of Clarkston*, a cavalcade of century-old county books, is a font of invaluable information.

Clarkston will always be fortunate that Susan Basinger called the village home. Among her countless community contributions, Basinger and her husband, Bill, created an in-depth website detailing the history and architecture of the Clarkston Historic District, which was far ahead of its time. More than a decade after her death, Susan Basinger's positive impact remains.

Continually building upon the foundation set by these Clarkston preservation pioneers is Toni Smith, director of the Clarkston Heritage Museum. Smith works tirelessly to acquire and record meaningful artifacts and design exemplary exhibits from which the entire community benefits.

Along with the aforementioned sources, another useful CCHS book is Catherine Passmore's *The Way We Remember It*, which includes personal narratives by longtime area residents.

On a personal note, I want to thank my own close-knit coterie for their acts of kindness. I especially must pay tribute to Sharron and the late Clarence Catallo, for being uncompromisingly stellar examples for both their children when it comes to preservation and service to community.

Finally, to those who take the time to interview Clarkston neighbors, realize that a great-aunt's photographs might have value beyond the family photo album, seek out or luckily happen upon ephemera at antique shows, or contribute to the CCHS from making donations to serving on its board, a thousand thanks. Every effort to preserve Clarkston's heritage, great or small, matters. This book honors and applauds those admirable efforts. Unless otherwise noted, all images are provided by the Clarkston Heritage Museum.

INTRODUCTION

The story of Clarkston is one of early pioneers determined to tame the wilderness and harness its waterways with hope that a village might grow from it. These risk takers forged ahead into the unknown, hauling hopes and know-how into unfamiliar territory.

In the early 1800s, this was no easy task in a place considered almost uninhabitable. Travel was challenging. Nearly impassable coach roads thick with wheel-jarring ruts jolted wagon riders. To risk a loved one's well-being for such a long and arduous journey—many came from as far as the East Coast—farmers and tradesmen had to believe wholeheartedly that this still-wild land would provide opportunities to carve out a better life.

With the completion of the Erie Canal in 1825, the West became reasonably within reach, and the flow of Easterners became steadier, including New York native Linus Jacox. In 1830, Jacox built the first permanent structure, a cedar shanty, in what was to become Clarkston. A few others followed Jacox's lead, and in 1832 Butler Holcomb bought Jacox's shanty plus 2,000 acres of land from the government for 50¢ an acre.

Holcomb built a small dam across the Clinton River to run a sawmill that would help build Clarkston, board by board, from wagons to plank roads and frame houses to barns. Soon, word of land availability enticed more and more people to venture north. One such family happened to be the Clarks, upstate New York natives who had relocated to Detroit where they operated a bakery near the shore of the Detroit River, roughly where Cobo Hall now stands. The Clarks' business thrived as they sold baked goods to boats passing through, needing to restock. While the bakery was a success—popular for plate-sized cookies—the enterprising brothers Nelson and Jeremiah Clark III had other plans, and in 1838 they purchased much of Holcomb's land, including his sawmill and milling rights. They promptly built a bigger dam and added a gristmill. With those mills came prosperity and economic security for the village the Clarks soon platted. The townspeople held the brothers in such high esteem that they opted to name the new village Clarkston in their honor.

The Clarks were by no means alone. William and John Axford opened the first store in 1838; Albert Birdsell, the first blacksmith shop; William Blake was the first shoemaker; Horace Foster became the local harness maker; and John Hertwig opened a tailor shop-turned-tavern. By 1840, Nelson Clark built the village's school, as other rural schools started to appear around Independence and Springfield Townships, educating the children when they did not have farm work calling.

In 1851, the landscape changed again when the train depot opened two miles outside of Clarkston center, leading to great debate about whether to move the village nearer to the railway. The community decided against it. Clarkston was, after all, a mill town. Cartage trucks and livery wagons would transport freight and people to and from the depot.

All along, the village's early prosperity and allure seemed linked with its waterways. The mill town's residents built simple, yet impressive, Greek Revivals and stately Victorians, reflections of that time, along the Mill Pond and Parke Lake. The homes mirrored the village's success, as Clarkston became a small economic hub. It was also becoming a vacation destination, with inns on Deer Lake and the Mill Pond. At times, trains pulled as many as 12 passenger cars slated for Clarkston's depot, where families would gather or reunite from nearby cities for rest and relaxation.

Shortly after the turn of the 20th century, modern times made the waterpower that previously fed the community's livelihood less essential. Once having a reputation for the finest flour around, the mill closed in 1917, and a company from Detroit disassembled the building, leaving bakers lamenting the loss of miller Thomas Farmer's fine flour. Likewise, tourism diminished, as reaching points farther north became easier, though Clarkston remained a worthwhile stop for travelers to stretch their legs and enjoy an ice cream before continuing on Dixie Highway or M-15.

Around the 1930s, recognizing the same pioneering possibilities that Holcomb and the Clarks did before him, Henry Ford reignited Clarkston's waterpower promise. With the motto "one foot on the soil and the other in industry," Ford hoped to add Clarkston to his Village Industries program, which worked to make factory jobs available in more rural areas, rather than depleting the community's young workforce with jobs in big city factories. Ford refurbished the dam and built a small factory where the mill once stood and retrofitted the former Clarkston School on Main Street as a textile factory. He also bought Deer Lake Hills Farm, not far from the village, which became Dearborn Motors' Sales Training School, a proving and training ground for dealers and salespeople to learn more about Ford tractors and Dearborn implements.

Today, waterpower no longer fuels the town, but thanks in part to its spot in the National Register of Historic Places, the village retains its mill town identity. Hints of the pioneer era remain: the horseshoe still imbedded in the concrete outside blacksmith Frank Yeager's old house, the Main Street stone wall that once lined the outside of Linabury Livery, and scattered coach steps and hitching posts in front of a few lucky houses. The well-preserved historical homes and storefronts that line modern-day Main Street and others within Clarkston's quaint historic district make it easy to imagine the village 100 years ago and earlier. Many of these buildings stood when farmers guided their horses and wagons into the village carrying grain to the mill along dusty dirt roads.

The bells in the two old churches still ring sometimes, though rarely. Now deconsecrated and purposefully reused, these buildings and others in Clarkston remain subdued reminders of those who dared to tame the wilderness and built a village, as well as those who followed and kept Clarkston's history alive through insightful preservation and deep-seated appreciation in what is now a thriving 21st century village.

One

Life in Early Clarkston

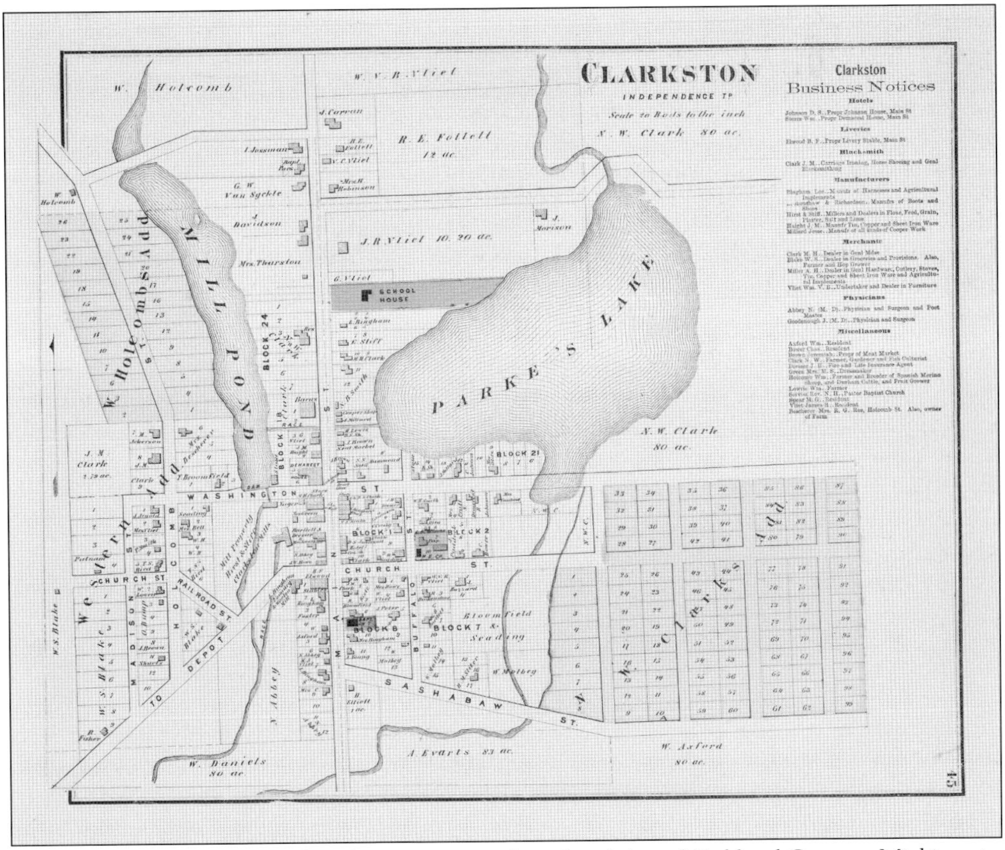

Clarkston Map, 1872. The plat map printed in the *Atlas of Oakland County, Michigan* in 1872 shows early Clarkston and potential plans for the village. Through time some of the names changed—Sashabaw Street became Waldon Road and Parke's Lake became Parke Lake—while Railroad Street disappeared entirely and others did not change at all.

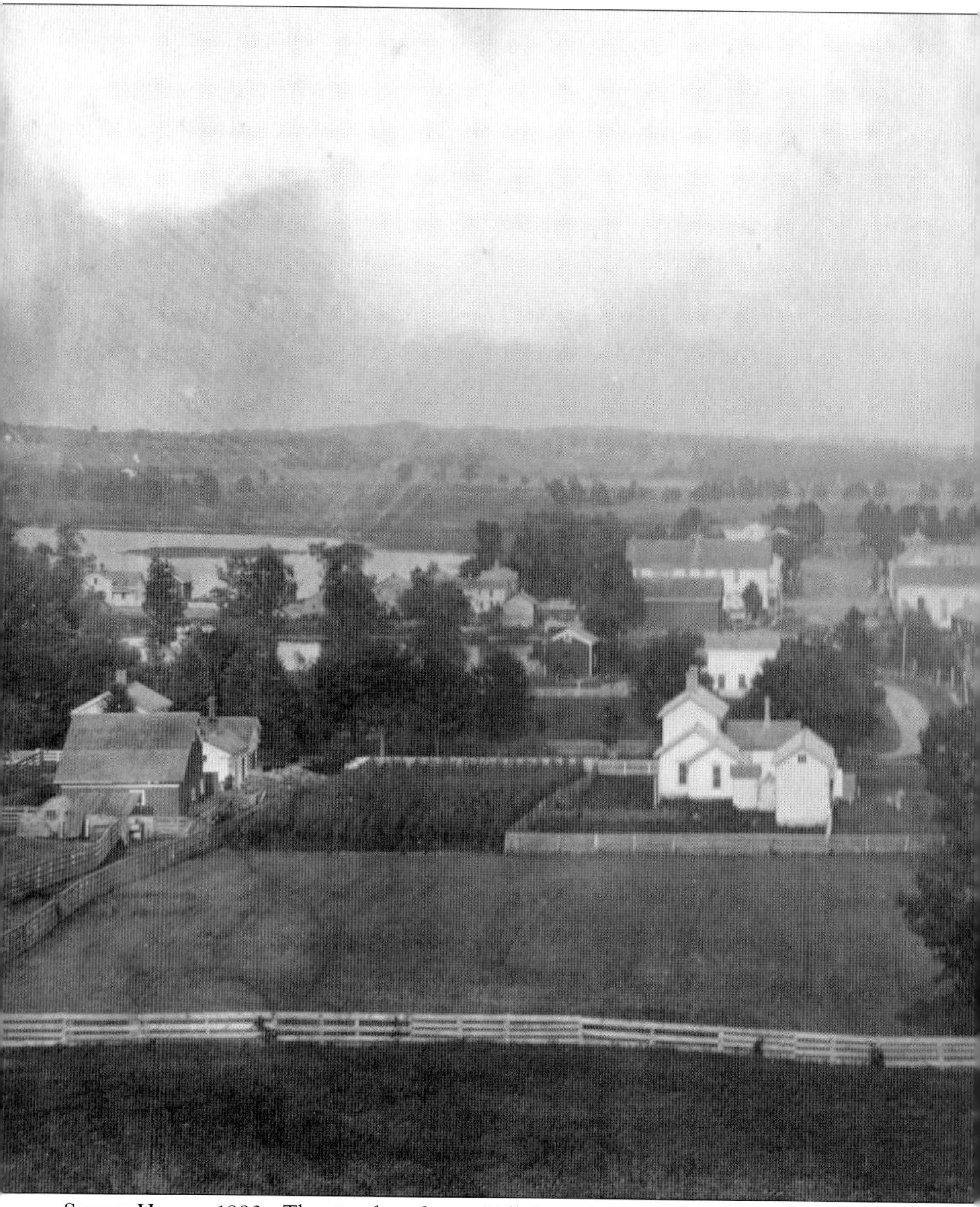

Sunset Hill, c. 1880s. The view from Sunset Hill shows familiar sights from Clarkston in the 1880s. Unpaved West Washington Street and Depot Road flank the white buildings that make up Clarkston Mills. The Demarest Hotel graces the northwest corner of West Washington and Main Streets, diagonally across Main Street from where the arched windows of tall Bingham Hall peek above other buildings, not long before it burned down around 1887. The two churches stand

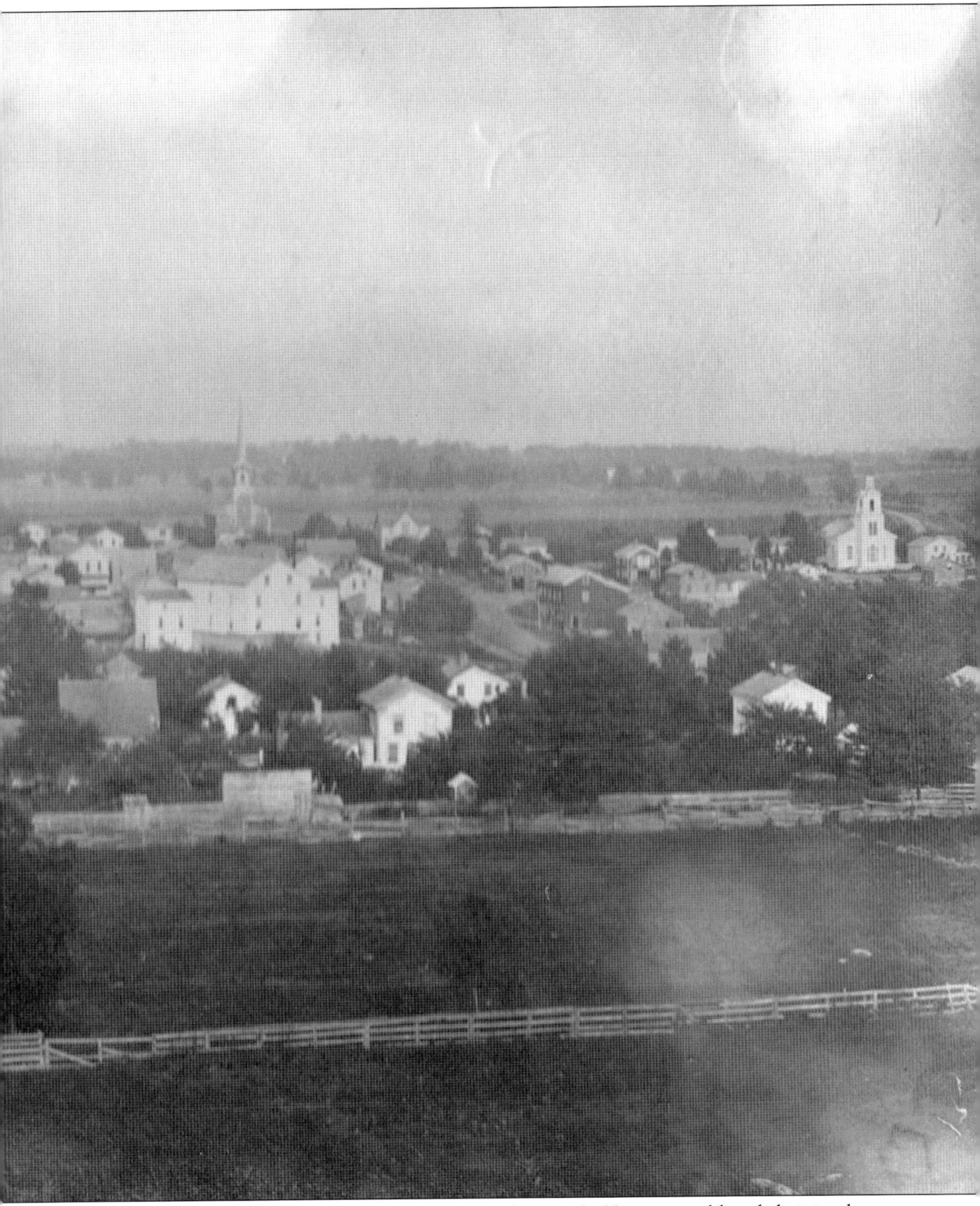

as place markers in the bustling village, by then almost a half-century old and thriving because of its mills. The next century saw the open fields beyond the churches fill, becoming the new site of the growing Methodist church and Clarkston High School, later known as Clarkston Junior High School and Renaissance High School.

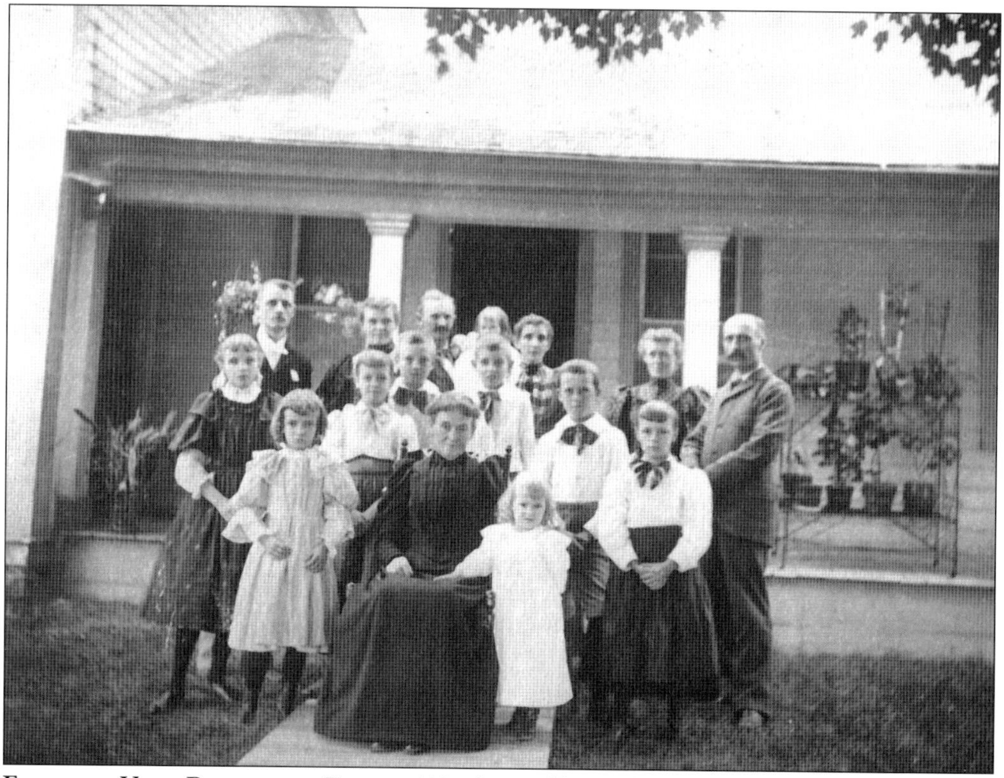

ELIZABETH VLIET BOWER WITH FAMILY, 1891. Legend has it that when Nelson Vliet left to serve in the Civil War as a private in Company D of the 22nd Regiment, Michigan Infantry, he walked back to Clarkston from Pontiac to kiss his heartbroken wife goodbye one more time. The two never saw each other again. Captured, Vliet died of dysentery and malnutrition at Andersonville Prison. Although his remains are buried at the national cemetery there, a second gravestone commemorates Vliet at Lakeview Cemetery, and his widow, Elizabeth Vliet (seated, wearing mourning clothes), began to decorate soldiers' graves, bringing Decoration Day, later known as Memorial Day, to Clarkston. Pictured are, from left to right, (first row) Beth Vliet, Elizabeth Vliet Bower, Josephine Vliet, and Bessie Clark; (second row) Gertrude Vliet, Leone Smith, Walter Smith, unidentified, and Lee Clark; (third row) Charles Smith, Josephine Smith, Joshua Vliet, Florence Vliet, Helen Vliet Clark, and Edwin Clark.

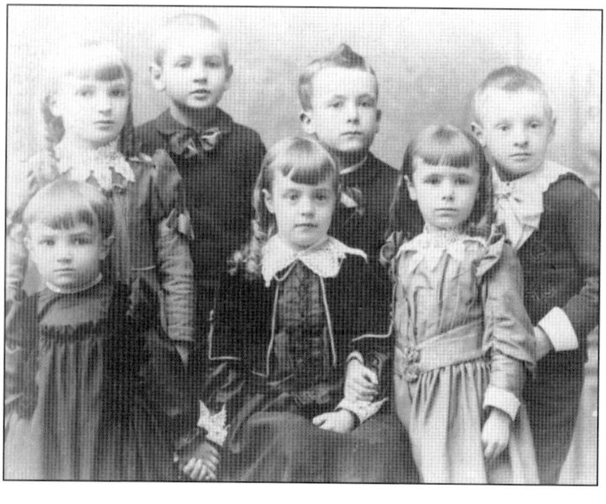

VLIET, SMITH, AND CLARK CHILDREN, C. 1891. Several of the children pictured above with Elizabeth Vliet Bower pose here. From left to right are (first row) Beth Vliet, Leone Smith, and Bessie Clark; (second row) Gertrude Vliet, Nelson Vliet, Lee Clark, and Walter Smith. Leone Smith died of diphtheria at the age of seven, shortly after this photograph was taken.

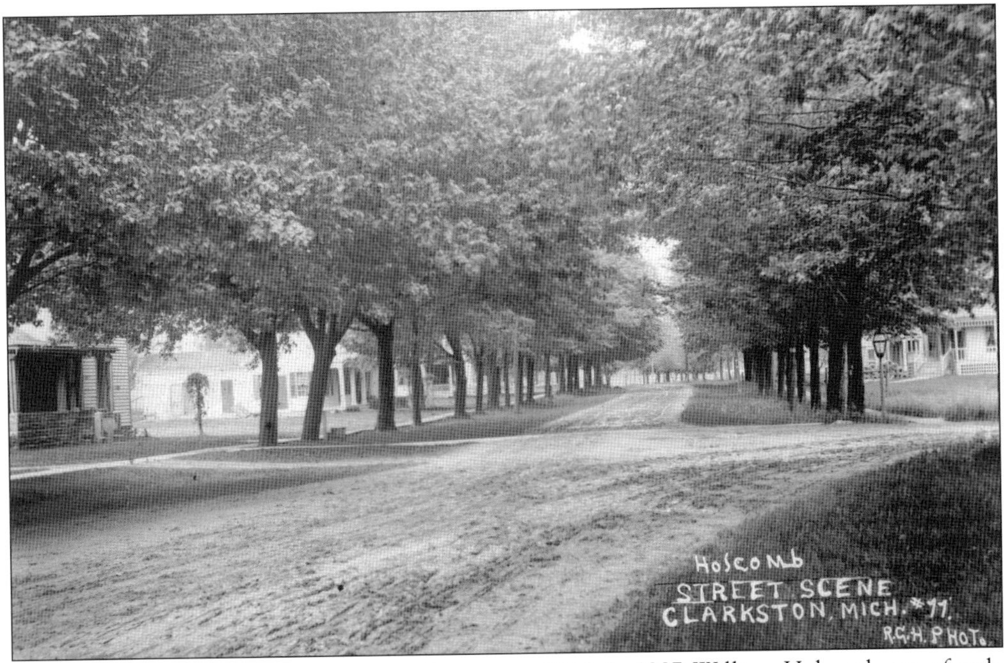

HOLCOMB ROAD AT WEST WASHINGTON STREET, C. 1915. In 1887, William Holcomb, son of early settler Butler Holcomb, gave a swath of land to honor his father's contribution to the community. Both William and Butler Holcomb had farms in the far northwest corner of the village. Long before the paving of Holcomb Road, hitching posts were plentiful, some of which remain today, scattered throughout Clarkston.

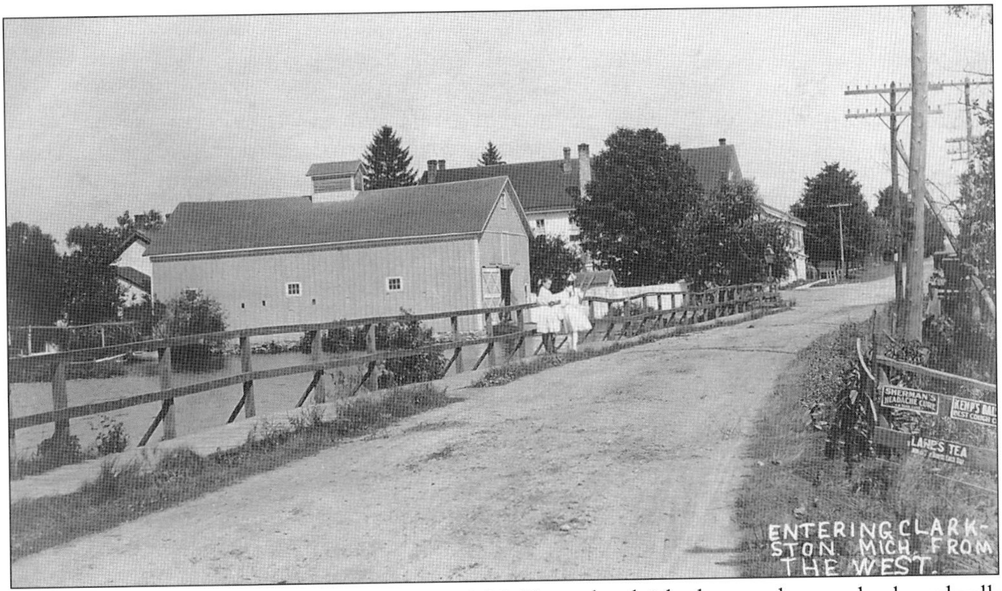

ENTERING DOWNTOWN FROM THE WEST, C. 1900. Two schoolgirls chat on the wooden boardwalk between West Washington Street and the Mill Pond. Note the wooden railings and fences on both sides of the street and the early advertisements on the fence at lower right.

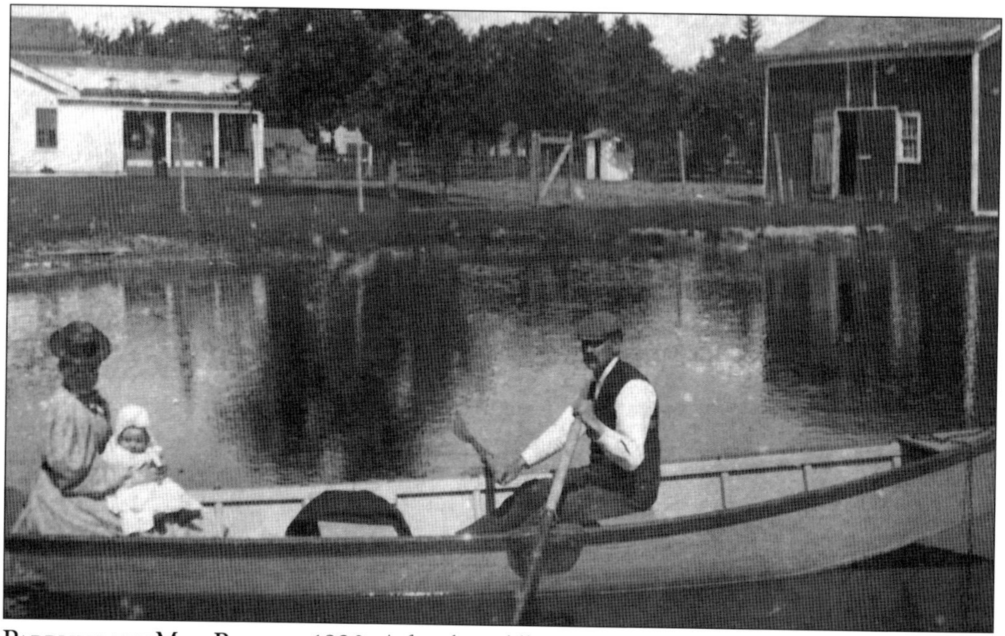

Paddling the Mill Pond, c. 1890. A family paddles across the south end of the Mill Pond. The house in the background is 49 West Washington Street, before construction of a neighboring house separated it from the pond.

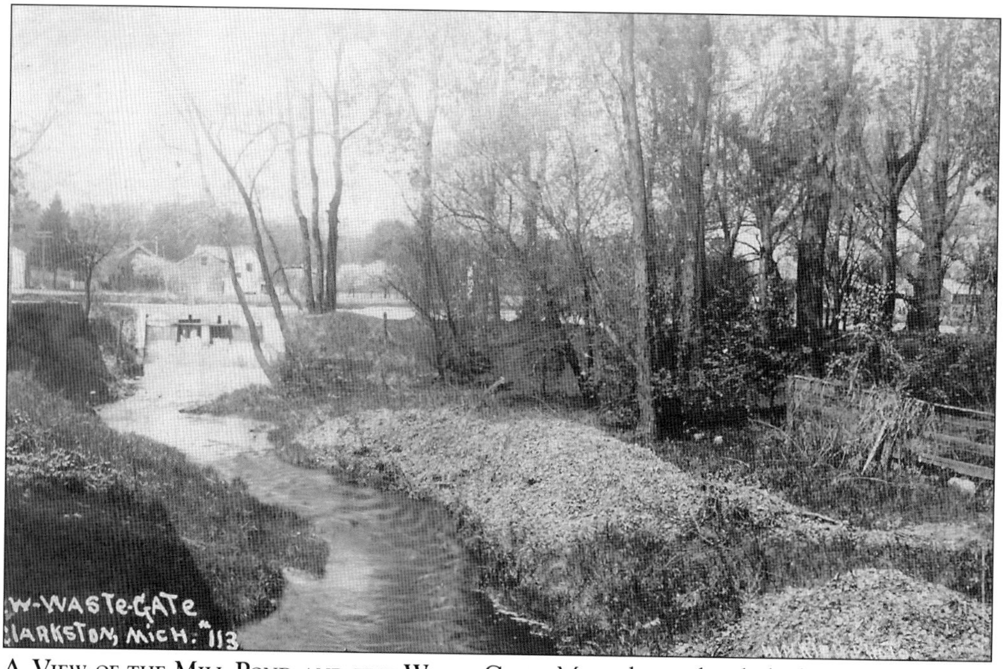

A View of the Mill Pond and the Waste Gate. More than a lovely little waterfall tucked north of Main Street's business district, the Mill Pond's waste gate controls the water's flow. By damming the Clinton River, water from the Mill Pond turned the all-important wheel at Clarkston Mills. Much of Clarkston's livelihood depended on the mill in those early days.

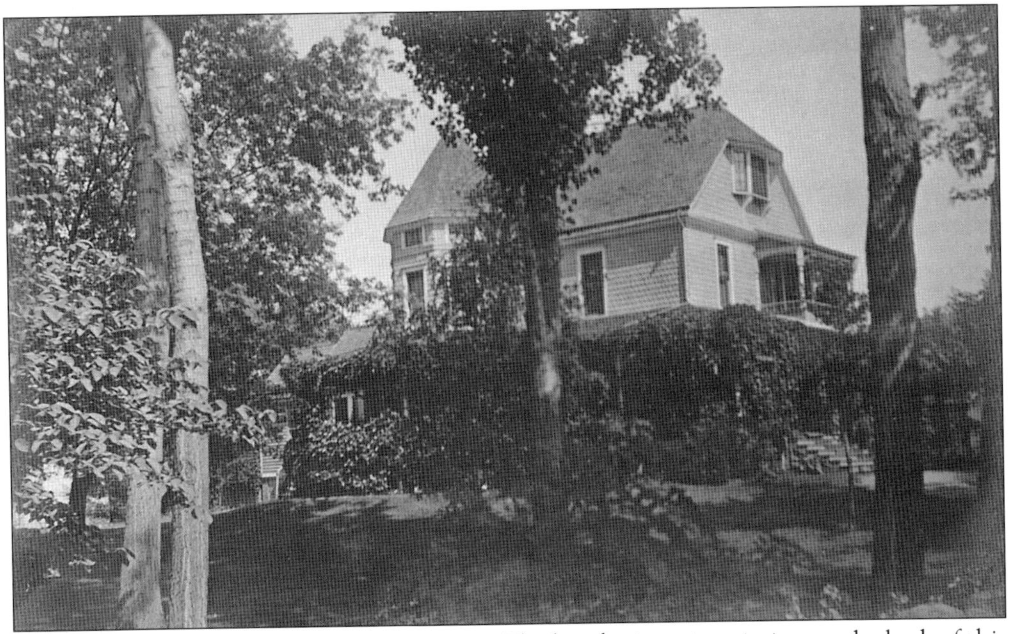

43 North Main Street, Postmarked 1910. The handwritten inscription on the back of this postcard describes this as "one of our summer homes." Located just north of the waste gate, this property was the site of Nelson W. Clark's barn prior to making way for one of Clarkston's most stately homes, a proud Queen Anne–style house built in 1883 for Henry and Ellen Kingsley. By then, Ellen Kingsley's parents, the Hursts, had already purchased the Clarkston Mills from the Clark brothers in 1859. In 1910, this home housed the Charles and Nettie Vliet Lambert family, of the Clayton & Lambert Manufacturing Company, makers of the Regal touring car. The Lamberts' son Frank later lived in the Main Street house, where he raised a family with his wife, Elizabeth Edmonson Lambert, one of the founders of both the Clarkston Farm and Garden Club and the Clarkston Community Historical Society.

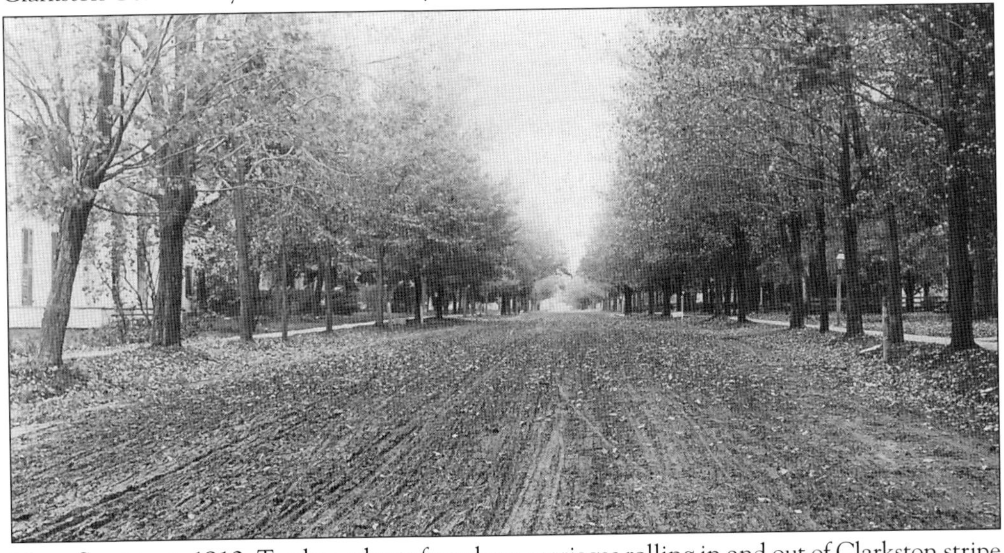

Main Street, c. 1910. Tracks and ruts from busy carriages rolling in and out of Clarkston stripe the expansive tree-lined Main Street, still unpaved. Notice the commanding columns of the Clark house to the left, while several carriage steps and hitching posts line the main thoroughfare.

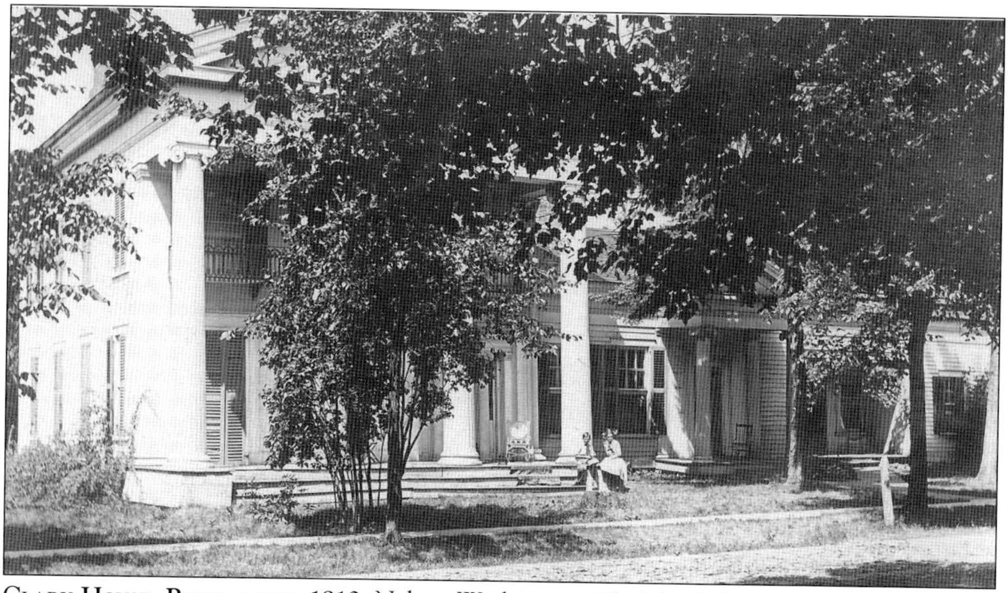

Clark House, Postmarked 1910. Nelson Washington Clark built the original portion of this Greek Revival home on the Mill Pond around 1855. Clark also built the school across the street and planted many trees on that property. He and his brother Jeremiah owned the mill and in 1842 platted the village, which residents named Clarkston in honor of the civically active and esteemed siblings.

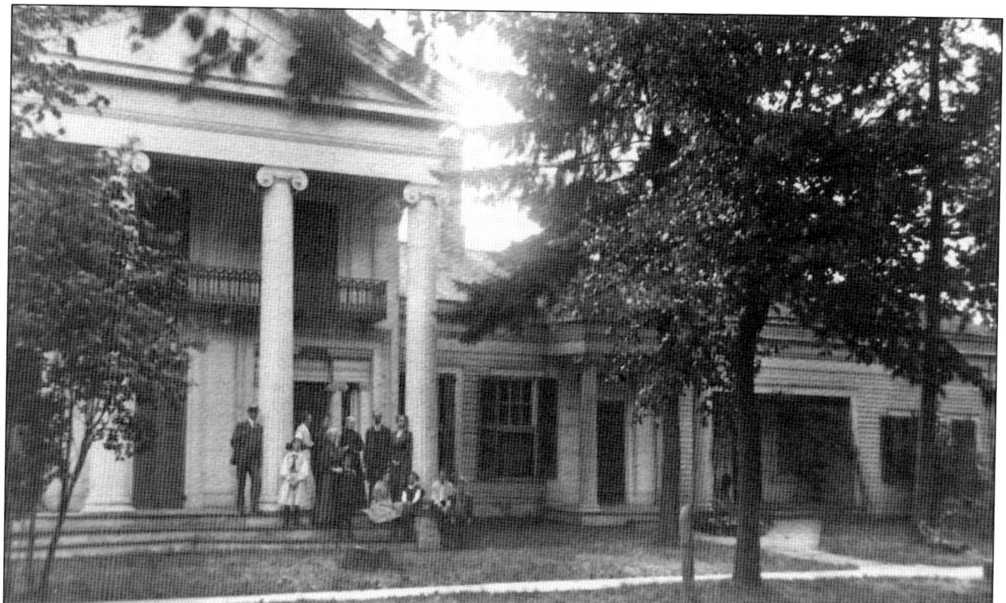

Congregating at the Clark House. As township supervisor, Nelson Clark often conducted village and mill business in his home's beautiful front parlor room or in the adjoining study. He had another business, though, that he could not so easily bring home: fish culturist. Clark recognized that the fish supply should not be considered unending and started a fish hatchery, where he successfully hatched fish from spawn, downtown near the mill. The government recognized Clark's methods, hoping to adopt his practices for better conservation. In 1873, Clark moved to Northville to focus on the hatchery business.

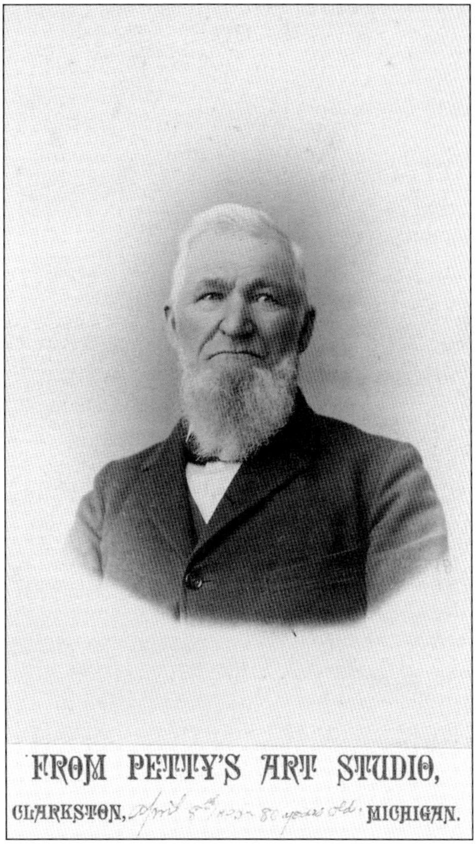

E.G. Clark, c. 1895. Born April 8, 1815, to Jeremiah Clark III and Phoebe Holdridge Clark, Edwin G. Clark settled on a farm in Independence Township in 1845 and followed his father's footsteps into politics, serving as a representative in the Michigan legislature in 1876. In 1883, he traded farm life for village living when he purchased the home his uncle built at 71 North Main Street, and lived there until his death in December 1908.

The Milton Clark House. Across the street and slightly south stands a different Clark House at 62 North Main Street. Built in 1855, this somewhat less grandiose Greek Revival belonged to Edwin G. Clark's brother Milton H. Clark and his wife, Hannah. Milton owned Clark & Stearns (later just Clark) General Store at the corner of West Washington and Main Streets. Clark loved politics and invited friends to gather above his store on election night 1892, to await word about Grover Cleveland's reelection bid. His store was next to an early telephone in Clarkston, so Clark ran downstairs to call Detroit to get vote tallies on the half hour. When Cleveland seemed certain to clinch victory, Clark excitedly raced upstairs to share the news, only to collapse once he reached the top, dying suddenly of a heart attack.

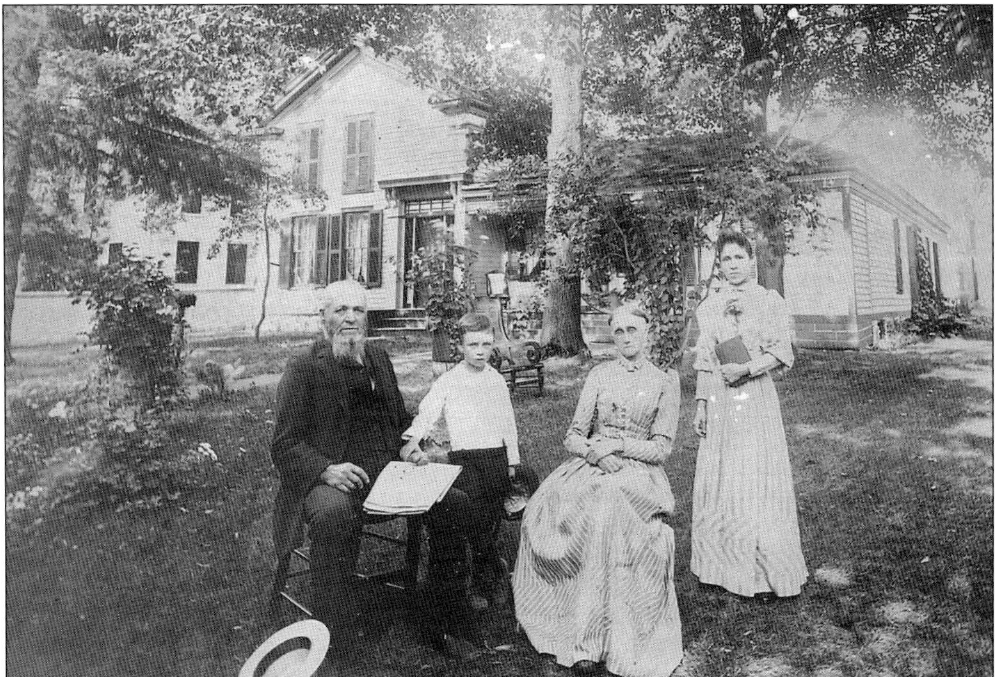

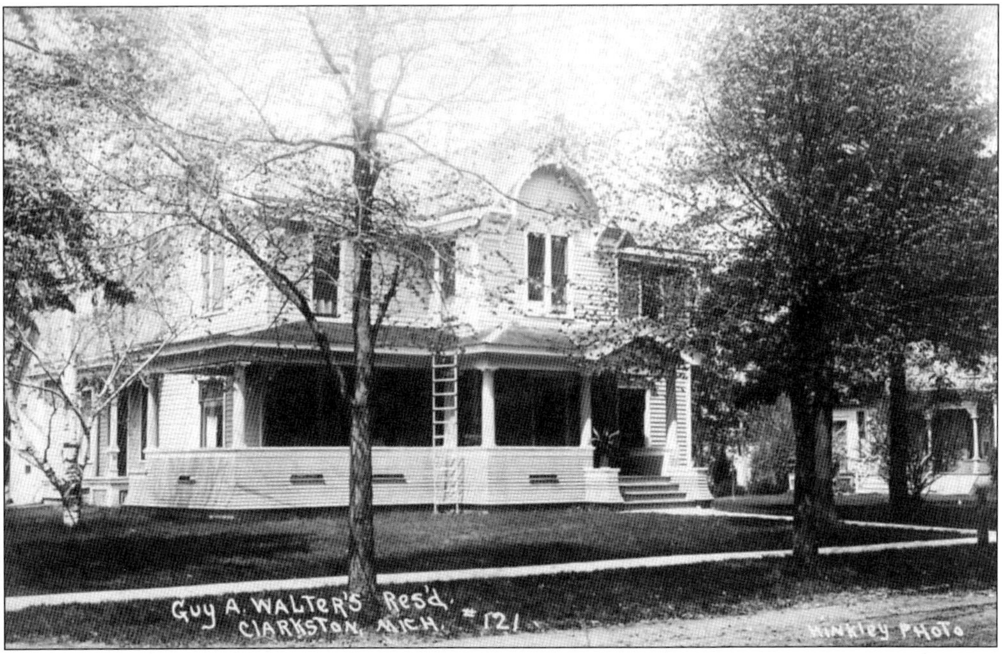

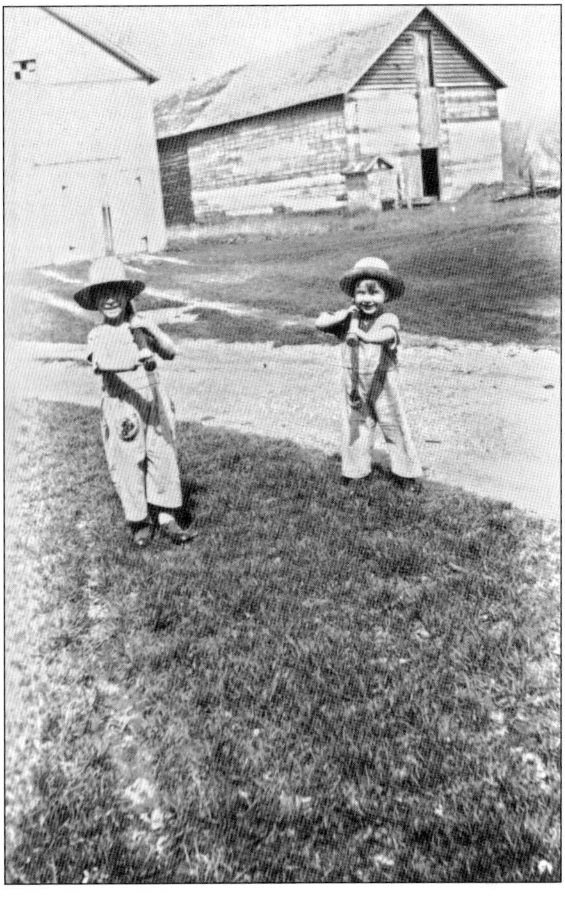

Guy Walter's Residence. Built in 1883, this Gothic Revival house was the home of Nelson and Josie Ainsworth Walter. Nelson and his son Guy operated Walter and Walter general store in a wooden building that stood on the site of 9 South Main Street, and later Guy Walter and Co. across the street at the Maccabee Temple building, where he organized programs at the opera house upstairs. The house became Guy and Viola Alger Walter's home in 1909.

Ronk Brothers near Icehouse. Clarkston brothers John (left) and Frank "Tink" Ronk stand outside a Clarkston icehouse, most likely the Walters'.

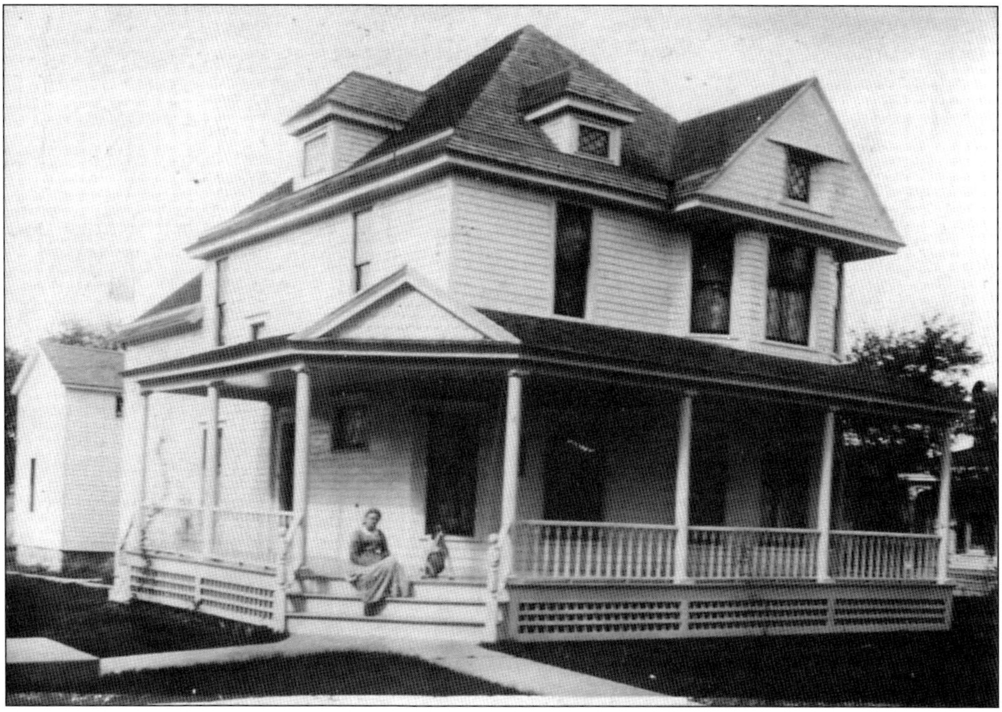

THE CLARKSTON ELLIS HOUSE. Because his wife, Esther, (pictured alongside their work dog Doc) longed to have a home in town, Norman Ellis, owner of 750-acre Ingomar Farms roughly four miles away in Springfield Township, built this late Victorian-style house at 99 North Main Street in 1902–1903. Ellis hired Franklin "Frank" Beardsley to guide the construction and mason Jerome Vliet to handle stonework. Much later, the home underwent renovations that transformed its original look considerably.

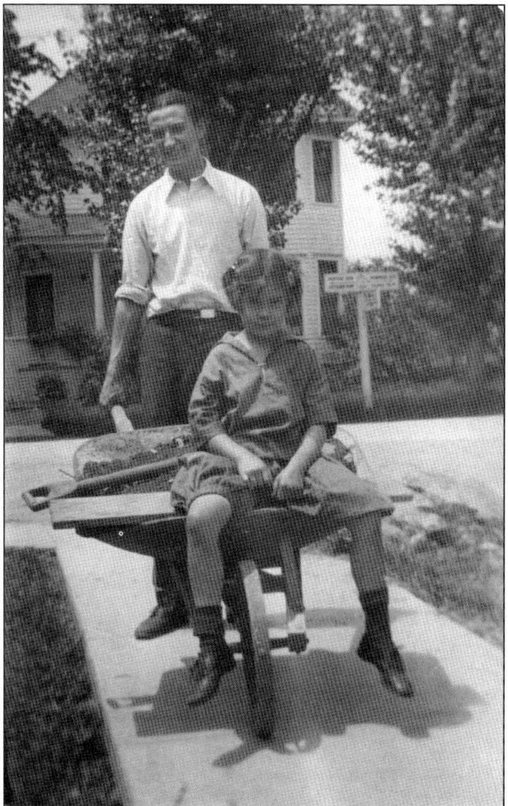

ROY ALGER AND NIECE, C. 1929. Roy Alger pushes his niece Sybil Picket in a wheelbarrow across the street from the Alger home at 135 North Main Street. The sign in the back points out the distances to Pontiac, Detroit, Ortonville, and Flint, among other places. Alger's father, Joseph, opened Alger hardware store in the Maccabee Temple building, which Roy later ran.

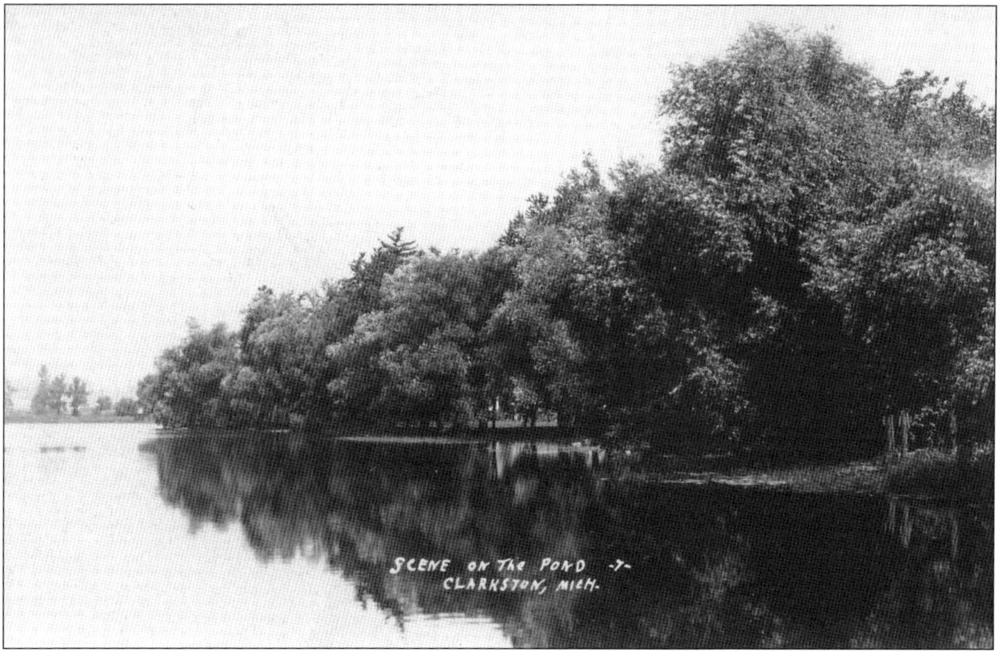

Scene on the Pond. The northern end of the Mill Pond provides a tranquil setting in this photograph, likely shot from Miller Road. It was a rare summer's day when the pond's surface was not broken by a swimmer's stroke or a boat's paddle.

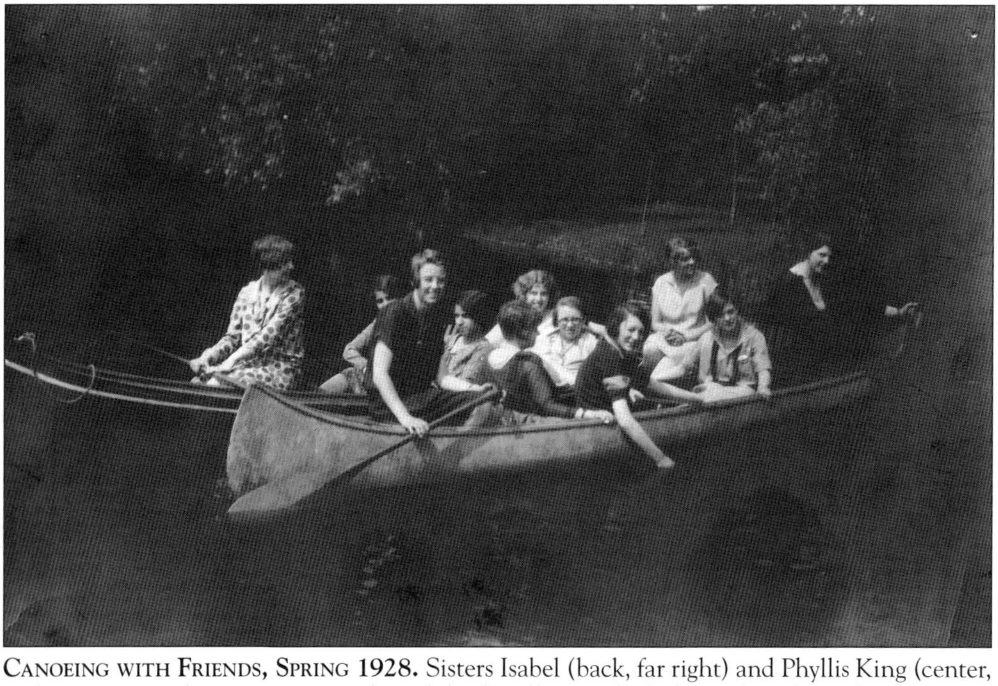

Canoeing with Friends, Spring 1928. Sisters Isabel (back, far right) and Phyllis King (center, with arm in water) enjoy a canoe ride with both college and Clarkston friends on the Mill Pond in 1928. Isabel King would later marry in the backyard of her childhood home at 55 North Main Street, overlooking the pond she so enjoyed as a child.

THE DOCK, PARKE LAKE, POSTMARKED 1907. The opposite side of Main Street offers its own wealth of water recreation with Parke Lake (sometimes referred to as Park Lake, as in these two postcards). The private lake stretches across the village to the township border.

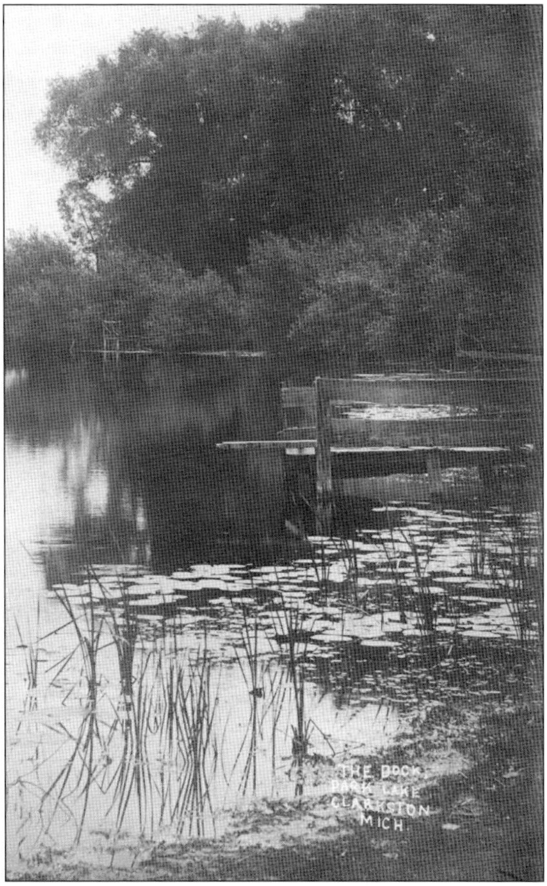

PARKE LAKE AND THE SCHOOL. This view across the water shows the original white schoolhouse on Main Street. Clarkston's longtime postmistress Elizabeth Hammond Ronk recalled how people passed time in the winter by racing their horses on frozen Parke Lake. Her family's workhorse would break into a canter as he rounded the Clarkston Road curve approaching the lake, as if it were time to race again.

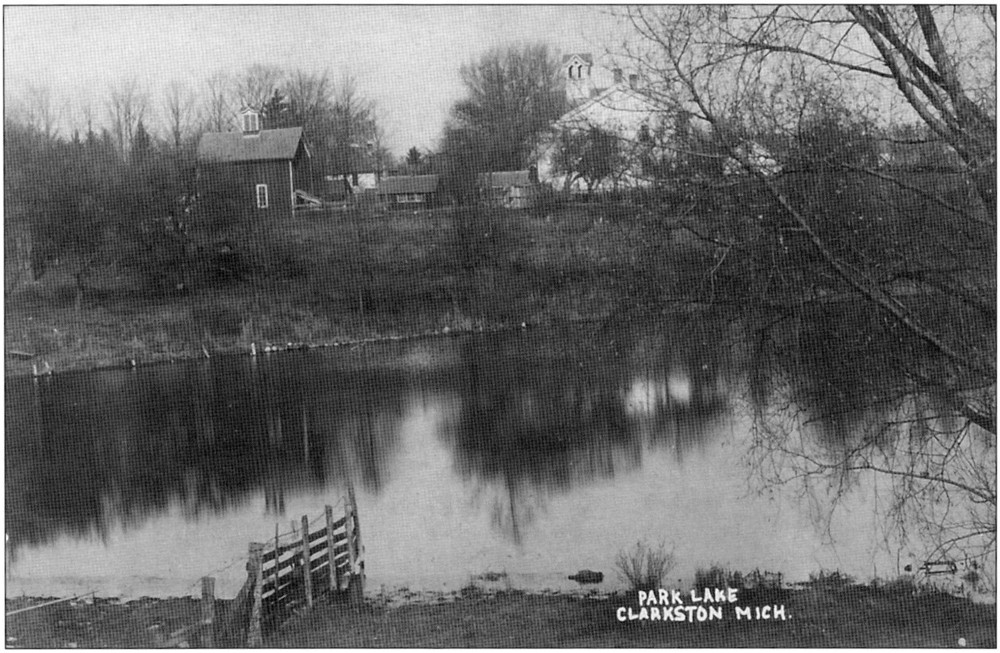

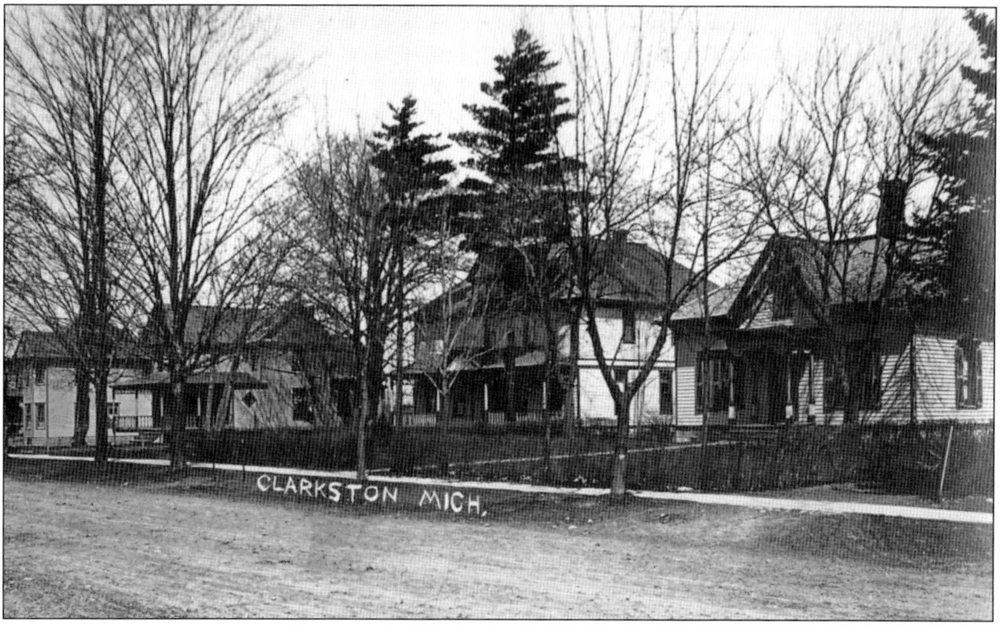

THE ROBERTSON HOUSE ON MAIN STREET. The house on the far right is the home of Dr. Charles Gray Robertson. In the early 1880s, Robertson and his wife, Jessie, bought eight acres that bordered Main Street on the west and Parke Lake on the east. They built this Main Street home and used the rest of the land as pasture, except for a small portion mined for road gravel.

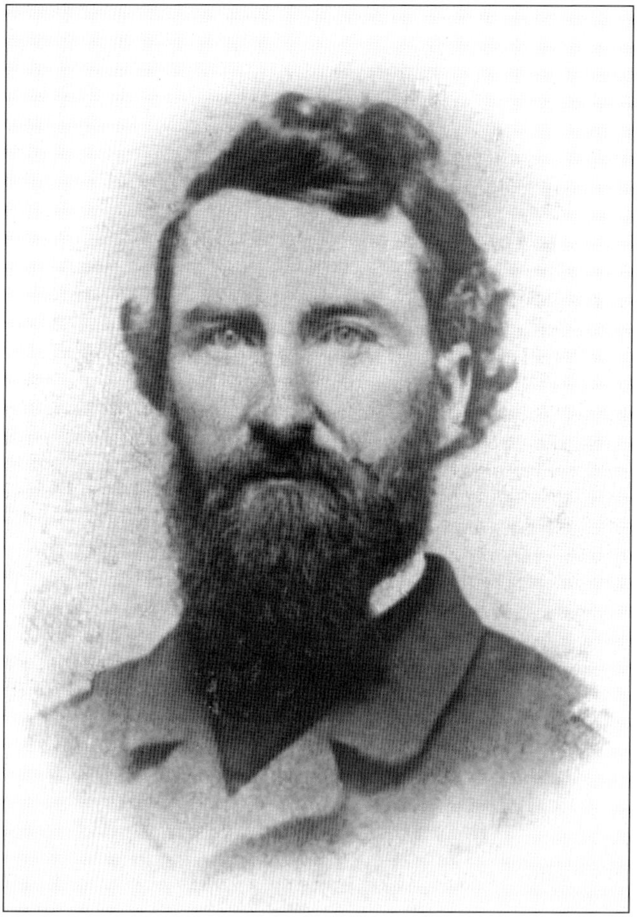

DR. CHARLES GRAY ROBERTSON. Born in Glasgow, Scotland, in 1829, Charles Gray Robertson became a celebrated surgeon with the Michigan cavalry during the Civil War. He moved to Clarkston to work alongside Dr. Josephus Goodenough.

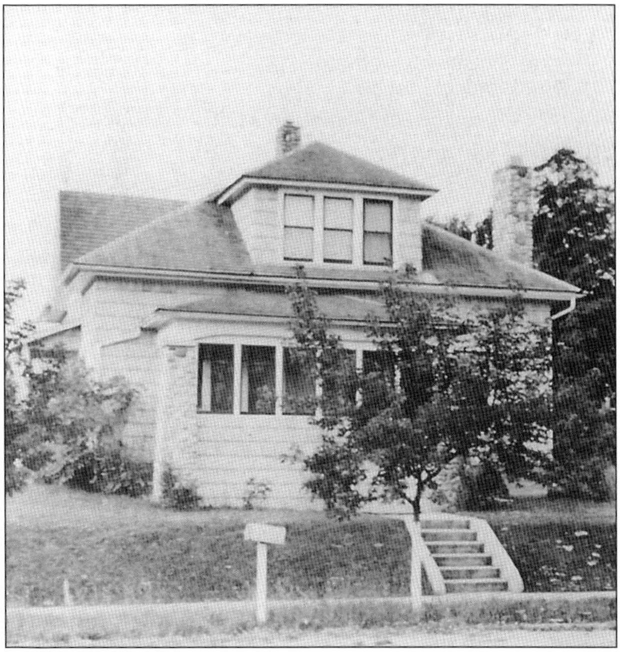

THE ROBERTSON HOUSE ON ROBERTSON COURT, MID-1920S. In 1923, following the deaths of his parents, Dr. Charles and Jessie Robertson, Milton Gray Robertson had his family's Main Street house moved to make way for Robertson Court and the new 37 residential lots that make up Park Lake Subdivision. Rotated about 90 degrees, making the front of the house the side, the house now sits at 10 Robertson Court. The original home's one-story kitchen,which had occupied the rear of the house, made a move of its own, becoming an addition to the home at 16 Clarkston Road. One of the homes Milton Robertson built on Robertson Court remains in the family today.

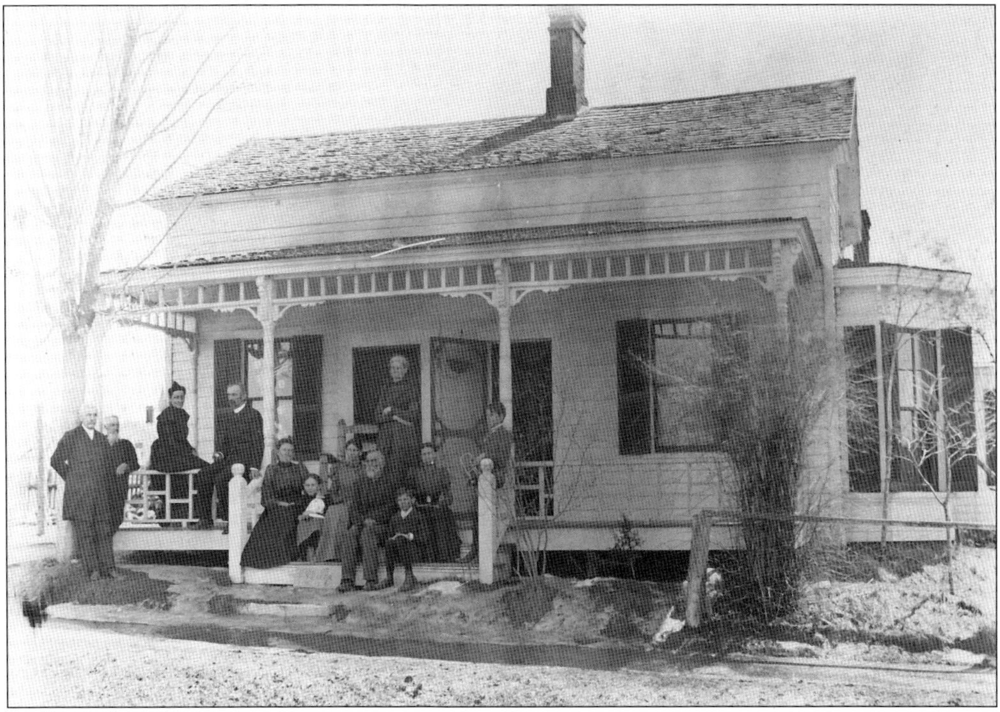

THE YEAGER HOUSE, 1899. Across Parke Lake at 8 East Washington Street, Civil War veteran Francis Follett (bearded) sits on the steps, while his wife, Sarah Jane Bates Follett, stands behind him. Others on the porch include the Follett and Green families, and likely blacksmith Frank Yeager and family, who lived at the house. A sign on the stoop states: Home of F. Yeager, April 12, 1899. Concrete steps leading to the home feature an embedded horseshoe, which still exists today, marking the blacksmith's home.

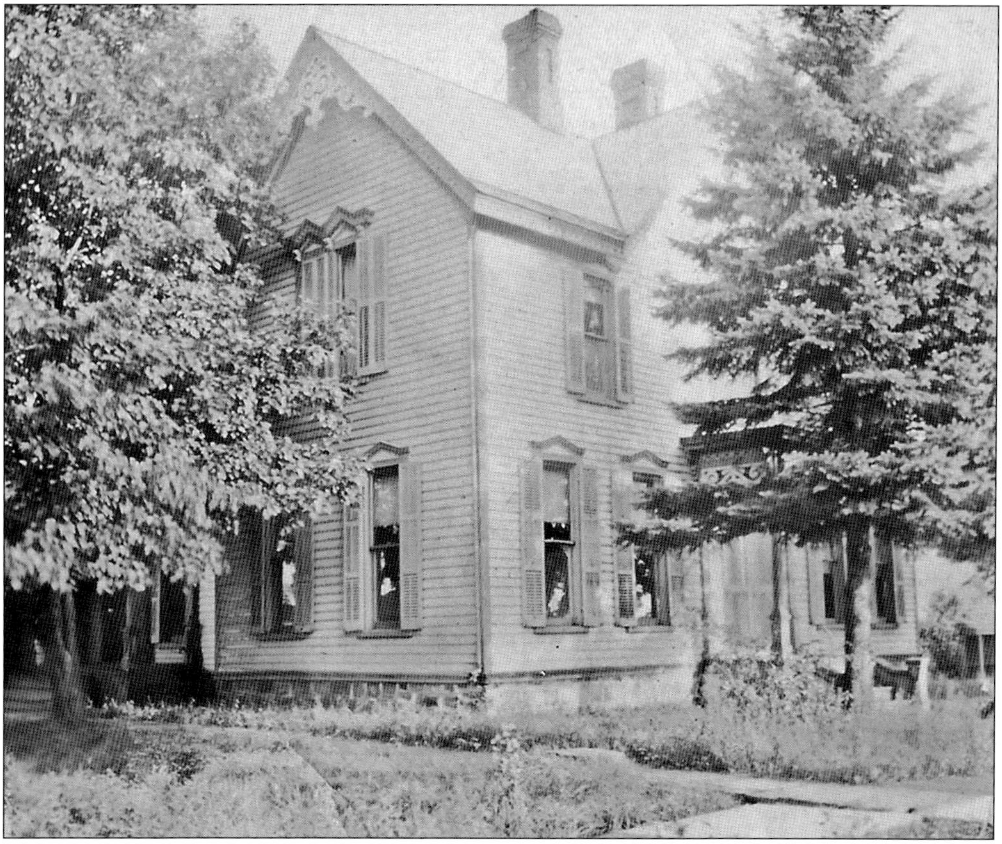

The Morley House. Built in 1860, most likely for William V.B. Vliet, this Gothic Revival house at the corner of Buffalo and Church Streets stands majestic. (From the collection of Marilyn Hanson, courtesy of Polly Hanson Remke.)

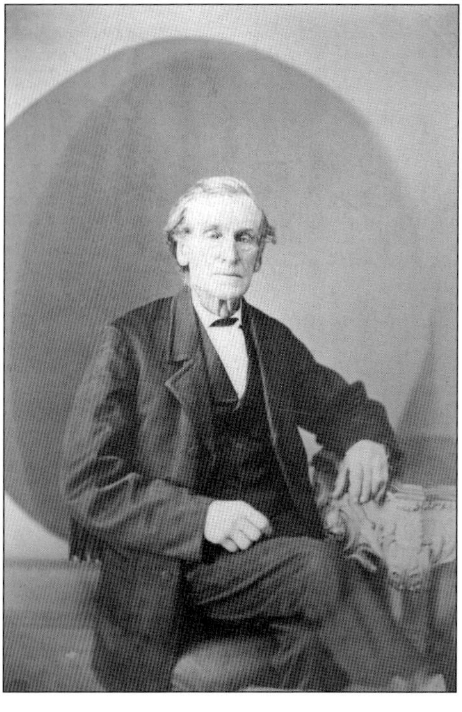

William V.B. Vliet. An undertaker and cabinetmaker originally from New Jersey, William V.B. Vliet either built or vastly altered 35 Buffalo Street. He was also the original Vliet of Vliet's-on-the Hill, the popular inn that overlooked Deer Lake on Church Street's westernmost corner.

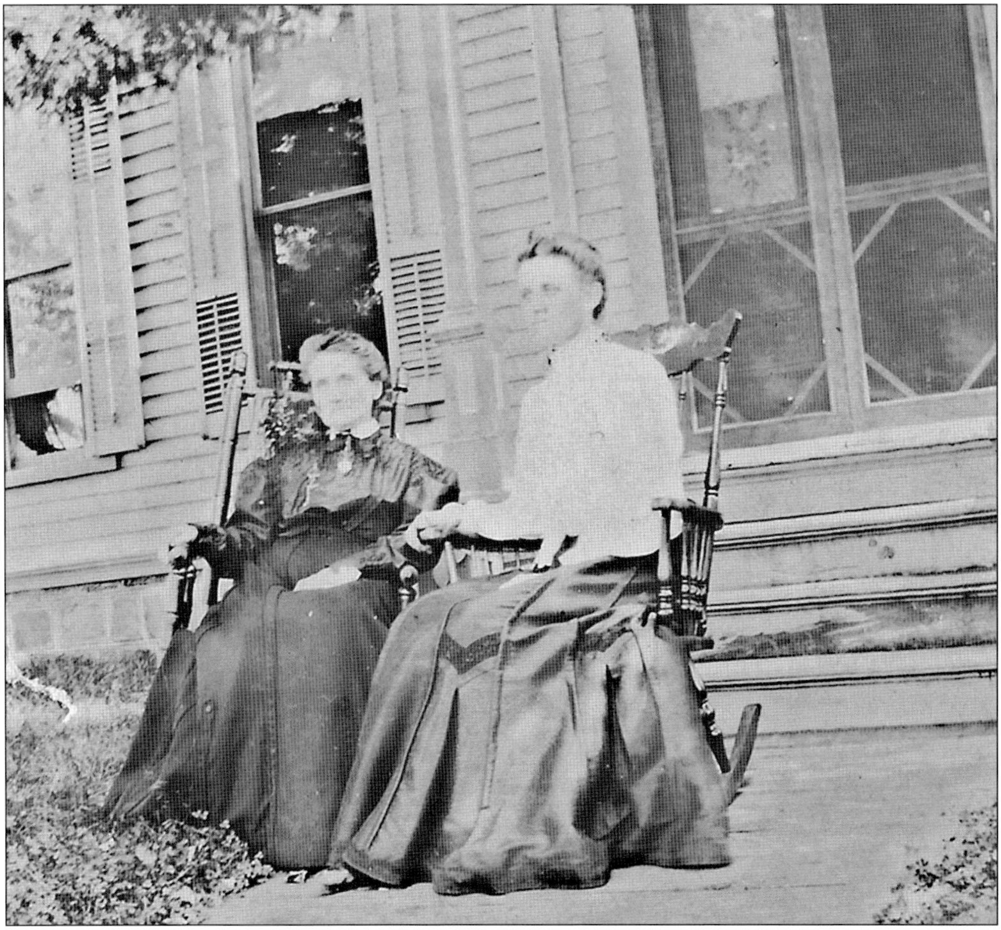

Juliette Morley. Above, Juliette Morley (left) relaxes in front of her home at 35 Buffalo Street. A widow, schoolteacher, and mother to John and Warren, Morley bought the house in 1890 for $1,000, admiring its proximity to the school and the churches. After his mother died, John Morley kept the family house. By that time, he was a judge, so he used the Buffalo Street entrance as his office and another nearby room to hold consultations, perform wedding ceremonies, and deliver judgments. The home reportedly also had a cell on the second floor to hold prisoners awaiting transfer to the jail in Pontiac. (Both, from the collection of Marilyn Hanson, courtesy of Polly Hanson Remke.)

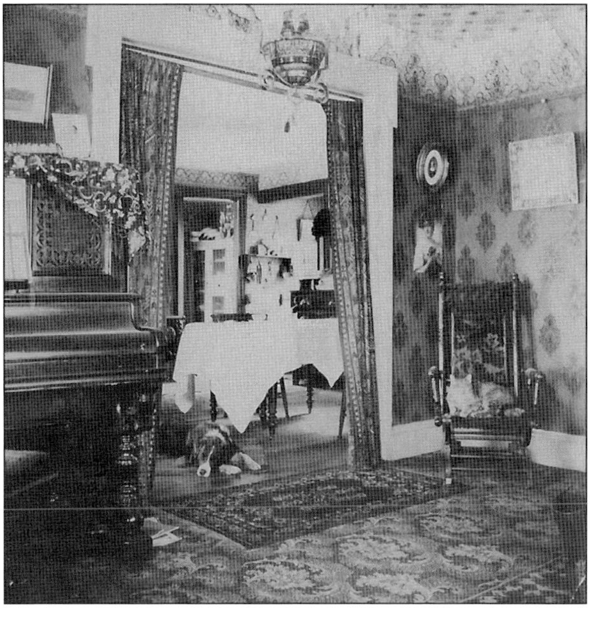

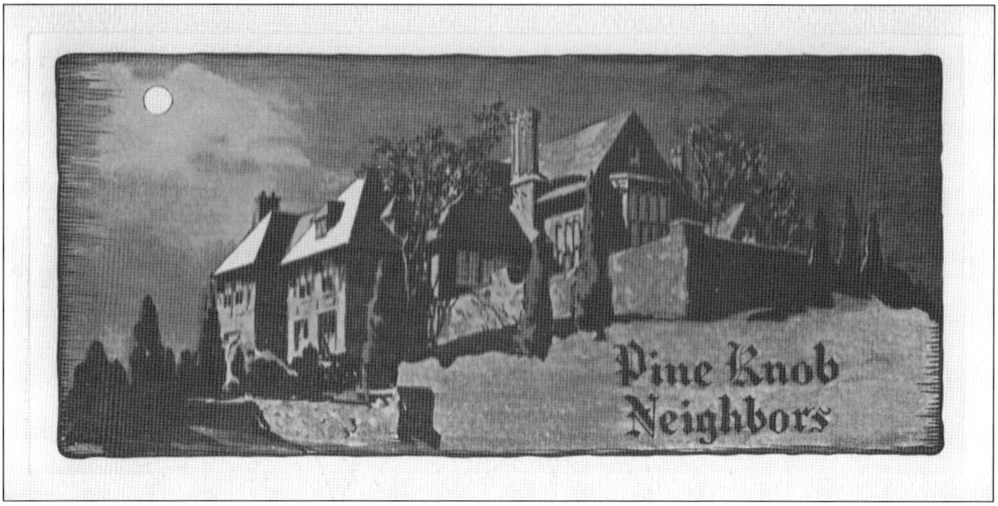

COLONEL WALDON'S PINE KNOB, C. 1930. Col. Sydney Waldon always fashioned personalized and poetic Christmas cards like this one featuring an image of his home, Pine Knob. The vice president of Packard Motor Company and later of Cadillac Motor Company commissioned H.A. O'Dell to build the 19-room Tudor home on 840 acres of land he purchased in 1927. An avid aviator, Waldon knew the Wright brothers and helped establish the landing strip that became Selfridge Air Force Base. The Waldons called Pine Knob home until 1947. It then became a branch of Henry Ford Hospital, a nursing home, the Hamburger Mansion restaurant, and finally the Pine Knob Mansion, an event rental facility.

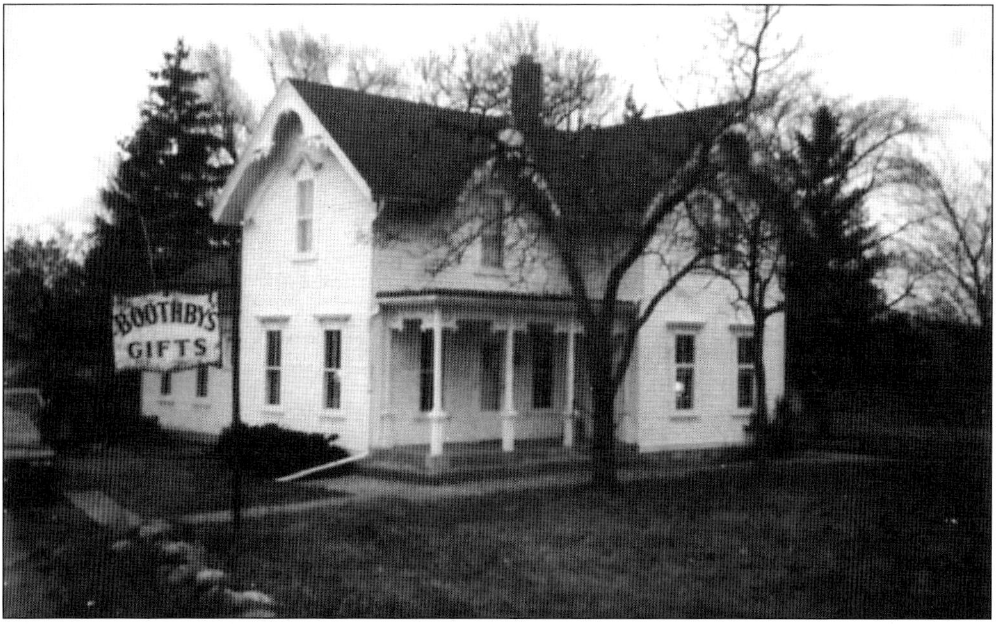

THE ADDIS/BOOTHBY HOUSE. Ephraim and Jane Addis built this house in 1876 at Addis Corners, at what is now the corner of Dixie Highway and White Lake Road. It later became home to the Boothby family. By the 1950s, it also served as Boothby's Old Farm Shop gift store. In 1988, after a developer bought the property and the home was slated for demolition, Independence Township resident Jon Abbott moved it to 180 North Main Street in the village and restored it to a residence.

Two

Clarkston Works

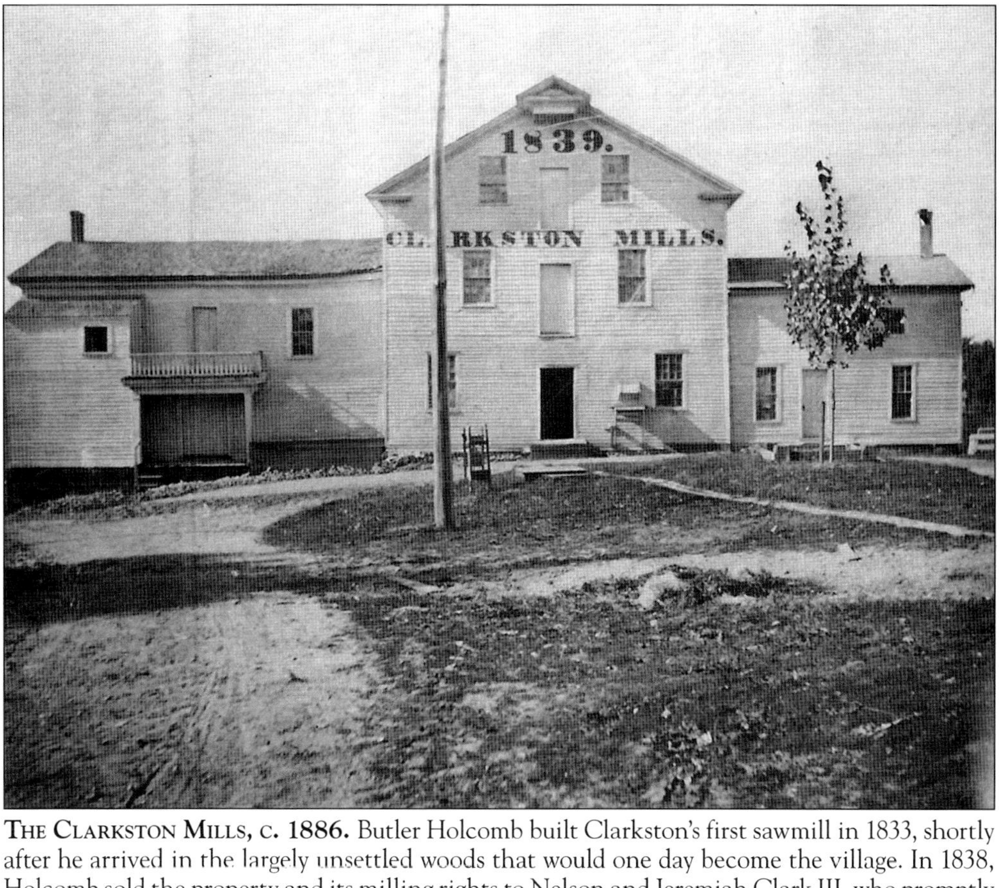

The Clarkston Mills, c. 1886. Butler Holcomb built Clarkston's first sawmill in 1833, shortly after he arrived in the largely unsettled woods that would one day become the village. In 1838, Holcomb sold the property and its milling rights to Nelson and Jeremiah Clark III, who promptly built a 200-foot dam with a 22-foot fall to power a 20-foot-diameter overshot and a 40-by-50-foot, two-story gristmill that would be known as Clarkston Mills.

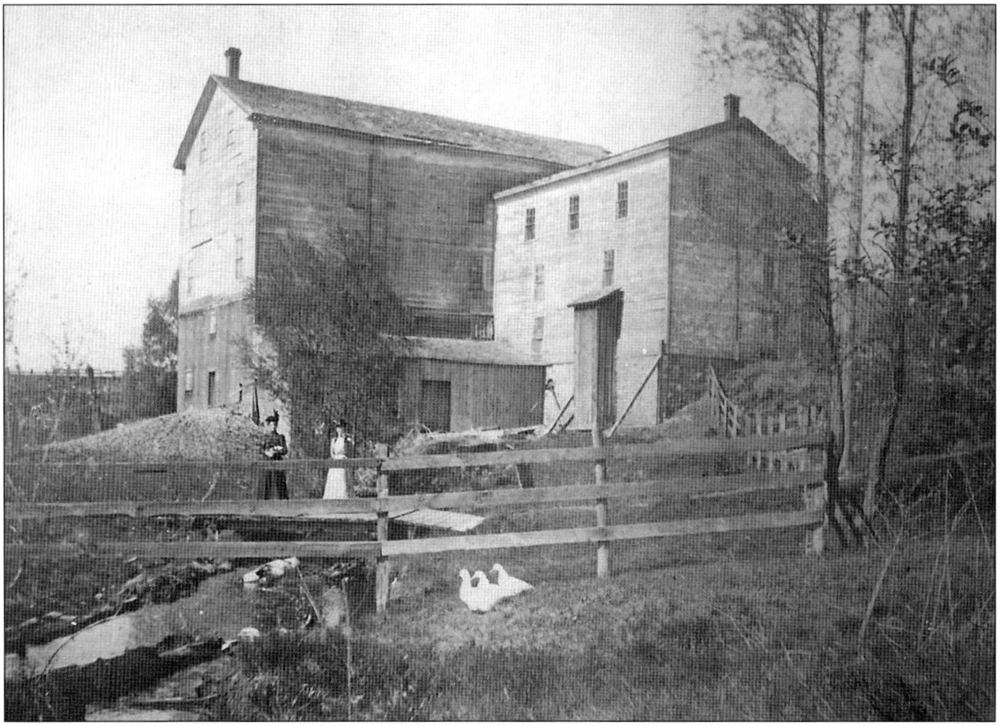

The Mill from Depot Road and Interior, c. 1900. Long credited with the village's prosperity, Clarkston Mills drew people with its reputation of purchasing local wheat, providing customers with much-loved fine flour, and helping establish Clarkston as a thriving mill town. Bakers loved miller Tom Farmer's flour, and within a few years, the mill reportedly could turn out 350 bushels every 10 hours. The exterior view above is from the standpoint of Depot Road. The distant fence at upper left is West Washington Street. Below is an image of the mill's interior.

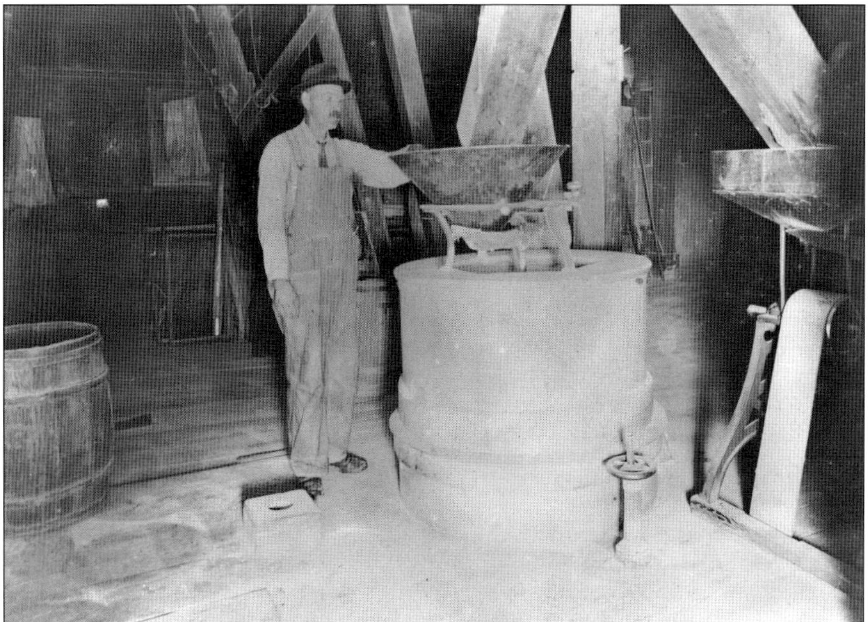

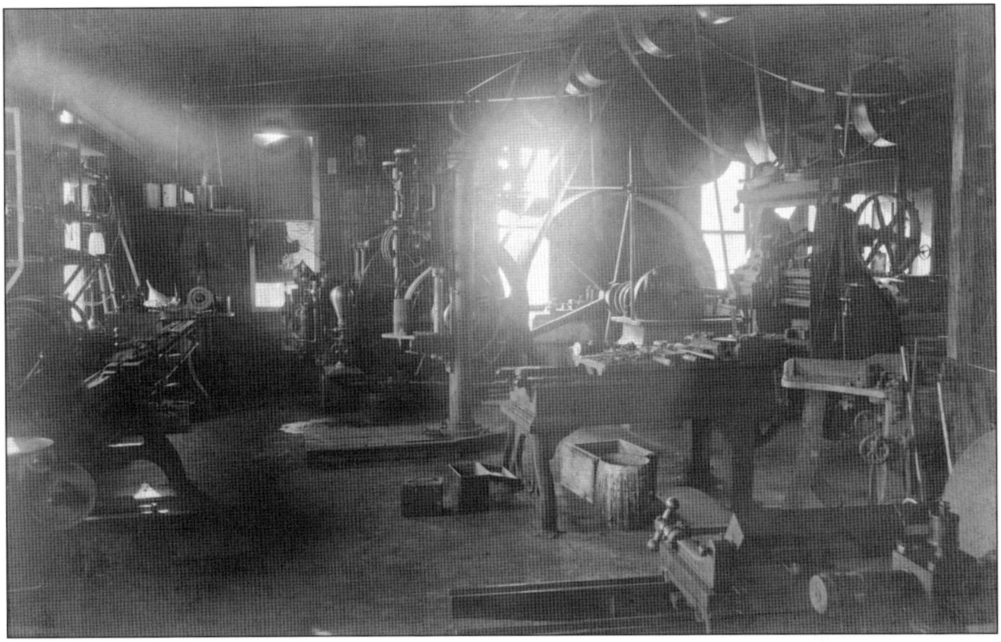

Butler J. Holcomb's Workshop. The Clarks sold the mill in 1859. In the late 1800s to early 1900s, Butler Holcomb's grandsons Charles and Butler J. Holcomb owned the mill property. A carpenter, Butler J. Holcomb kept his workshop inside the mill. In 1917, after falling into disrepair, a Detroit salvage company demolished the building, by then known as the Clarkston Roller Mills.

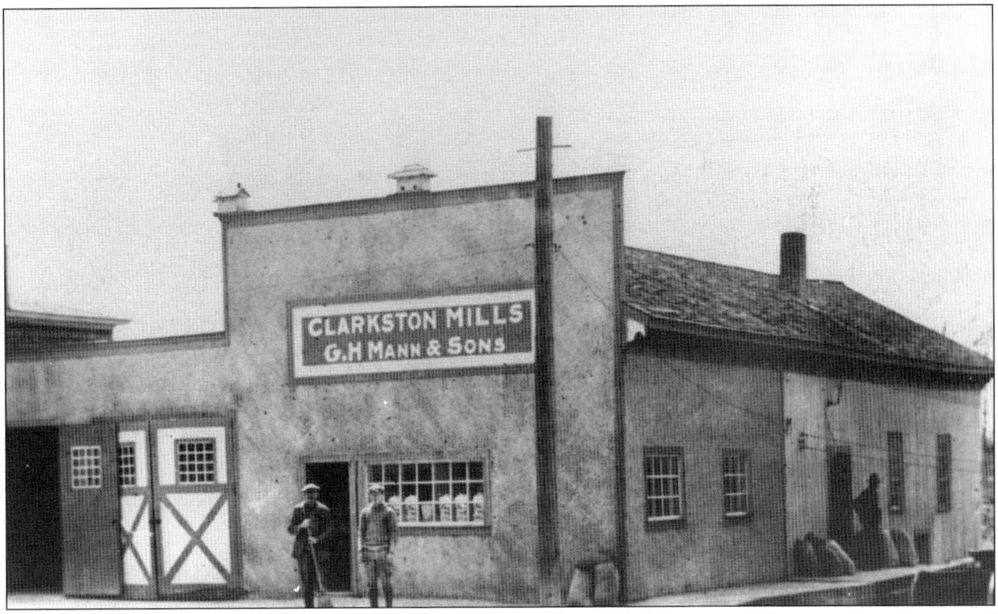

Clarkston Mills, G.H. Mann and Sons. The George H. Mann and Sons mill at the top of Livery Hill, where Depot Road and South Main Street meet, ground grain for farmers to use as animal feed. Previously a livery, the Mann building also housed Dr. Clark Sutherland's horses. Sutherland would pull his horse and buggy in through the Main Street doors. Once unhitched, the horse knew to head back out the doors, take a sharp left, turn to go down the Depot Road hill, and make another left to enter the building's lower level and his basement stall.

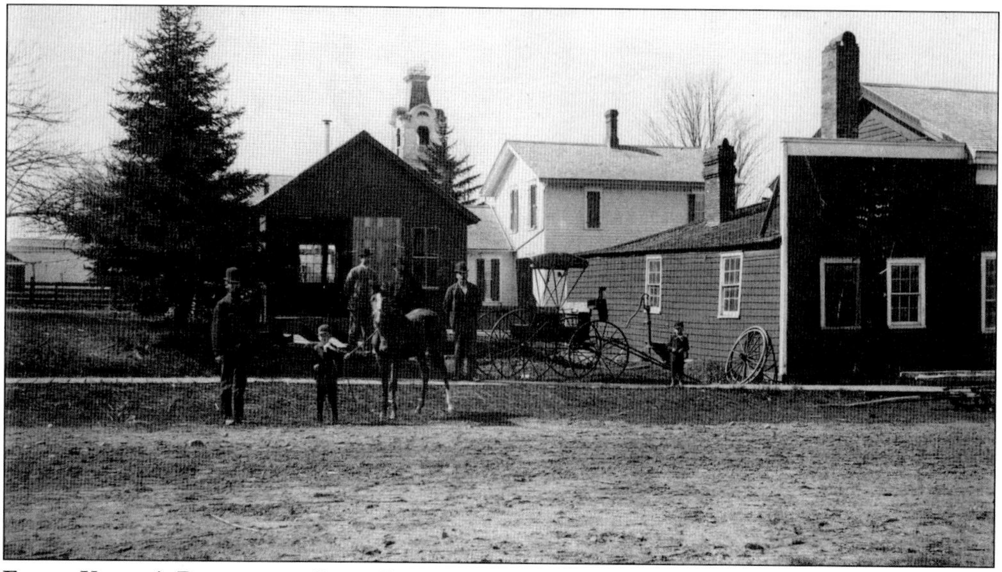

Frank Yeager's Blacksmith Shop, Church Street, 1877. Frank Yeager was just a one-year-old boy when he and his parents, Sarah and Jedediah, arrived in Clarkston by ox cart from New York in 1854. Jedediah Yeager was a blacksmith who, along with other Clarkston men, left in 1861 to serve in the Civil War for four years. Frank Yeager attended the private academy run by Isaac C. Cochran at 90 North Main Street, but he knew he wanted to follow in his father's footsteps and began blacksmithing at age 14. Taken from Church Street, this photograph shows the shop to the right and the nearby bell tower of the Baptist church. (Courtesy of the Collection of The Henry Ford.)

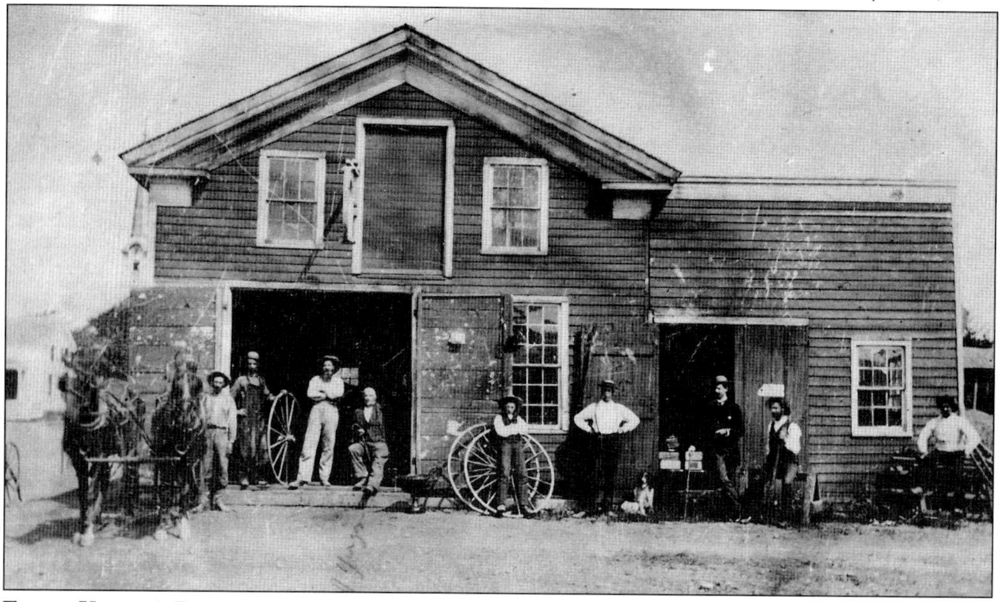

Frank Yeager's Blacksmith Shop, Main Street, 1877. Frank Yeager stands at the far left of the doorway, near the wagon wheel, while his father, Jedediah, sits holding his cane, leg outstretched, at Frank Yeager's blacksmith shop on the southeast corner of Main and Church Streets. The vessel that resembles a trophy near Jedediah Yeager reportedly was used to repair wagon and buggy wheels. While the blacksmith building is long gone, the Church Street home on the left and the first Methodist Episcopal church visible in the background remain.

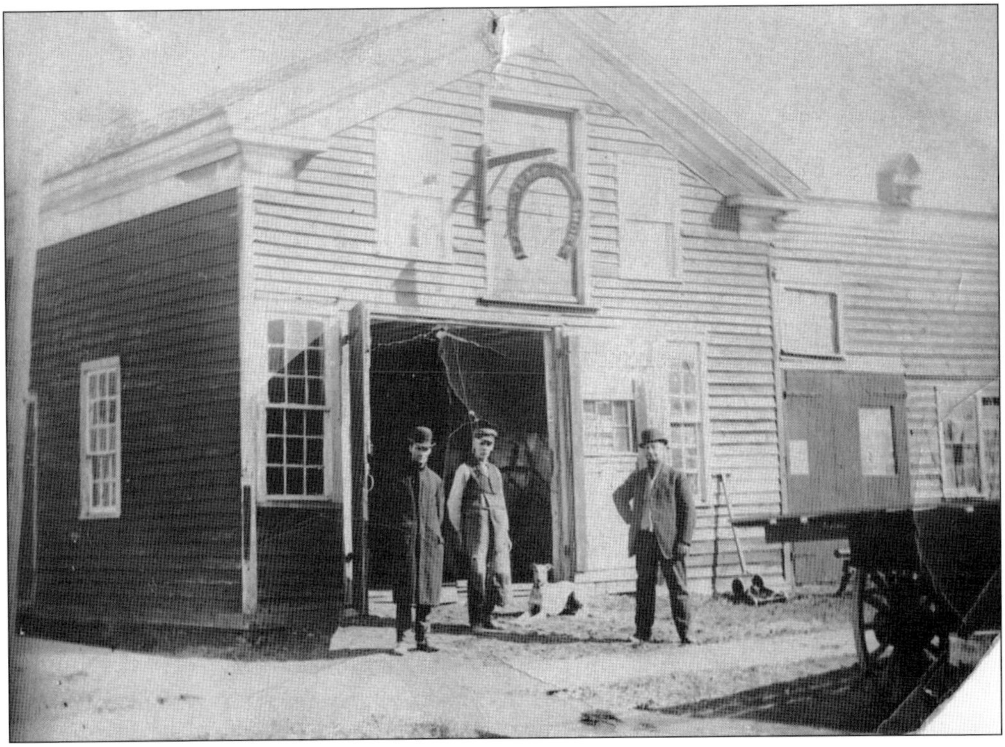

FRANK YEAGER WITH CUSTOMERS. Frank Yeager (center) chose to put his blacksmith shop directly across Main Street from customer Peter Green's livery. Yeager was reportedly so good at his job that he once shoed 80 horses in a single day. Clarkston resident Ada Scrace once recounted how sparks would fly when Yeager shoed horses. He was also an artist, creating decorative wreaths and other iron pieces. (Courtesy of Robert E. Donohue Jr.)

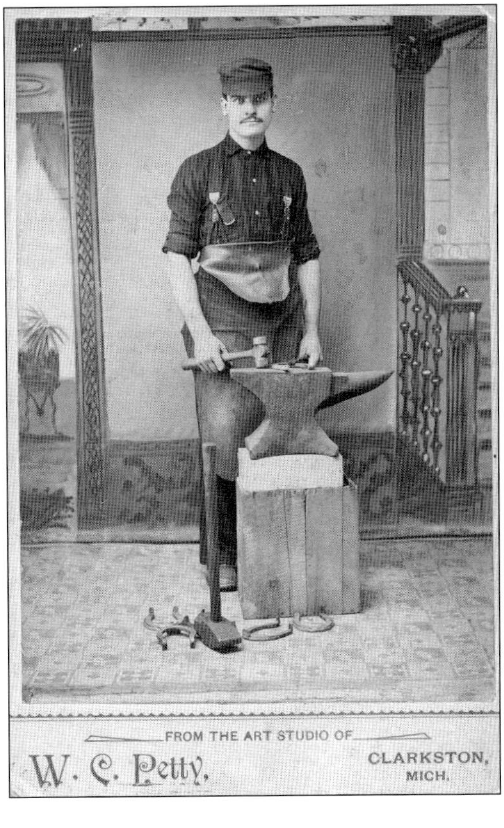

BLACKSMITH, 1893. The Yeagers were not the first blacksmiths in Clarkston. Around 1838, Albert Birdsell built a one-story board shanty as the first blacksmith shop, at the corner of Washington and Main Streets. Soon Demarest House took its place. By the 1850s, Clarkston had at least three busy blacksmiths, each reportedly with several workers on staff, including Clarkston-namesake Jeremiah Clark III. The blacksmith pictured here, whose surname is hard to make out on the back of the image beyond Joseph S—tzer, posed for this 1893 portrait by Clarkston photographer W.C. Petty.

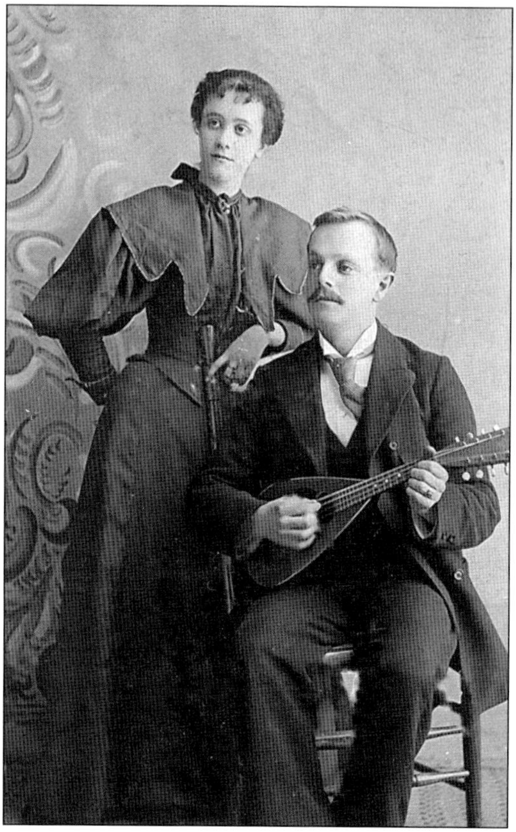

Petty Art Studios, Posing with Friends. Petty Art Studios, or Petty Photography, among other business names William Petty used, was on the second floor of Wilson "Wiltsie" Vliet's cabinet and boat shop at 21 North Main Street. Petty captured many portraits of area families, but these two images feature Petty himself. The one at left, reportedly with his wife, could well be a self-portrait or just Petty having fun with his camera. The shot below with Petty and his friends clearly seems to be the latter.

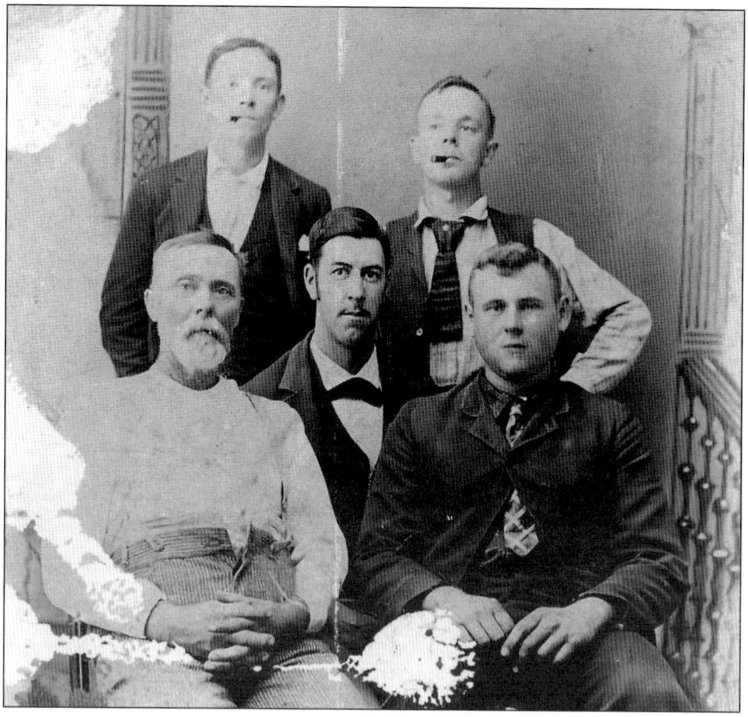

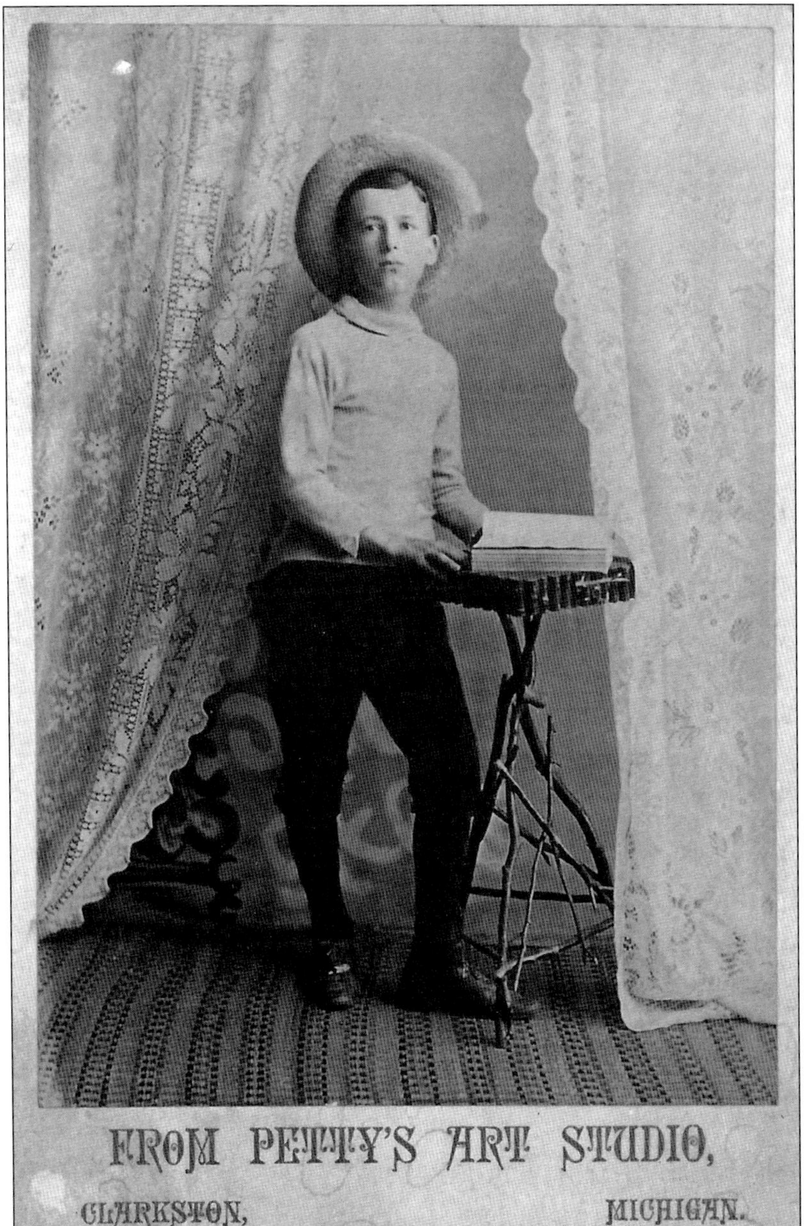

Lee Clark, Petty Art Studios. The young man in this Petty image is Lee Clark, grandson of Milton Clark and great-grandson of Jeremiah Clark III. He worked with his father, Edwin M. Clark, at their company, Phoenix Ironworks, later called Vulcan Company, in Detroit. Missing Clarkston, they moved the brass, bronze, and copper metal-manufacturing business back to the village in 1915, building the fieldstone structure at Waldon Road and Main Street. When the wooden arch at Lakeview Cemetery deteriorated, the new stone columns and gate came from these Clarks. Lee Clark created a memorial plate (which appears to no longer be there), which read: "In Memory of Pioneers of Clarkston—Jeremiah Clark, Nelson W. Clark, and Ebenezer Clark." He also reportedly made the war memorial tablet on the boulder that stands near Independence Township offices and printed a series of Clarkston postcards.

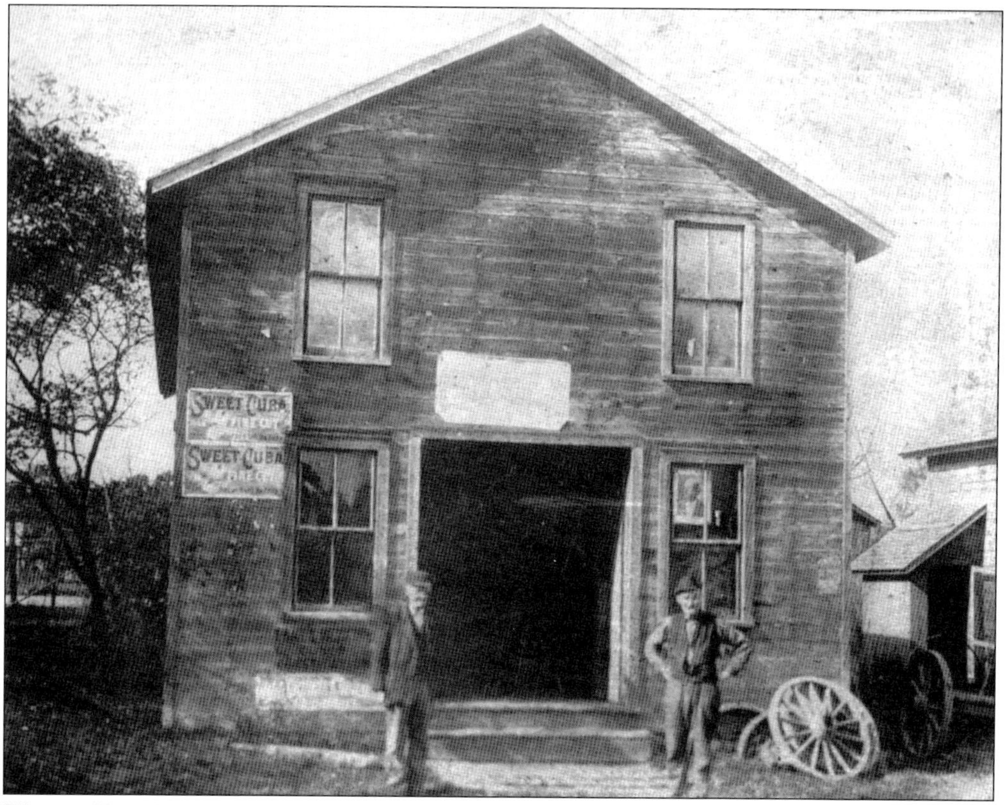

WILTSIE VLIET'S BUILDING, C. 1900. Wiltsie Vliet was an accomplished woodworker known to build wagons, cabinets, boats, and other wooden items. He lived and worked at 40 Buffalo Street before moving his business to 21 North Main Street (pictured) in the 1880s. A 1902 *Pontiac Post* item claimed Vliet was building the largest rowboat ever built in Clarkston for a customer in Windiate Park. This structure later became an antiques shop and remains one today, the Clarkston Country Store and Antiques.

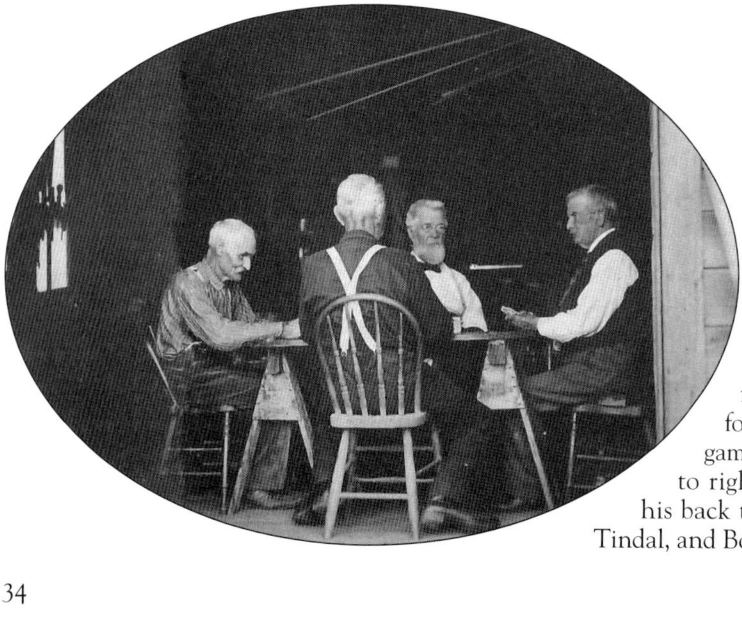

WILTSIE VLIET WITH FRIENDS. Wiltsie Vliet (far left) takes a break from his woodworking for one of his regular card games with friends. From left to right are Jake Petty (with his back to the camera), George Tindal, and Bob Reid.

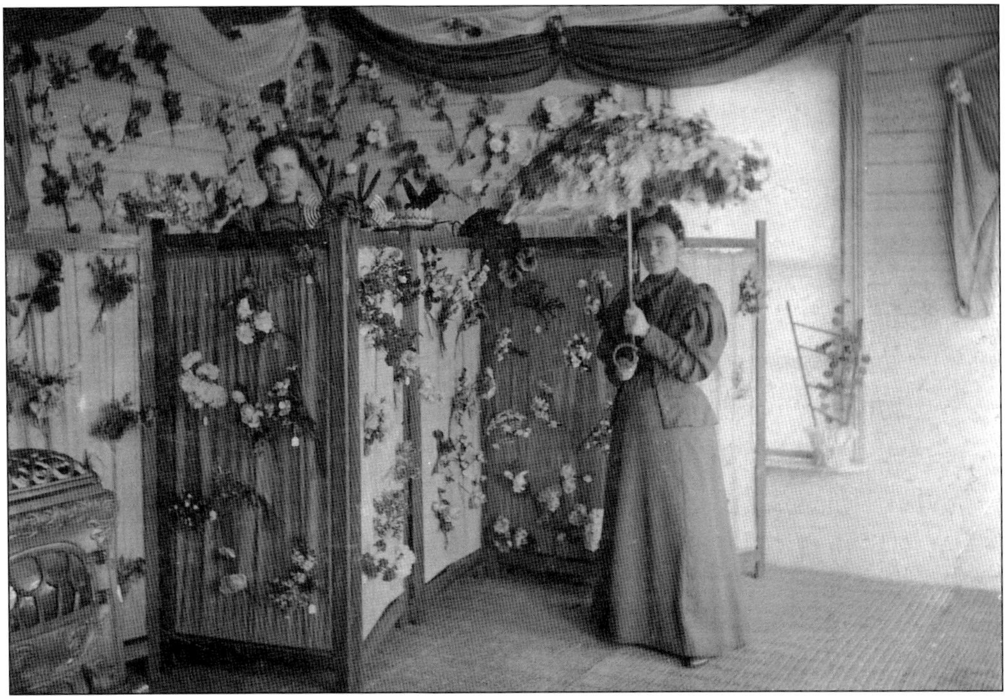

The Mason Sisters and the Millinery. Sisters Lucy Mason (behind the screen) and Mary Mason Taylor (holding parasol) opened their hat shop at 11 North Main Street in 1895. An average ready-made hat, one suitable for everyday use, ran about $2, but a custom-made original hat could cost as much as $30. The various decorations strewn about are likely embellishments the sisters used on their creations. The house was demolished in the 1960s. In 1984, property owners Hank and Jennifer Radcliff moved the historical John Green house from its original site on Dixie Highway near Maybee Road to the vacant spot, sparing it from demolition and being replaced by a fast-food restaurant.

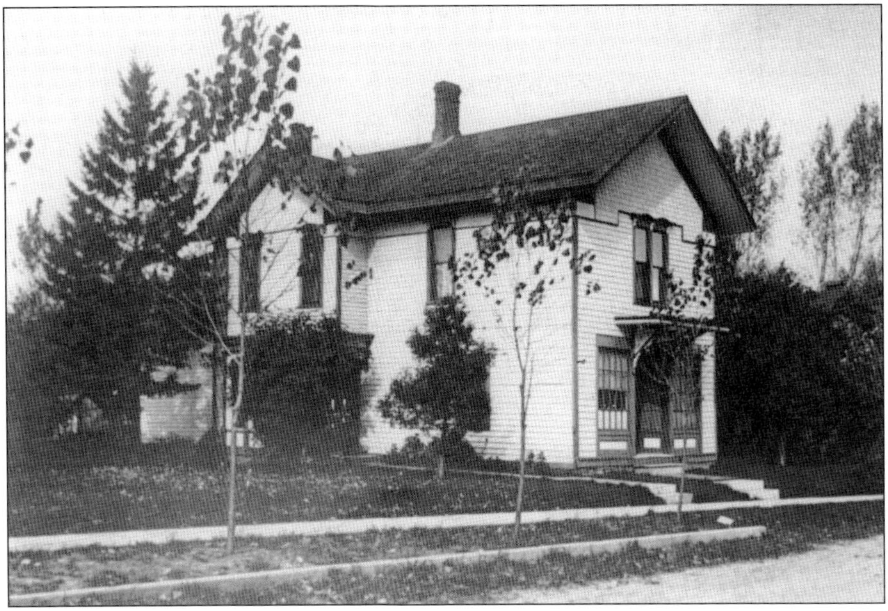

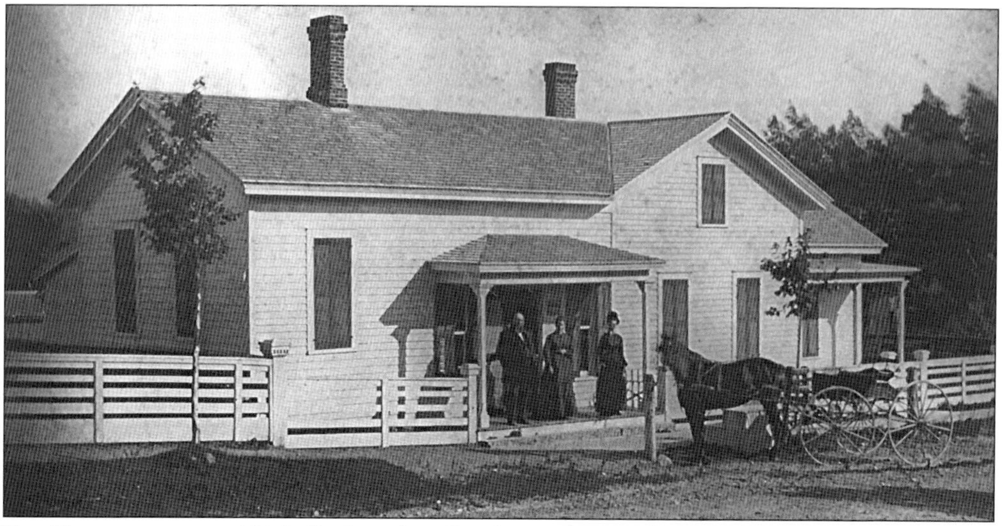

DR. GOODENOUGH, C. 1900. Dr. Josephus Goodenough moved to Clarkston in 1871 to live and practice medicine at 42 North Main Street, where a separate room upstairs served as his exam room. Initially, the house was street level, but street widening and paving through the years causes it to sit lower than much of Main Street. Dr. Goodenough wrote a remedies book, *Favorite Medical Receipt Book and Home Doctor*, published by the Dickerson Publishing Company of Detroit in 1902. Though an early Clarkston doctor, Dr. Goodenough was not the first. That credit likely goes to Dr. Nelson Abbey, who came in 1845 and remained until he died in 1873.

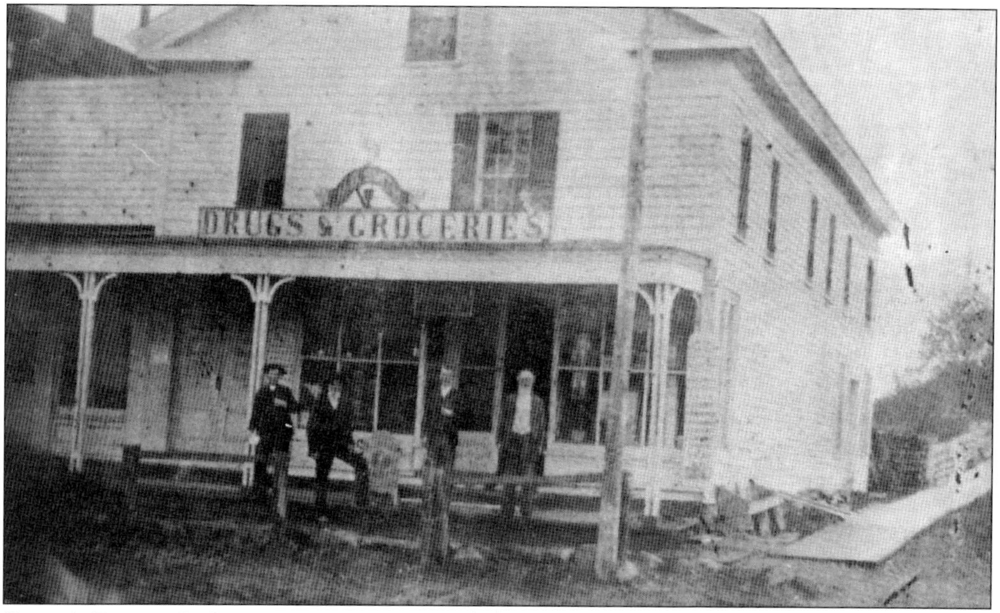

SMITH'S DRUGS & GROCERIES, C. 1890. Nicholas Bonaparte Smith (far right) stands with his son to his right, at Smith's Drugs & Groceries, where farmers shopped, bartered, and traded. The building also housed Leman Gulick's barbershop, and upstairs was the earliest site of Clarkston's Masonic temple. Some believe that Floyd Andrews moved this portion of the double building to join with 20 North Main Street, making the tavern there larger, and used the remaining portion for his blacksmith equipment, converting its second story into his family residence. The empty lot then became the site of the new Masonic temple building.

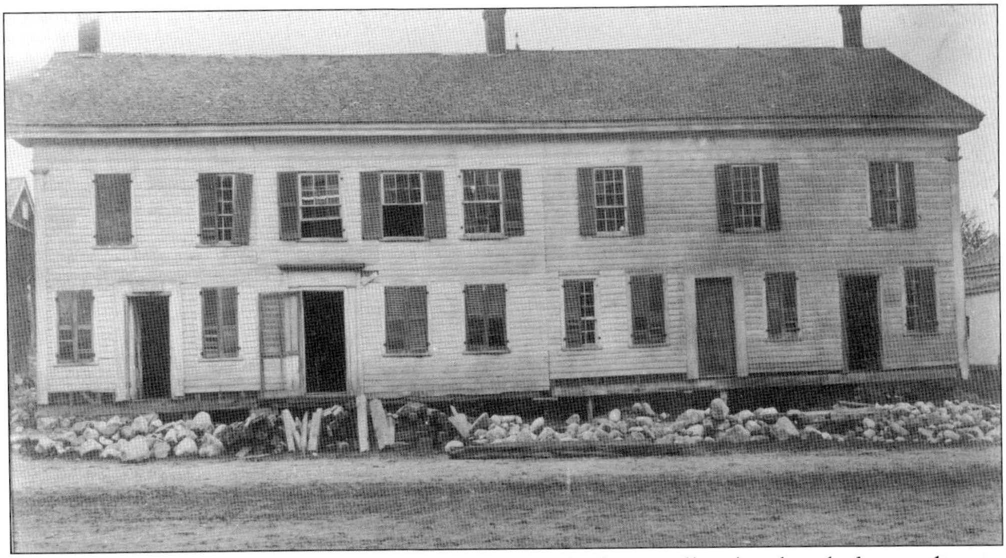

The Johnson House. In 1840, tailor John Hertwig built a small tailor shop before trading in his thread and thimble to transform the space into a tavern two years later. It was among the first places where weary travelers could find lodging in Clarkston. This oldest building in the business district comes with a few stories, including that a jail once occupied its north end and the building stretched to its current size when proprietor D.S. Johnson expanded it by adjoining another building, believed to be Nicholas Bonaparte Smith's shop moved from the northeast corner of North Main and East Washington Streets.

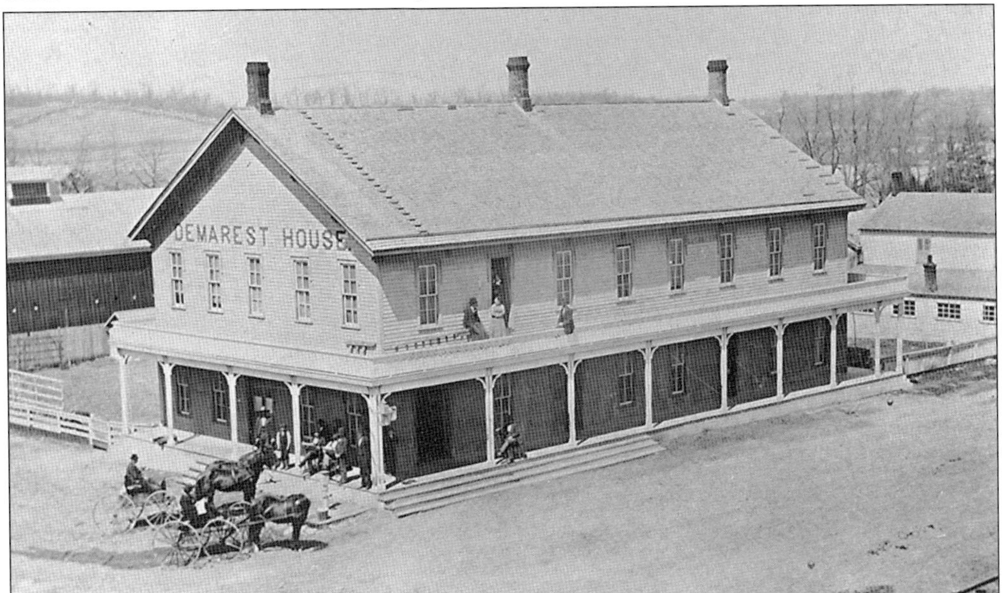

Demarest House, c. 1880. J.G. Demarest built the Demarest House in 1872. Among the first hotels in the village, it changed hands—and names—often in subsequent years, including the New Wooster in the late 1890s, the Caribou Inn in the 1920s, and the Clarkston House sometime between the two. It was the Caribou when it burned in 1958. Rather than working to salvage the damaged building, the community opted to demolish it, making way for the public parking lot there today.

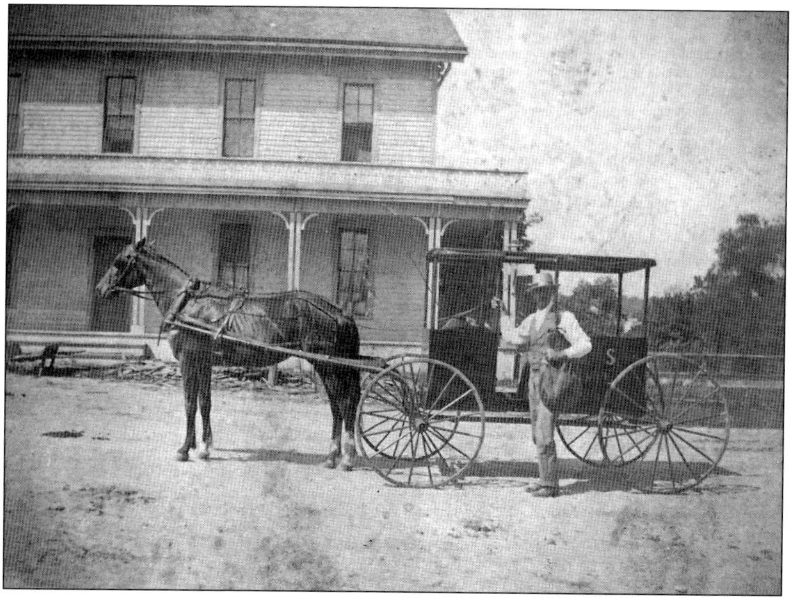

Elmer Vliet at Demarest House, c. 1910. With his mail satchel hanging from his shoulder, post rider Elmer Vliet stands next to his horse and buggy parked alongside the Demarest House.

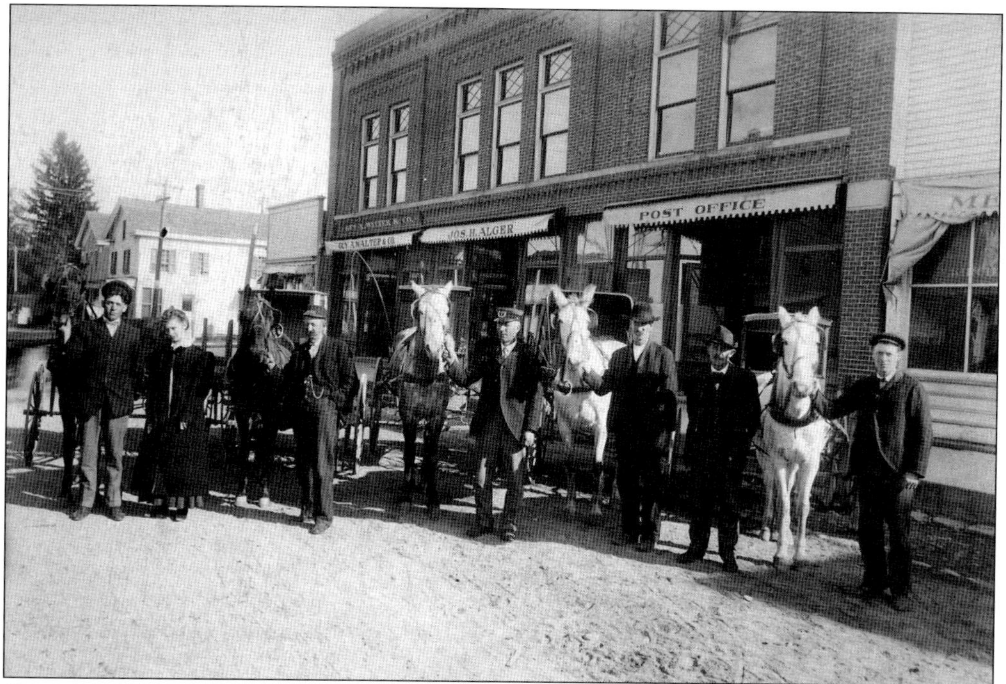

Clarkston Post Office and Post Riders, c. 1907. Clarkston's initial mail deliveries arrived several times a week by horseback from Pontiac. By 1846, mail traveled by four-horse stagecoach via Territorial Road, and in 1851 the railroad arrived at Clarkston Depot, making mail deliveries quicker and more frequent. Pictured here from left to right in front of the post office when it was in the Maccabee Temple building are Loren Chestnut (substitute carrier), Julia Smith Yeager (clerk), Albert Hammond (RFD carrier No. 1), E.S. Waterbury (RFD carrier No. 4), Elmer Vliet (RFD carrier No. 3), John T.P. Smith (postmaster), and John Hammond (RFD carrier No. 2). Interestingly, Albert and John Hammond were the grandfather and father, respectively, of Elizabeth Ronk, who served as Clarkston's postmistress from 1936 through 1970.

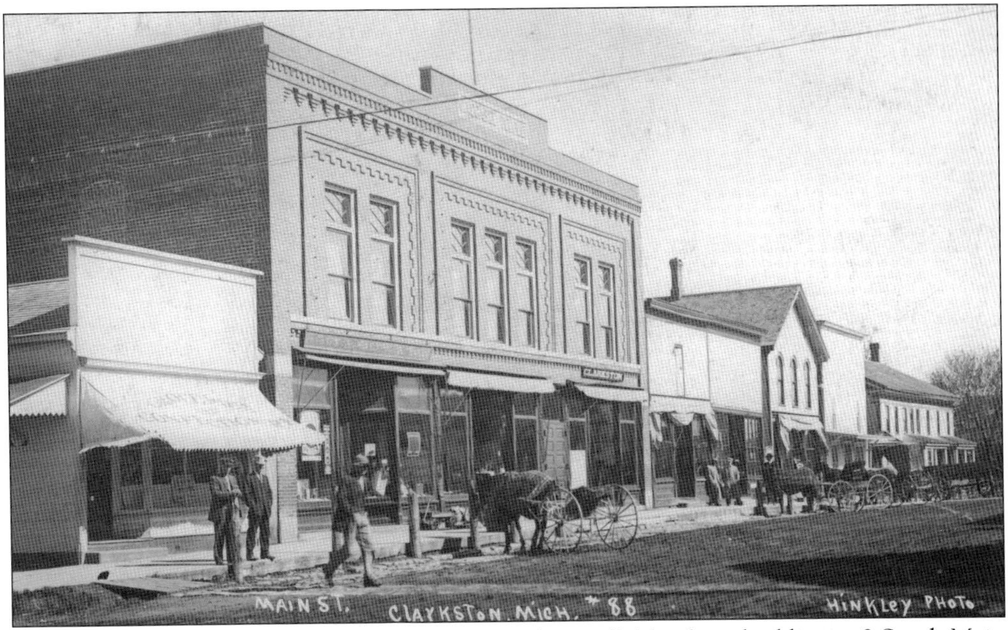

The Addis and Maccabee Temple Buildings. The small false-front building at 2 South Main Street (far left) is the Addis Building, which Daniel Addis purchased from Esidore Jossman in 1895. Formerly known as the Scranton Store, the building was moved from 3 North Holcomb Street. The Maccabee fraternal order stepped in to build the building next door in 1902, vacant since Bingham Hall burned around 1887. Seventy-four townspeople bought stock to form the Clarkston Building Association to help finance the building, which features clipper brick from Fort Street, Detroit, still visible on the second story. The Opera House was upstairs above the storefronts, bringing the community together for dances, musicals, and other events.

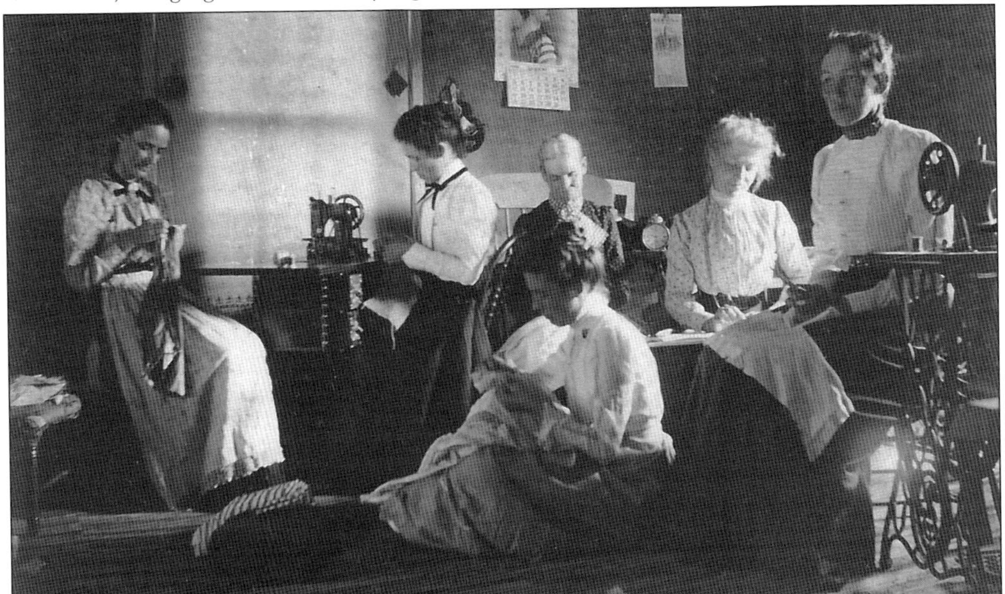

Seamstresses at Work. Roxy Lucille Tucker King (second from left) and other seamstresses diligently sew piecework, likely at Esidore Jossman's general store in 1900.

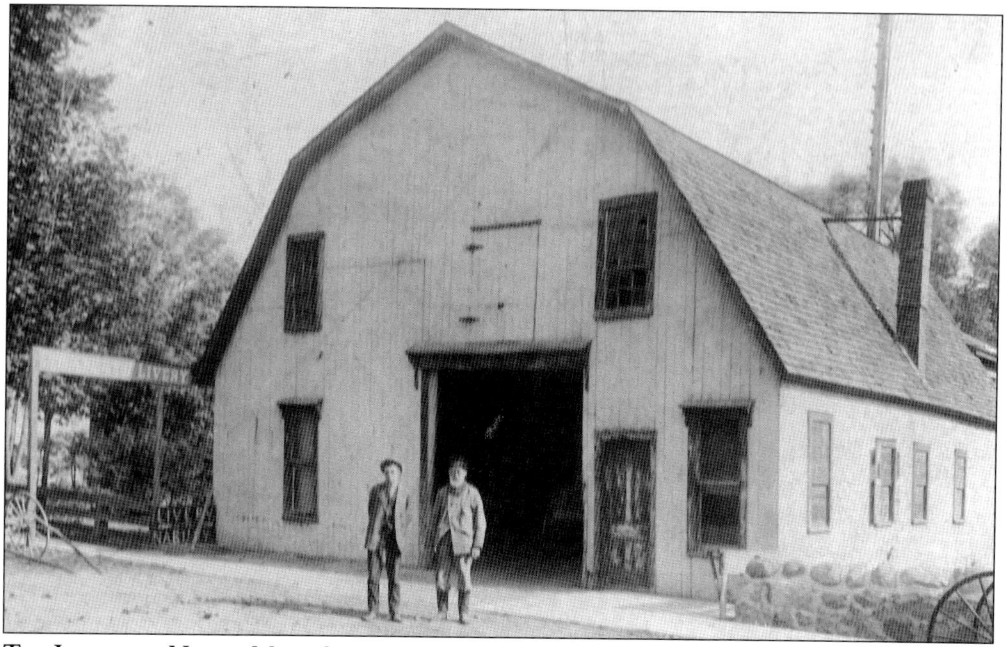

The Livery on North Main Street. Believed to be Jedediah Yeager's blacksmith shop at one point, the livery building tucked into the northern edge of the Main Street business district where the river and Parke Lake meet had various owners, including Cyrus Linabury (likely the bearded man pictured here). J.A. Skarritt purchased Linabury Livery in 1909 and operated it and a transportation business until 1921.

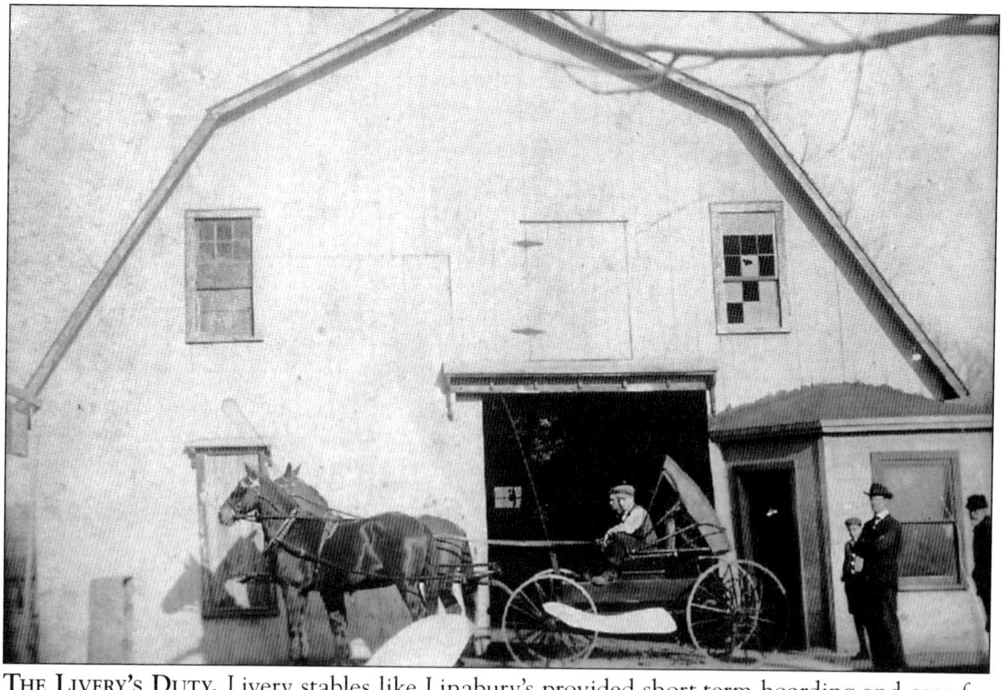

The Livery's Duty. Livery stables like Linabury's provided short-term boarding and care for horses when people rode into the village to work, shop, sell goods, lodge, or simply visit. They also provided horses and carriages for hire.

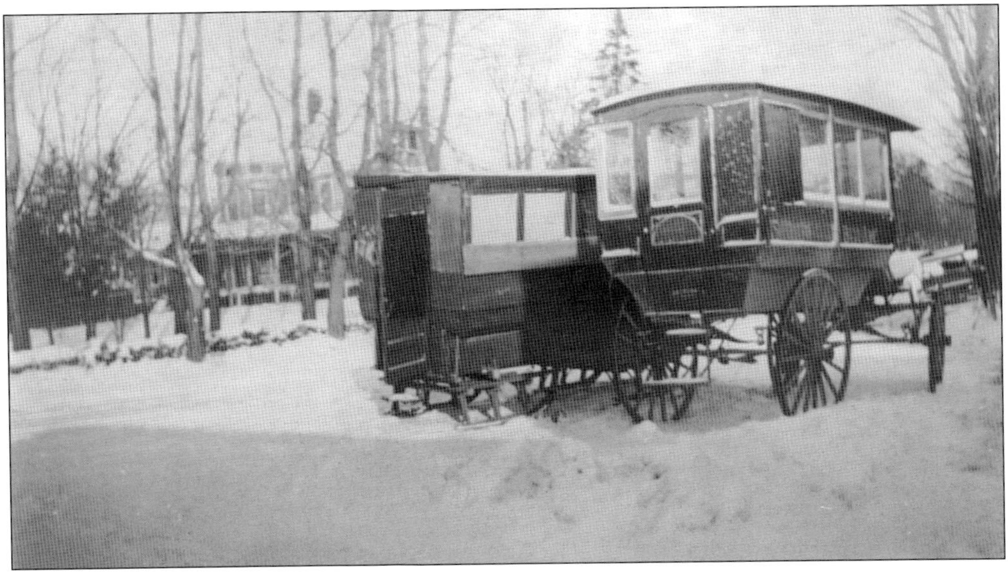

J.A. Skarritt Livery and Buss Line, 1917. The Skarritt Livery and Buss Line provided transportation to and from the train depot, the village, and area inns, first by horse-drawn "buss" and later by automobile. The home visible in the background above is 43 North Main Street.

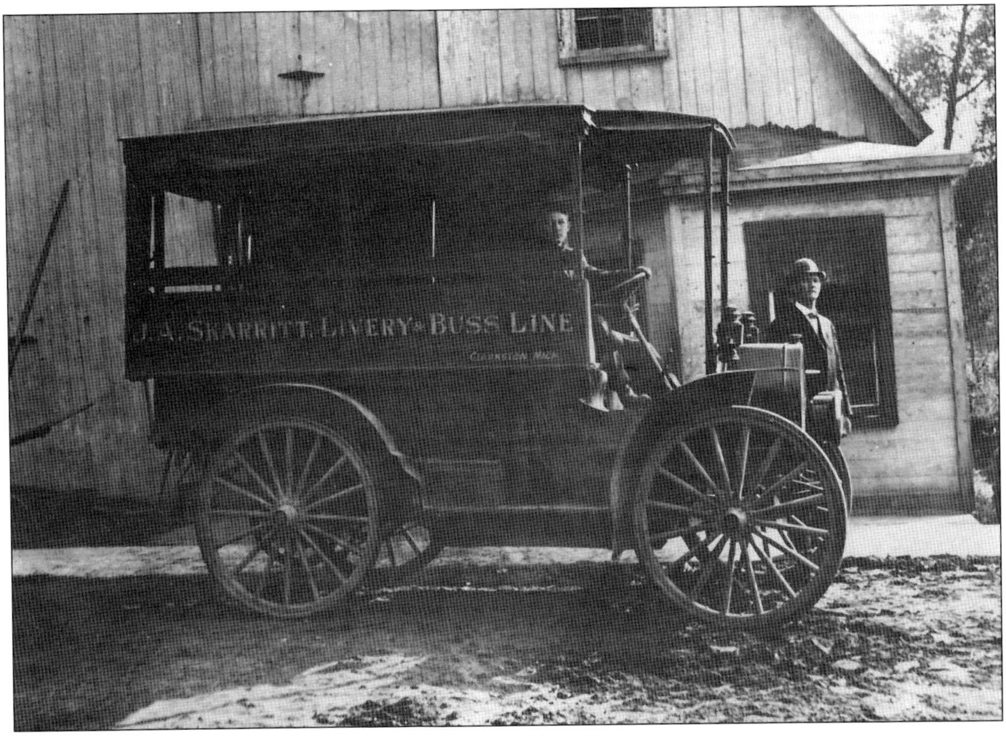

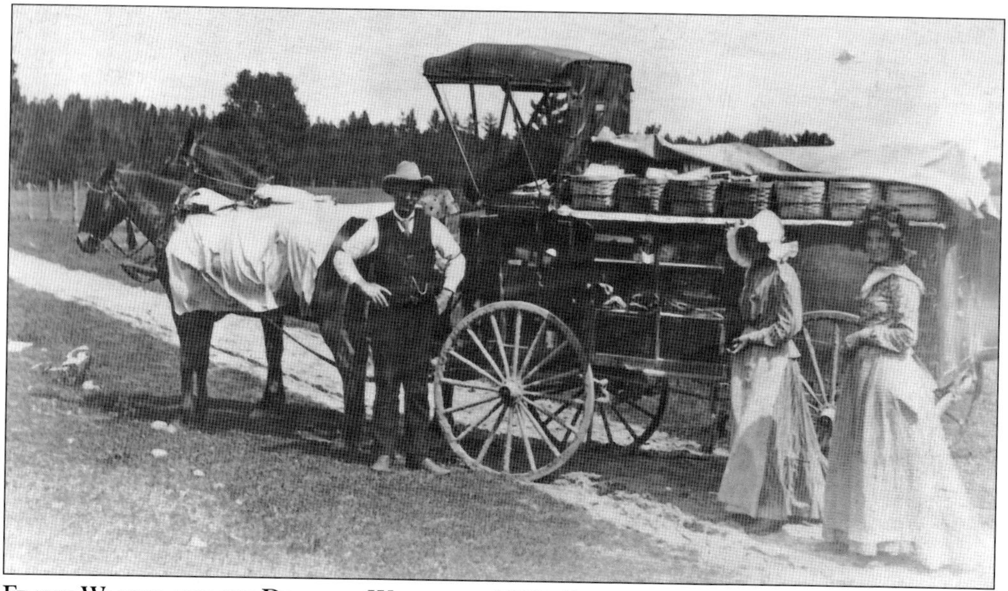

Frank Walter and his Delivery Wagon, c. 1890. Getting into town took valuable time out of a busy farmer's day, so Frank Walter (pictured with customers) traveled by wagon throughout Clarkston and Independence Township to deliver willow baskets full of necessities ordered a week earlier. Resident Ada Scrace once recalled that Walter would regularly visit her family farm on Pine Knob Road when she was a girl, often arriving conveniently at mealtime and welcomed to stay to enjoy it with the family. Walter carried more with him than dry goods; he brought news and rumors to delight the often-secluded farm families.

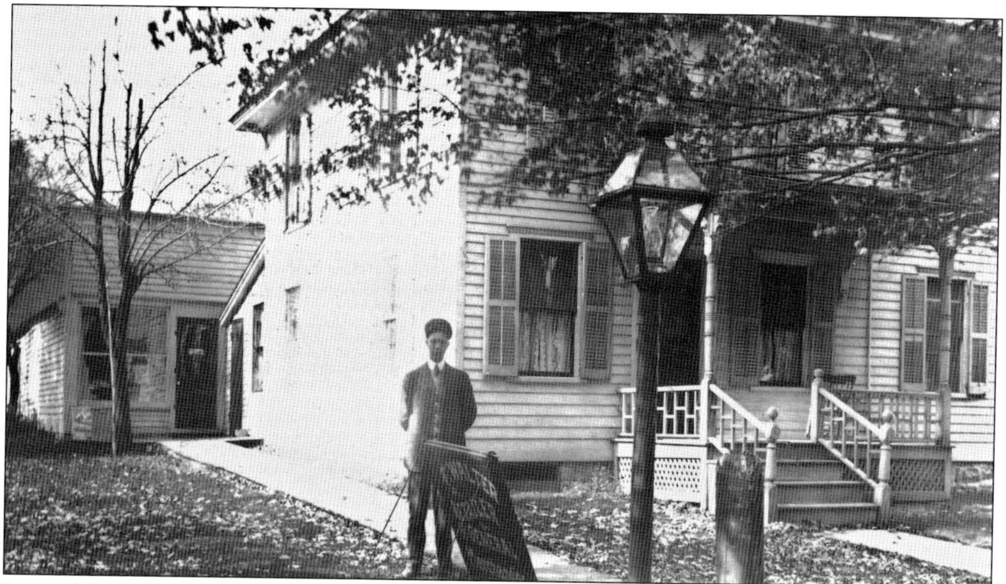

Louis Walter and Holcomb Storefront and Home, c. 1900. Louis Walter helped run his father's business, Frank Walter & Son General Store, from the small, wooden-frame storefront behind their home on Holcomb Street. They also used the barn as a wool station, where local sheep farmers would bring wool to bale. Earlier, Walter had a storefront in Bingham Hall, destroyed by fire in the late 1880s. In 1919, the store moved into the building at 5 South Main Street that became known as the Walter Building, which eventually housed the weekly *Clarkston News.*

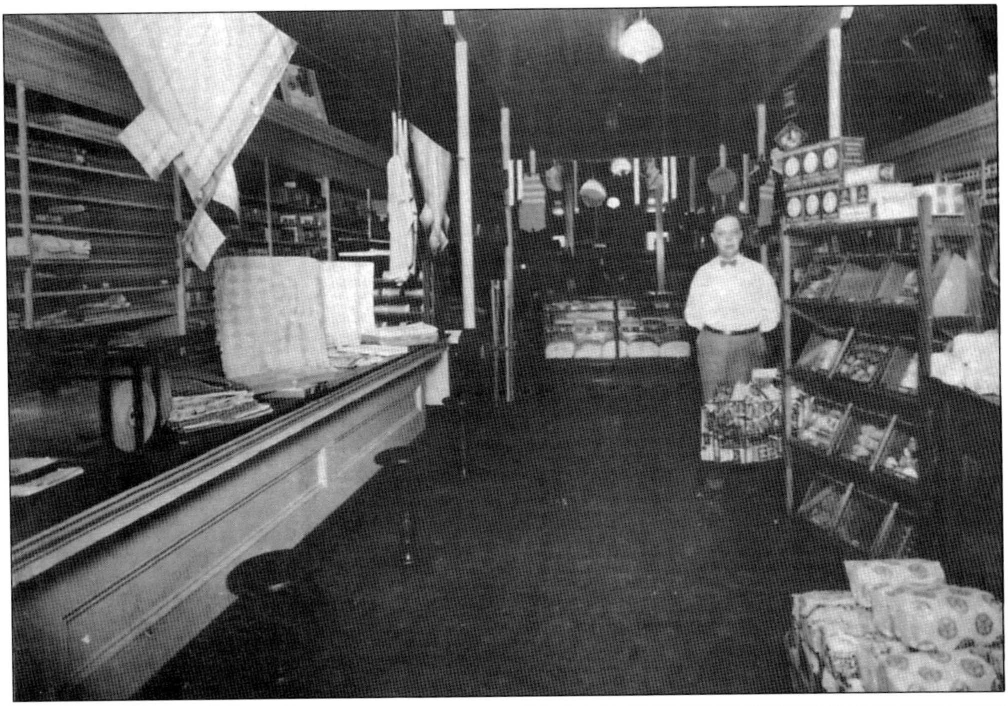

WALTER STORE ON MAIN STREET, C. 1910. Above, Louis Walter waits for customers at Frank Walter & Son Dry Goods, Footwear, and Groceries at 5 South Main Street. Locals often perched upon the store's wooden counter stools to catch up on happenings around town. Charlotte Maybee recalls coming into town to trade eggs and other items from the family farm for groceries at the Walters' grocery store.

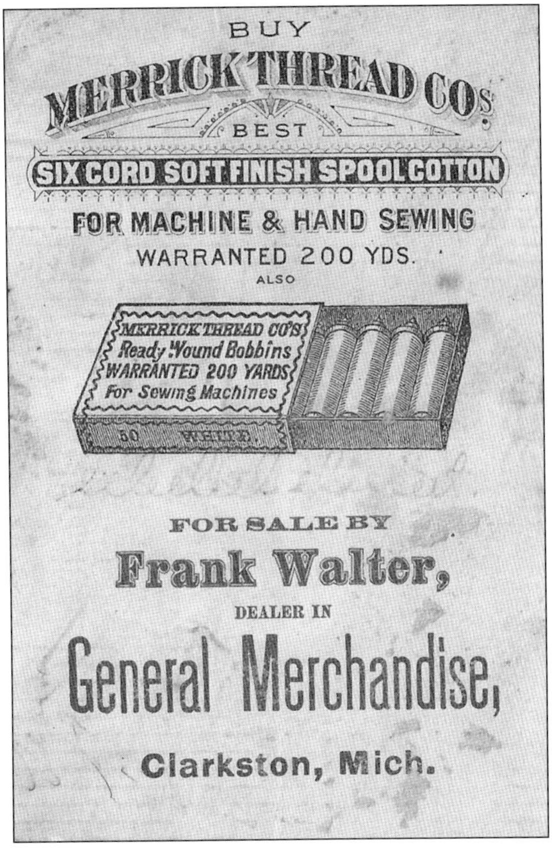

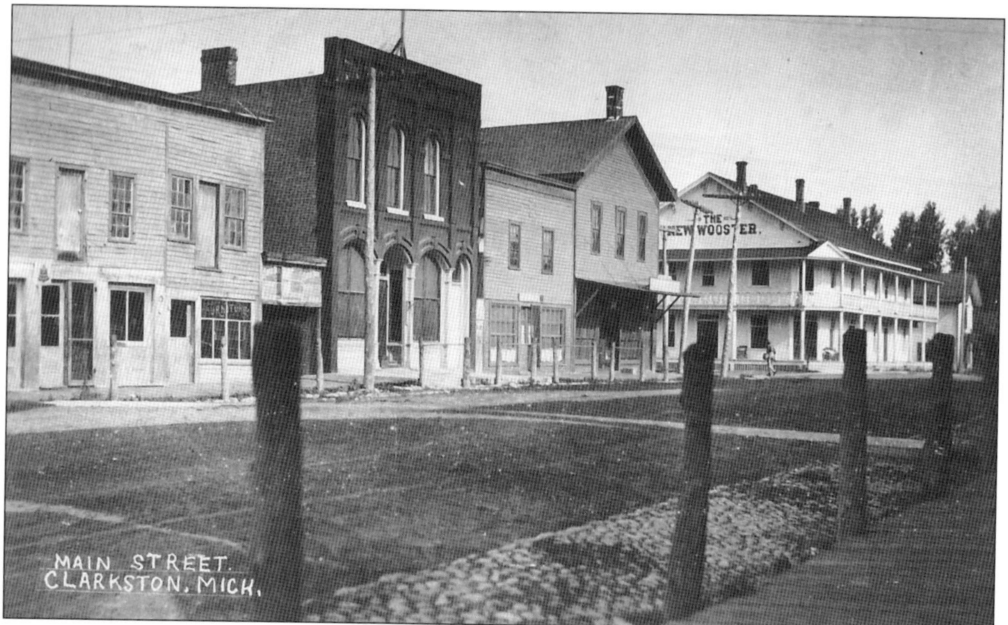

Northwest View of Main Street, c. 1907. The corner building across Washington Street from the New Wooster Hotel is M.H. Clark Dry Goods, Hardware, Boots, and Shoes, which Milton Clark opened in 1844 when he was 24 years old and went on to run for more than half a century. Clark distributed penny-sized Civil War tokens—coins bearing his store's name and redeemable toward a penny's worth of goods on a customer's next purchase. Often mistaken for a real penny, some of these tokens still exist. At left is Jasper Linabury's Furniture Shop. Notice that the street was still dirt, with an edging of cobblestone before reaching the hitching posts and wooden boardwalks.

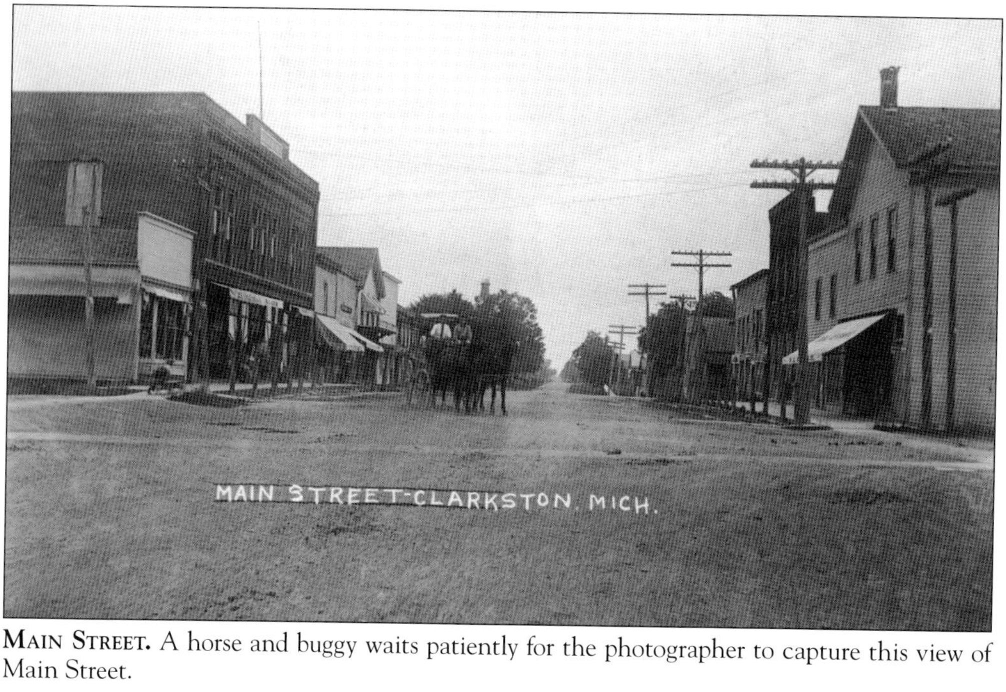

Main Street. A horse and buggy waits patiently for the photographer to capture this view of Main Street.

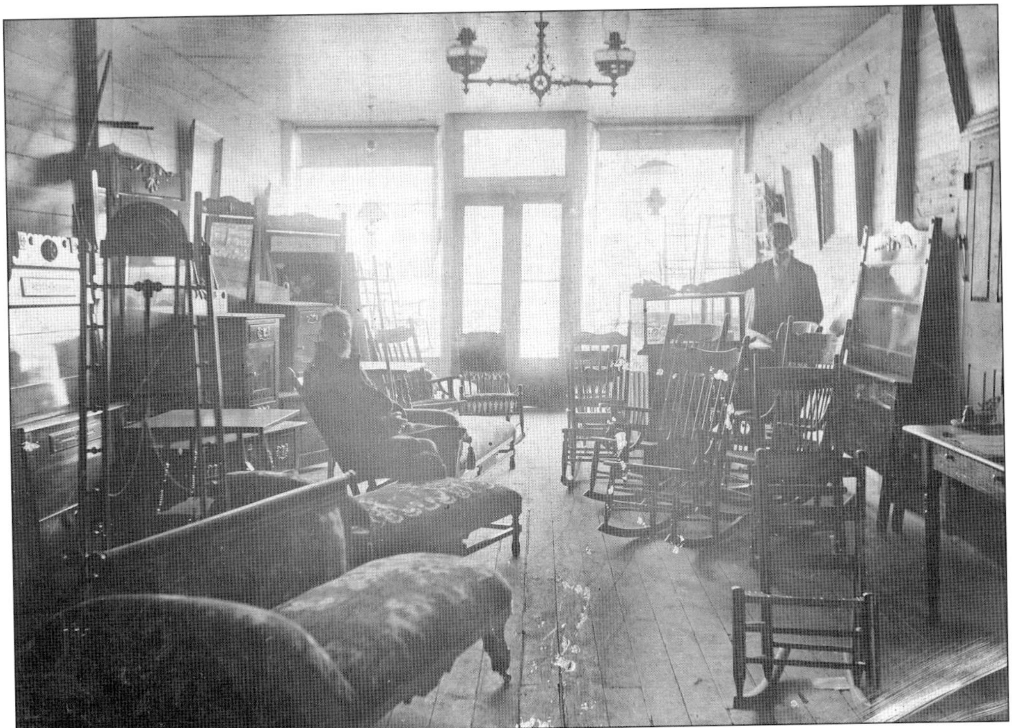

Jasper Linabury's Furniture Store, 1912. To the left of 5 South Main Street, on the corner where Mill and Main Streets meet, stood Jasper Linabury's furniture store. And of course, the former livery owner delivered. Before long, the building and a few of its neighbors would be gone, making way for native stone buildings and others that filled vacant spots and remain today.

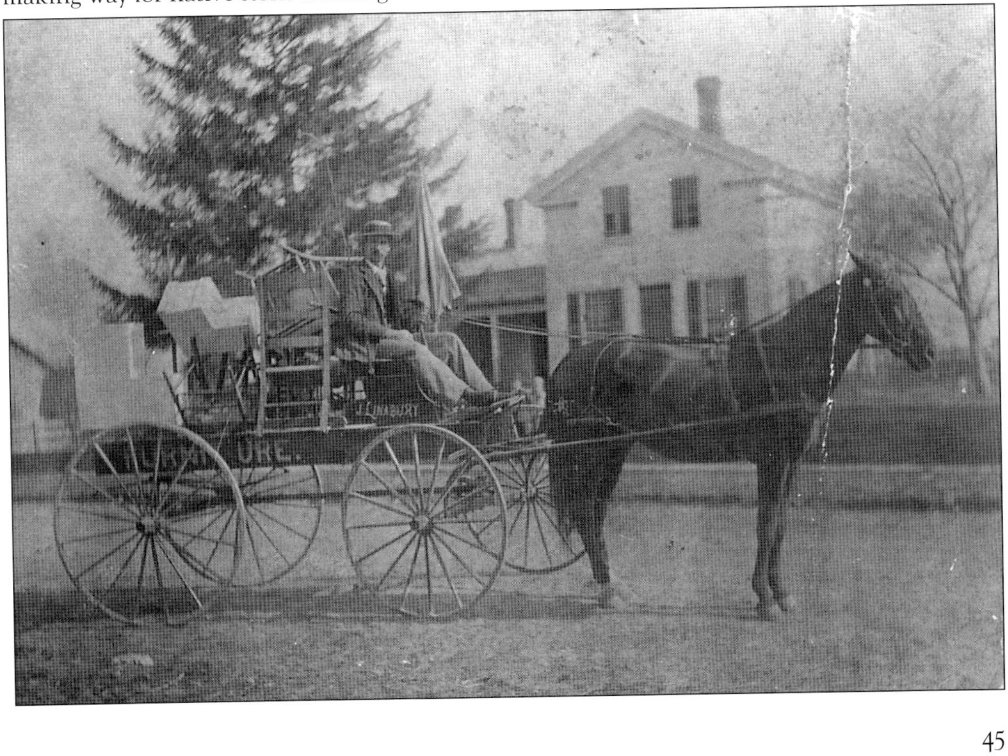

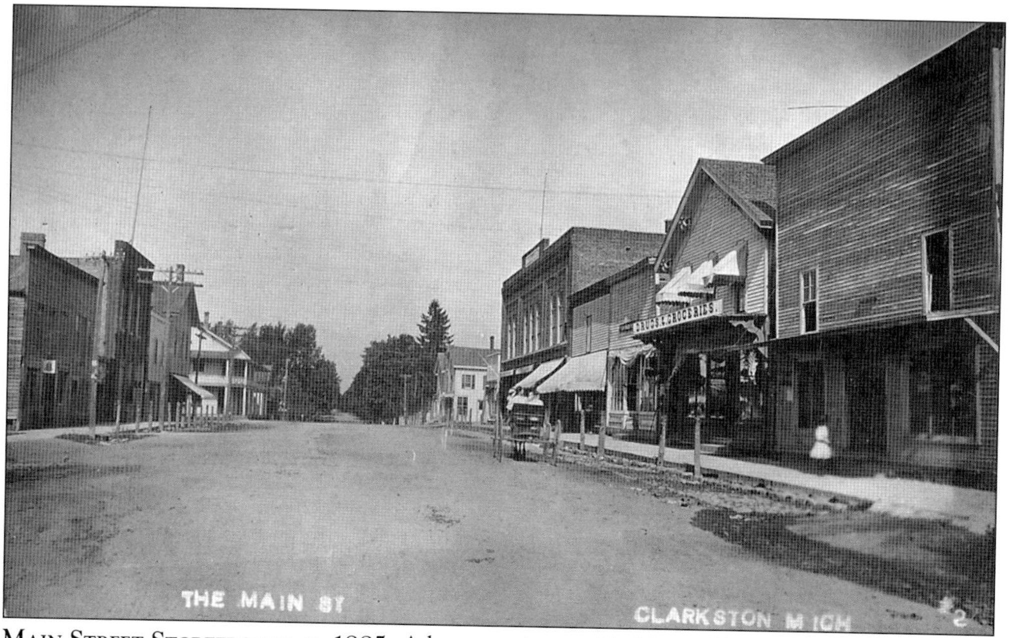

Main Street Storefronts, c. 1885. A buggy waits outside Floren Hammond's Italian Revival storefront (with three second-floor window awnings on the east side of South Main Street). This full-service drug and grocery store was typical of the era, when village residents and farmers ventured to buy or trade for common necessities. Although the person to the right below is unidentified, Albert Hammond stands in the doorway, with Lucy King to the left.

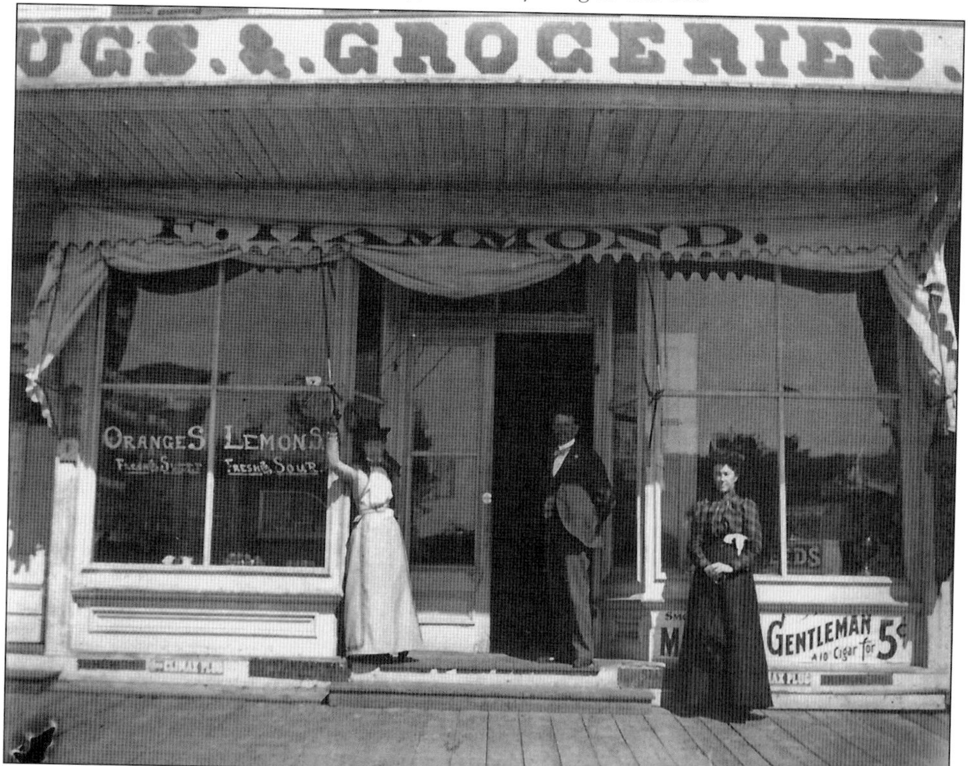

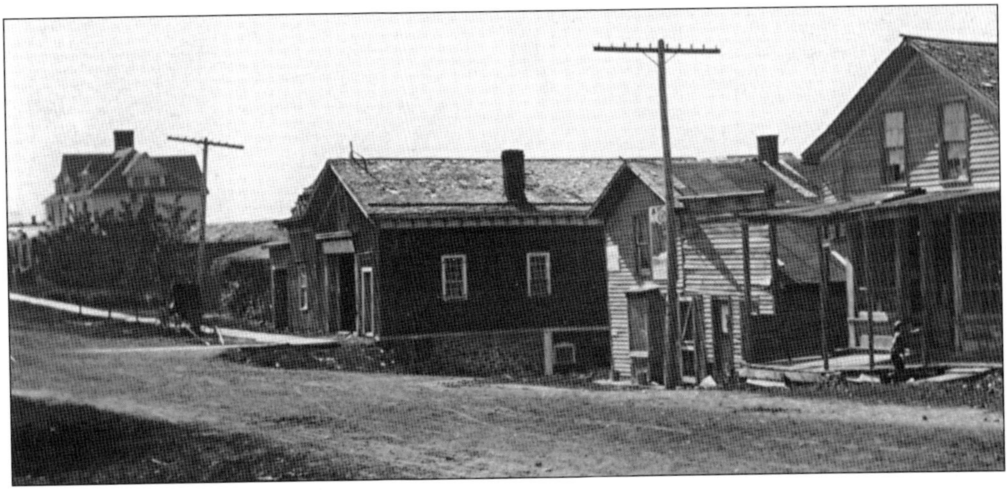

LIVERY HILL AND SOUTH MAIN STREET. The steep Livery Hill access to Depot Road—just north of the livery building that gave it its name—often closed in the winter to avoid the steep slope's treacherous travel and to become the village's favorite sledding hill. Notice the imposing Sutherland House in the distance above and hints of the building that much later became the Clarkston Conservatory of Music, while the buildings north of Depot Street, c. 1900, are less familiar and now long gone. The corner property belonged to J.W. Howe, but Oliver Smith, nicknamed "C.O.D." (Cash On Delivery) because of his business practices, ran a foundry and hardware in the back of the lot. In 1910, Howe sold the property to Henry Garter, who built the rusticated block Garter Building, opening the first of several hardware stores that initially filled the new building.

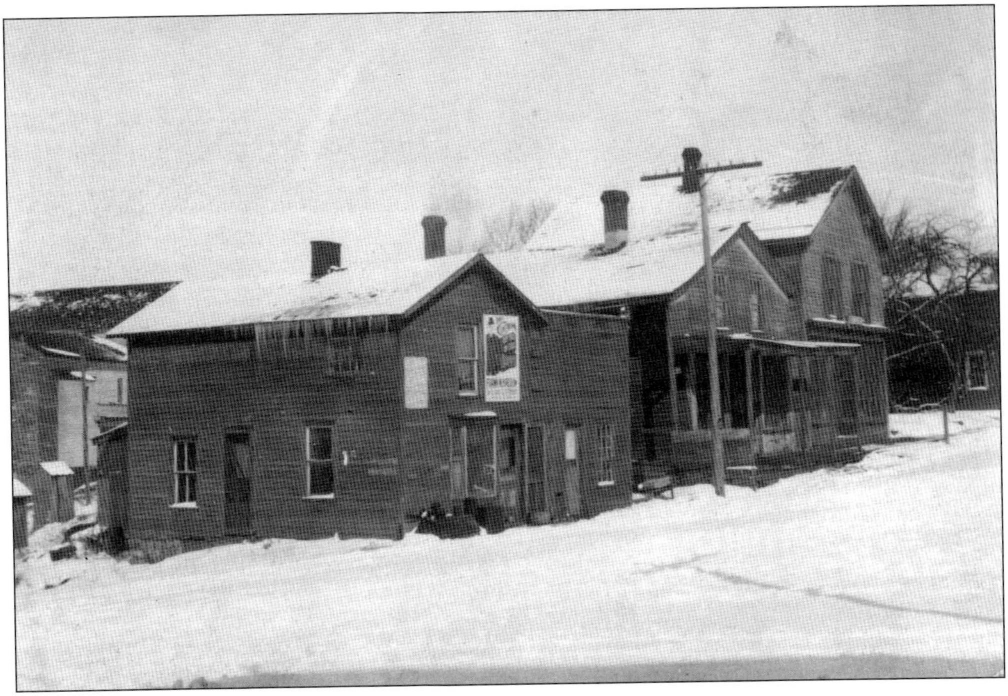

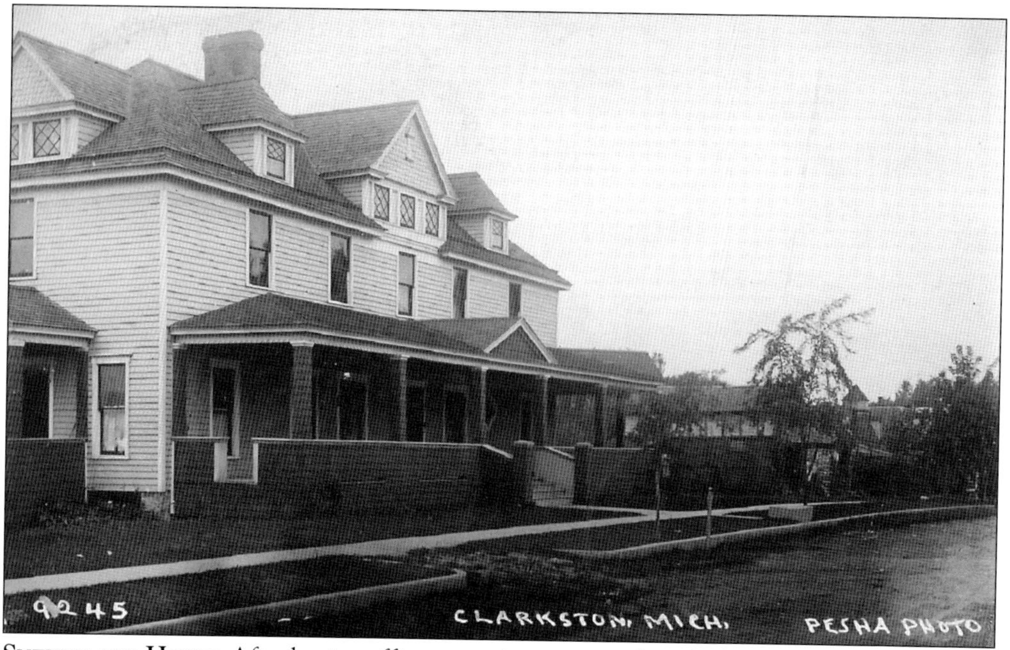

Sutherland House. After having offices at various spots within the business district, Dr. Clark Sutherland commissioned the large Queen Anne–style building at 59 South Main Street in 1903 to serve as his home and office. Even after his wife, Maude Rose, died, Dr. Sutherland continued to live in the home until his death in 1941. The home became apartments until the mid-1970s, when it briefly housed a boutique on the first floor and a basement restaurant, then returned to apartments within a decade.

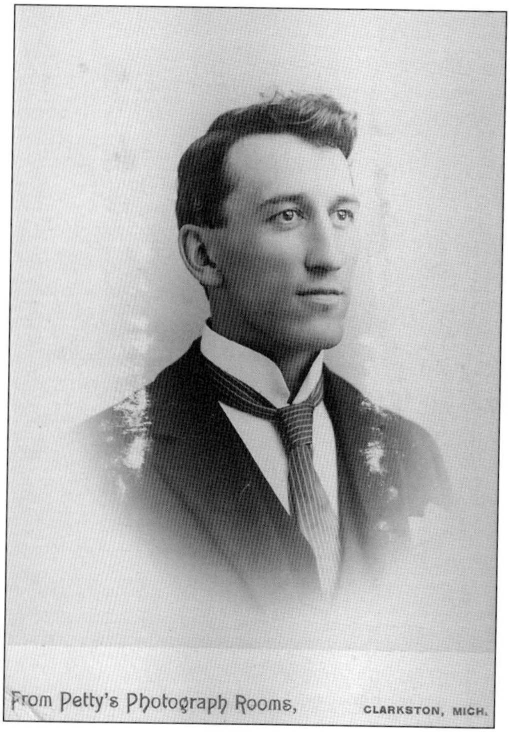

Dr. Clark Sutherland. Born in 1867, Dr. Clark Sutherland graduated from the University of Michigan medical program in 1891 and came to Clarkston to practice medicine with Dr. Charles Gray Robertson. The six-foot-four-inch Sutherland, a former football player at Michigan, created a lasting impression when he made house calls by horse and buggy, reportedly cutting wire fences to take shortcuts through fields. It is fitting that in 1906, Sutherland became the first person in Clarkston to own a car. In failing health for his final four years, Dr. Sutherland spent weeks at a time in bed. In the last year of his life, his guest log recorded 1,633 callers coming to visit the personable and well-liked doctor who cared for much of Clarkston. After nearly half a century of practice, Sutherland died on January 7, 1941.

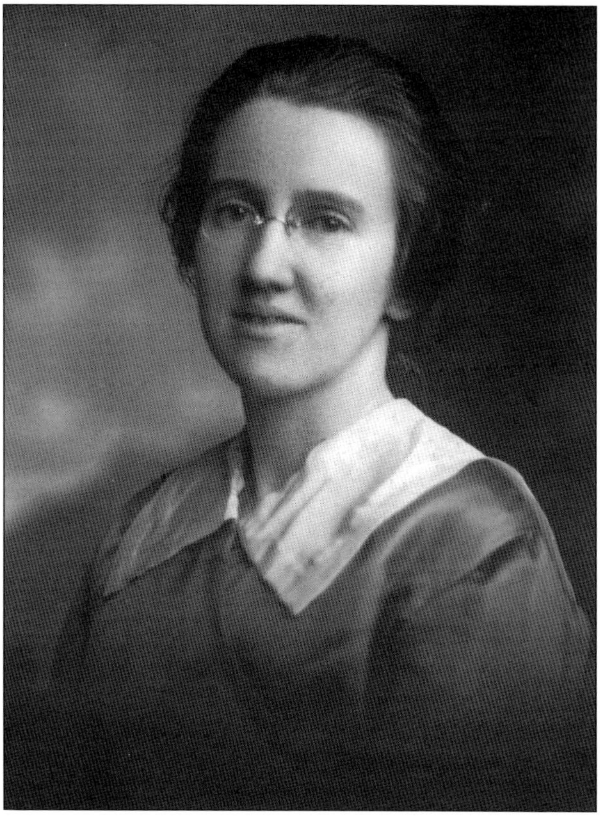

Ada Scrace. Ada Scrace worked alongside Dr. Clark Sutherland on and off for years, often acting as midwife, before she left Clarkston to work as a nurse in Goodrich. She later returned to care for her ailing sisters and eventually Dr. Sutherland himself until his death. Scrace went on to work at the post office for 15 years.

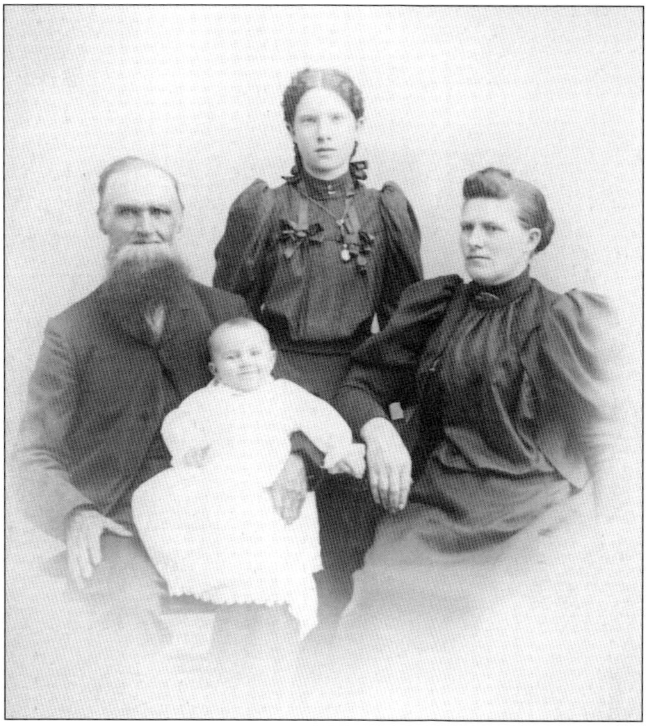

Grandma Green. At a time when most births took place at home, Mary Green opened and operated a licensed maternity home at 18 North Holcomb Street from 1922 to 1943. Known to many as "Grandma Green," she assisted in many Clarkston births. Pictured here from left to right are Green's husband, Rev. O.H.P. Green, infant son Arthur, daughter Ruth Gibbons Belitz, and Green.

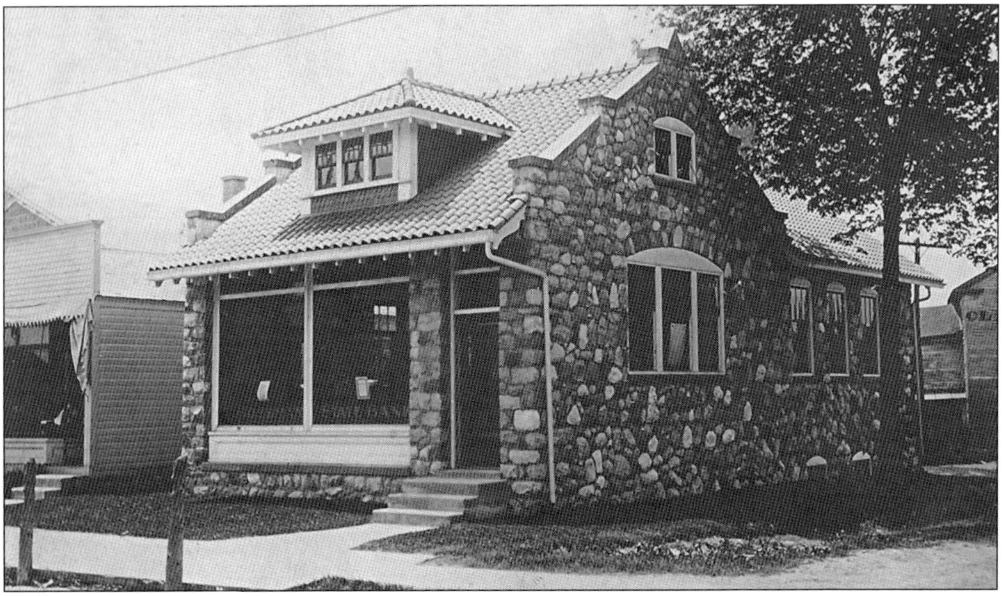

Jossman Bank, c. 1912. Esidore Jossman started Clarkston's first bank in the back of his Main Street store before moving into the new, cut-stone bank building at 15 South Main Street in 1910. Unfortunately, Jossman's nephew reportedly embezzled from the bank, sending it into ruin. Notice the hint of Clarkston Mills visible in the background at right.

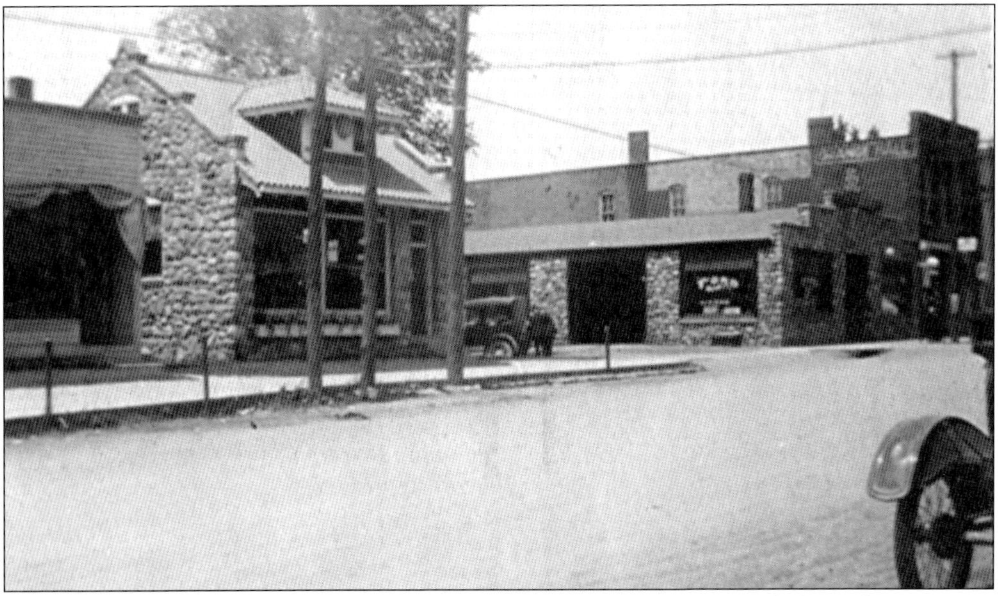

Clarkston State Bank, c. 1919. After Jossman Bank failed, a group of Clarkston businessmen organized the Clarkston State Bank in 1913. Subsequent banks filled the space until National Bank of Detroit closed its doors there in 1997. The following year, several local entrepreneurs again came together determined to bring a bank back to the building that had housed one for the better part of a century. The new Clarkston State Bank opened in January 1999 but closed that branch in 2015 and sold the building.

The Clarkston State Bank Condensed Statement, 1919. Numbers aside, the names on this condensed statement are an honor roll of prominent Clarkston businessmen and early families, including David Teggerdine, George King, Guy Walter, J.H. Alger, Washington Irish, Nelson W. Morgan, and others.

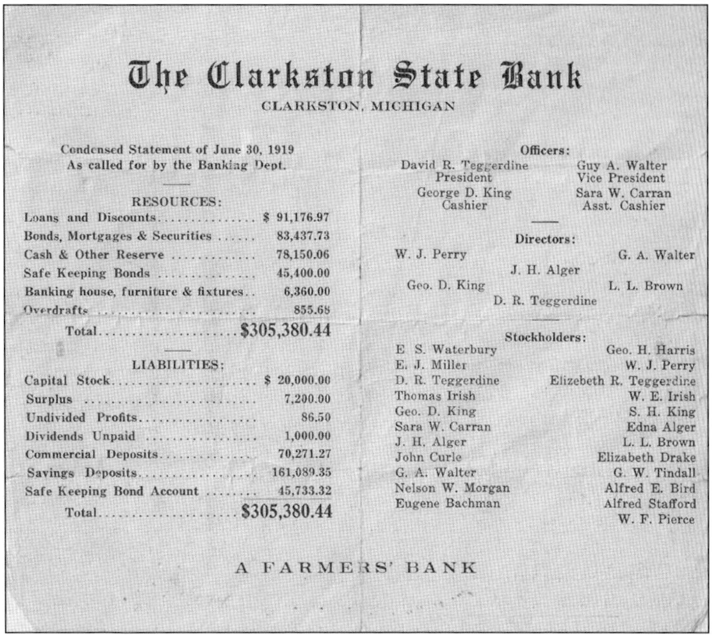

The Clarkston State Bank

CLARKSTON, MICHIGAN

Condensed Statement of June 30, 1919
As called for by the Banking Dept.

RESOURCES:

Loans and Discounts	$ 91,176.97
Bonds, Mortgages & Securities	83,437.73
Cash & Other Reserve	78,150.06
Safe Keeping Bonds	45,400.00
Banking house, furniture & fixtures	6,360.00
Overdrafts	855.68
Total	$305,380.44

LIABILITIES:

Capital Stock	$ 20,000.00
Surplus	7,200.00
Undivided Profits	86.50
Dividends Unpaid	1,000.00
Commercial Deposits	70,271.27
Savings Deposits	161,089.35
Safe Keeping Bond Account	45,733.32
Total	$305,380.44

Officers:

David R. Teggerdine, President
Guy A. Walter, Vice President
George D. King, Cashier
Sara W. Carran, Asst. Cashier

Directors:

W. J. Perry
G. A. Walter
J. H. Alger
Geo. D. King
L. L. Brown
D. R. Teggerdine

Stockholders:

E. S. Waterbury
Geo. H. Harris
E. J. Miller
W. J. Perry
D. R. Teggerdine
Elizebeth R. Teggerdine
Thomas Irish
W. E. Irish
Geo. D. King
S. H. King
Sara W. Carran
Edna Alger
J. H. Alger
L. L. Brown
John Curle
Elizabeth Drake
G. A. Walter
G. W. Tindall
Nelson W. Morgan
Alfred E. Bird
Eugene Bachman
Alfred Stafford
W. F. Pierce

A FARMERS' BANK

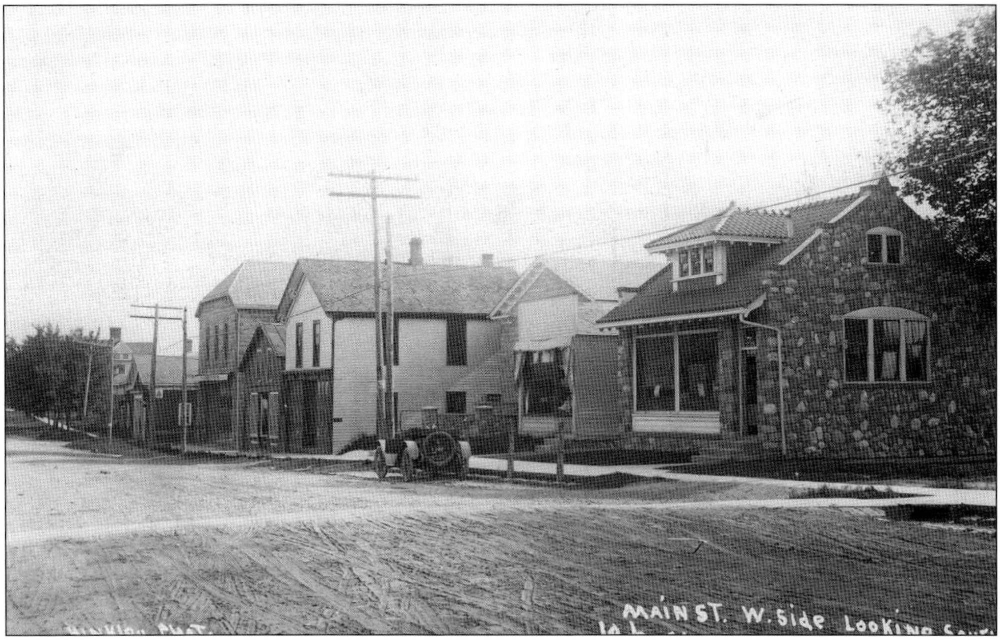

The Bank Robbery. On July 16, 1932, two young robbers held up the Clarkston State Bank. A chase ensued, but the robbers escaped with $5,000, disappearing entirely until early November, when police followed up on a Lapeer boy's tip. While police recovered the bulk of the money in the end, a robber and two police officers died. The magazine *Real Detective* covered the story with great fanfare in its March 1937 issue.

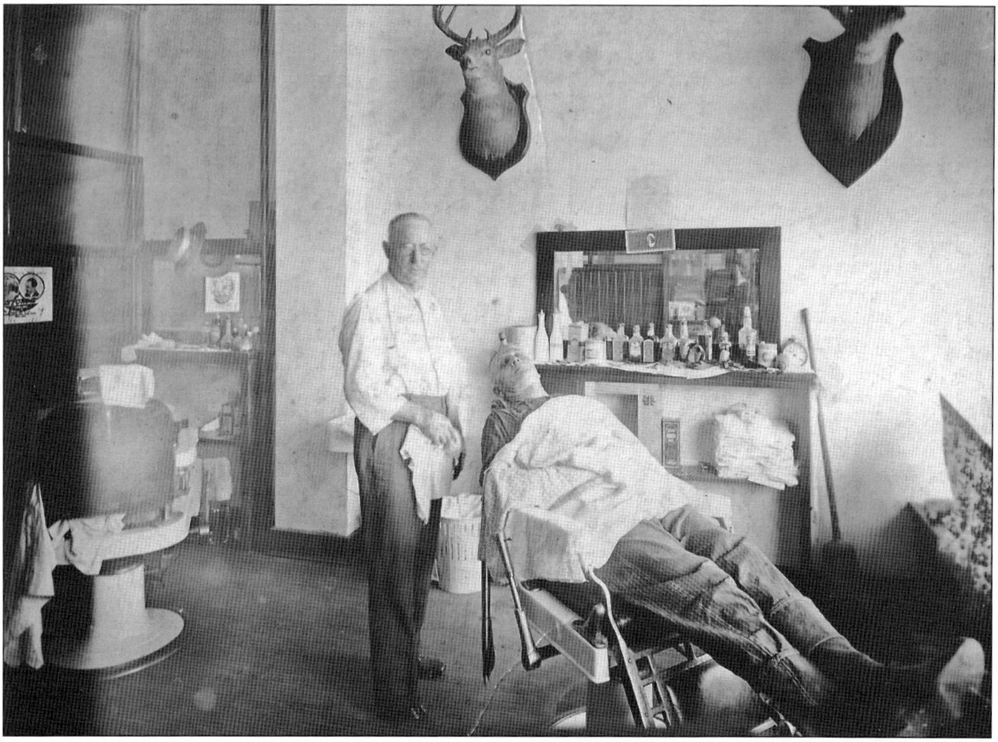

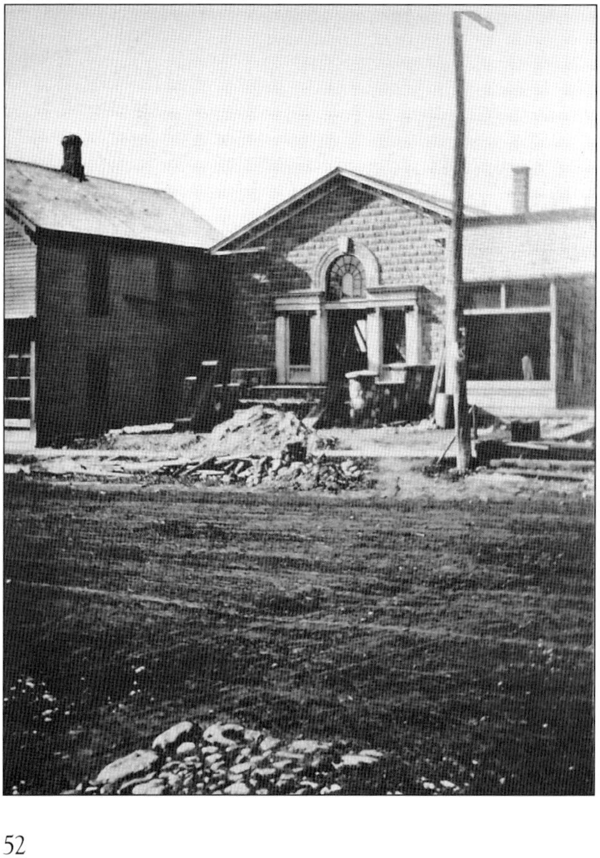

Jake Gulick's Barbershop, 1910. Saturdays were barber Jake Gulick's busiest days at his 19 South Main Street barbershop, when many of the farmers and their families would come into town for groceries, errands, and socializing. In 1921, Gulick traded his barber implements for a fishing pole, selling the business to Harvey "Dude" DeMond. On December 6, 1925, DeMond moved the barbershop, then sandwiched between the bank and township hall, out of town, enabling the bank to expand.

Township Hall, c. 1914. Built in 1914, the rusticated concrete block structure at 21 South Main Street started as Independence Township Hall. It later became Clarkston Village Hall and then the Clarkston branch of the US Post Office in 1942, helmed by well-loved postmistress Elizabeth Ronk, who held the post from 1936 to 1970.

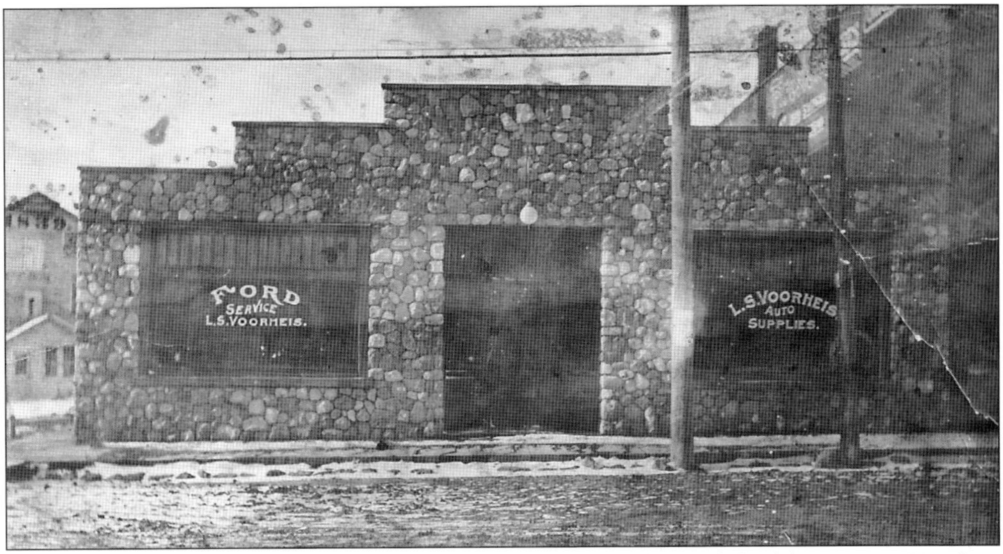

VOORHEIS FORD, C. 1915. Five years after construction of the bank building, Lewis Voorheis built L.S. Voorheis Ford Service and Auto Supply. Voorheis sold the building and dealership to Frank Leonard and Ben Miller in 1919. They operated there until 1934, when a Pontiac and Buick dealership followed until World War II. This building is best known as the final location of Rudy's Market years later. Note the mill building peeking out at the end of Mill Street at left.

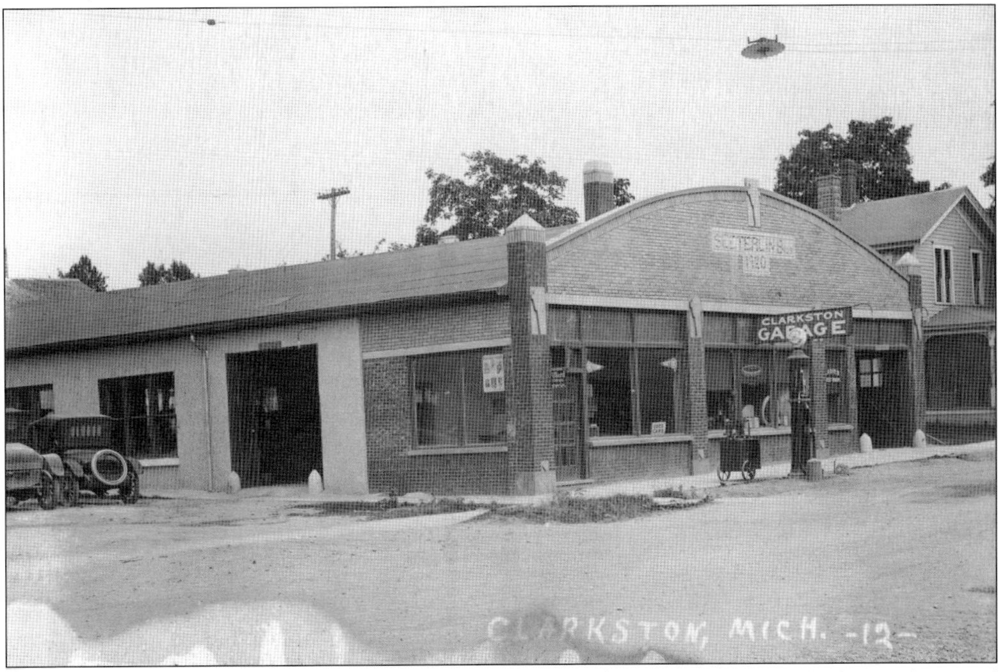

SEETERLIN BROTHERS AUTOMOTIVE. Once the site of Frank Yeager's blacksmith shop, Edwin and Joseph Seeterlin built this garage on the southeast corner of South Main and Church Streets in 1919 to house Seeterlin Brothers Chevrolet Sales and Service. The building became home to Clarkston Garage when the Seeterlins moved across the street to 3 East Church Street. Notice the house to the right of the garage building; movers relocated the Victorian-style home to 6129 South Main Street to make way for an addition to the garage.

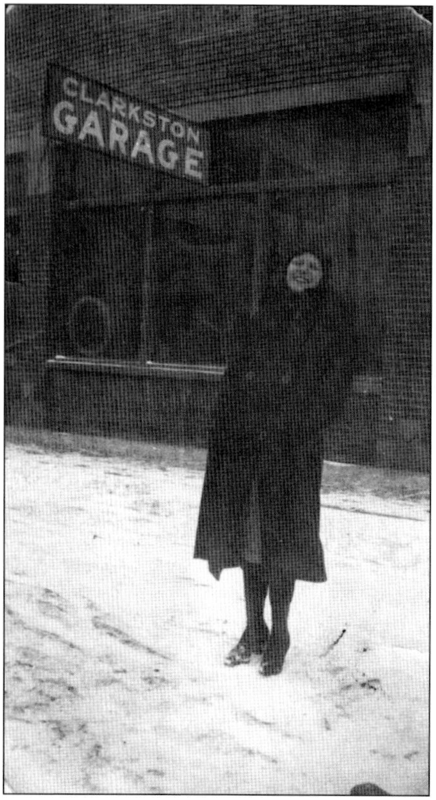

Clarkston Garage. A woman smiles as she stands near the sign for Clarkston Garage.

Beattie Brothers Ford Sales and Service, 1927. This image of Beattie Motor Sales shows the addition that came once the house next door moved. Sadly, a 1943 explosion and fire destroyed this interesting building. Beattie rebuilt his business on Dixie Highway at Andersonville Road, while another dealership, Bill Spence Rambler, rebuilt on this site, later the home of Haupt Bump Shop.

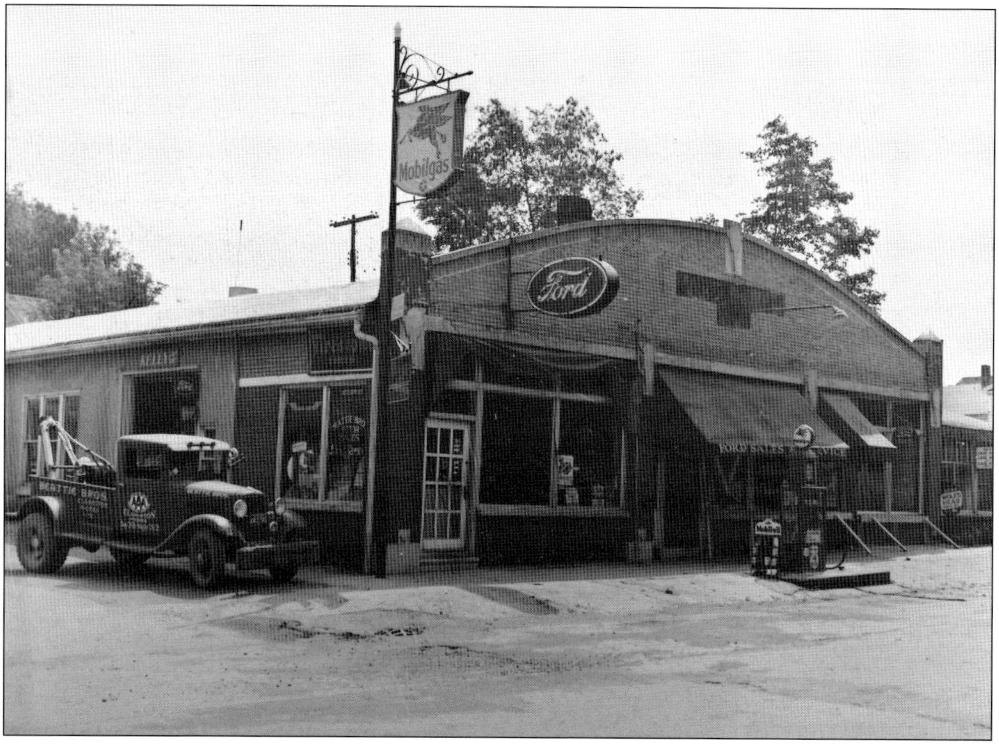

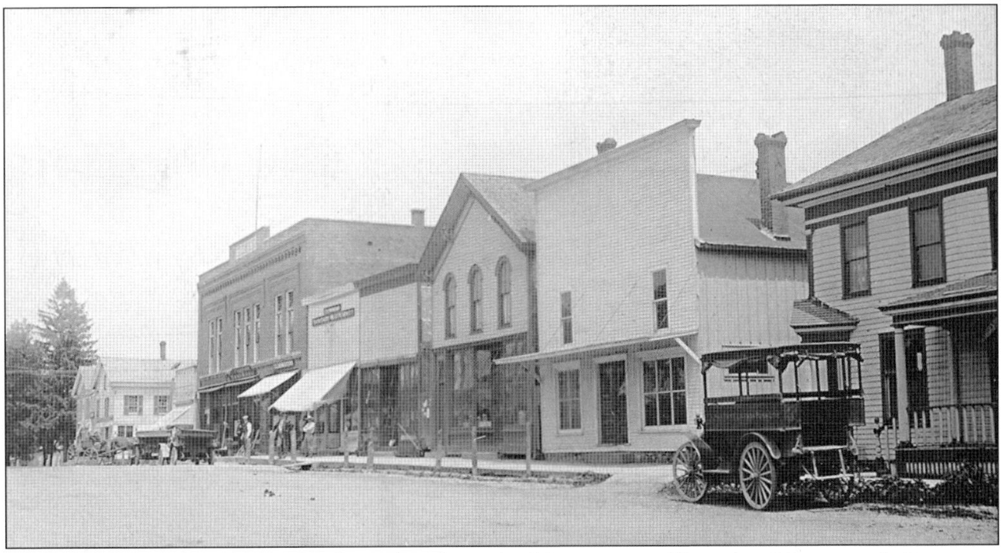

Dry Goods, c. 1910. The gabled wooden-frame building pictured here was Hammond's Groceries & Drugs before it became Frank Dunston's meat market in 1924. The building to the right is Hubble & Hopkins Pool Room. Notice the Skarritt coach parked in front of the Johnson House hotel building.

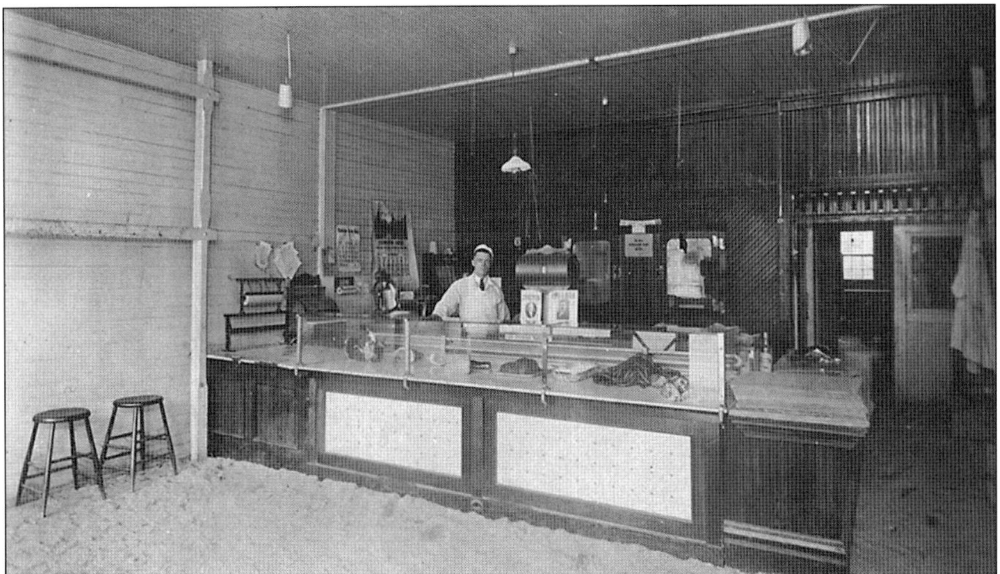

Crosby and Teggerdine's Meat Market, 1922. Crosby and Teggerdine's Meat Market occupied 12 South Main Street. Notice the sawdust floor and the large scale in the center of the counter.

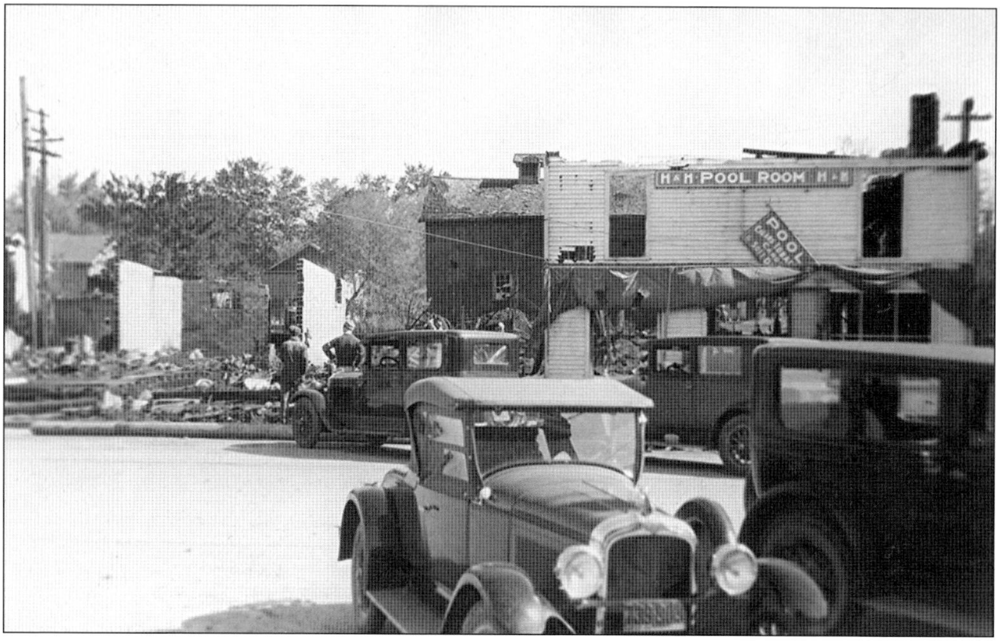

The 1927 Fire. In October 1927, a fire swept through the east side of South Main Street, destroying the four 1880s-era wooden frame storefronts that made up 12–18 South Main Street, including Frank Dunston's meat market and Hubble & Hopkins Pool Room. Townspeople formed a bucket brigade to extinguish the fire, which finally stopped before reaching the nearby Terrace Building, formerly the Johnson House, which survived in part because the small alleyway separating the buildings proved to be enough to prevent the flames from reaching it.

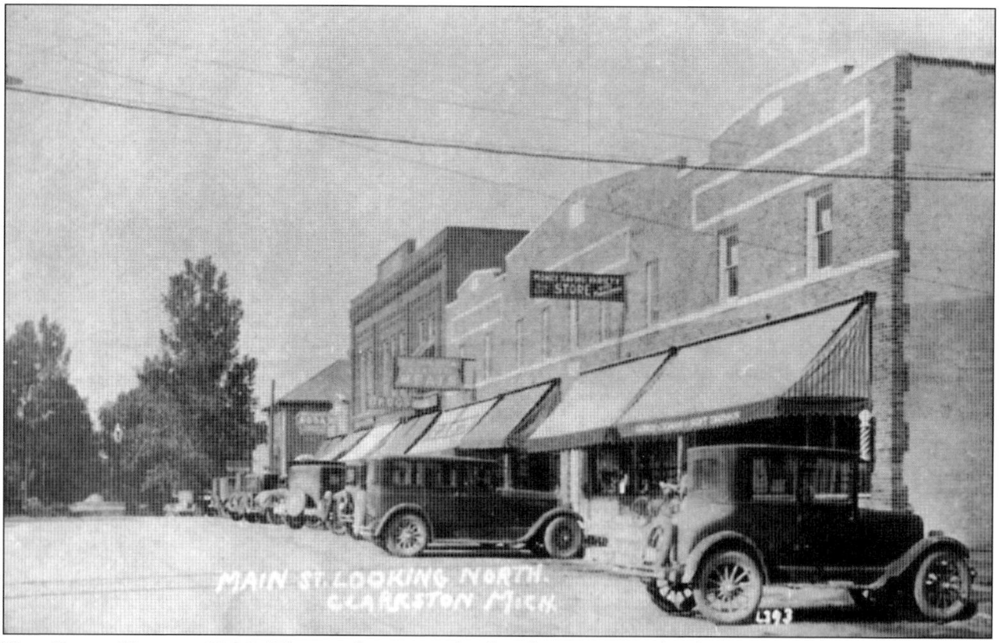

The Brick Block, 1929. The poolroom and other businesses rebuilt in 1928, constructing what became known as the Brick Block, named after the new building's distinctive yellow brickwork. The building's four separate storefronts stretch from 12 to 18 South Main Street.

Three

Henry Ford's Clarkston Connection

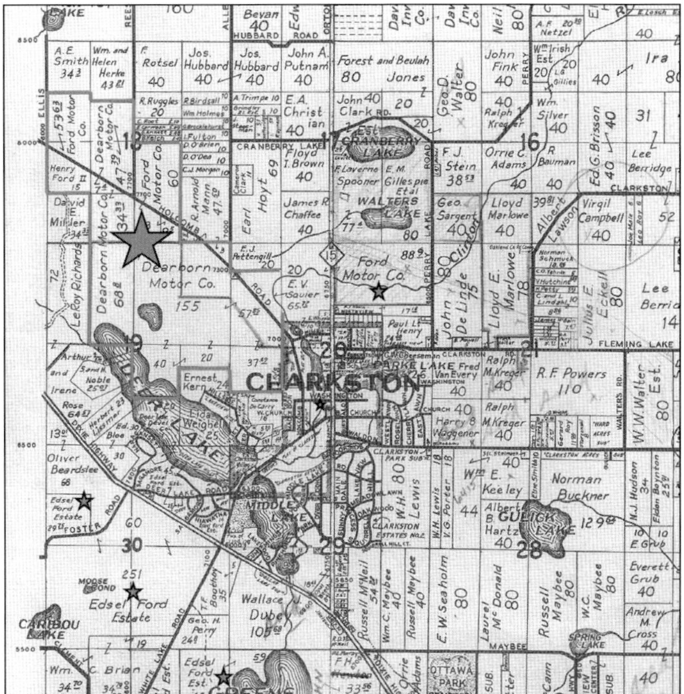

Ford Country. This 1947 map suggests how much land Ford and Ford Motor Company occupied in and around Clarkston. The largest star and outline denotes the property known as Deer Lake Hills Farms, which Dearborn Motor Company used as a Ford tractor and implement-training facility. Note that it lists both Ford Motor Company and Henry Ford II. The smallest star marks the location of Ford's village factory in the center of Clarkston. The other stars mark additional Ford property. Missing is 90 North Main Street, which Ford Motor Company had closed by then.

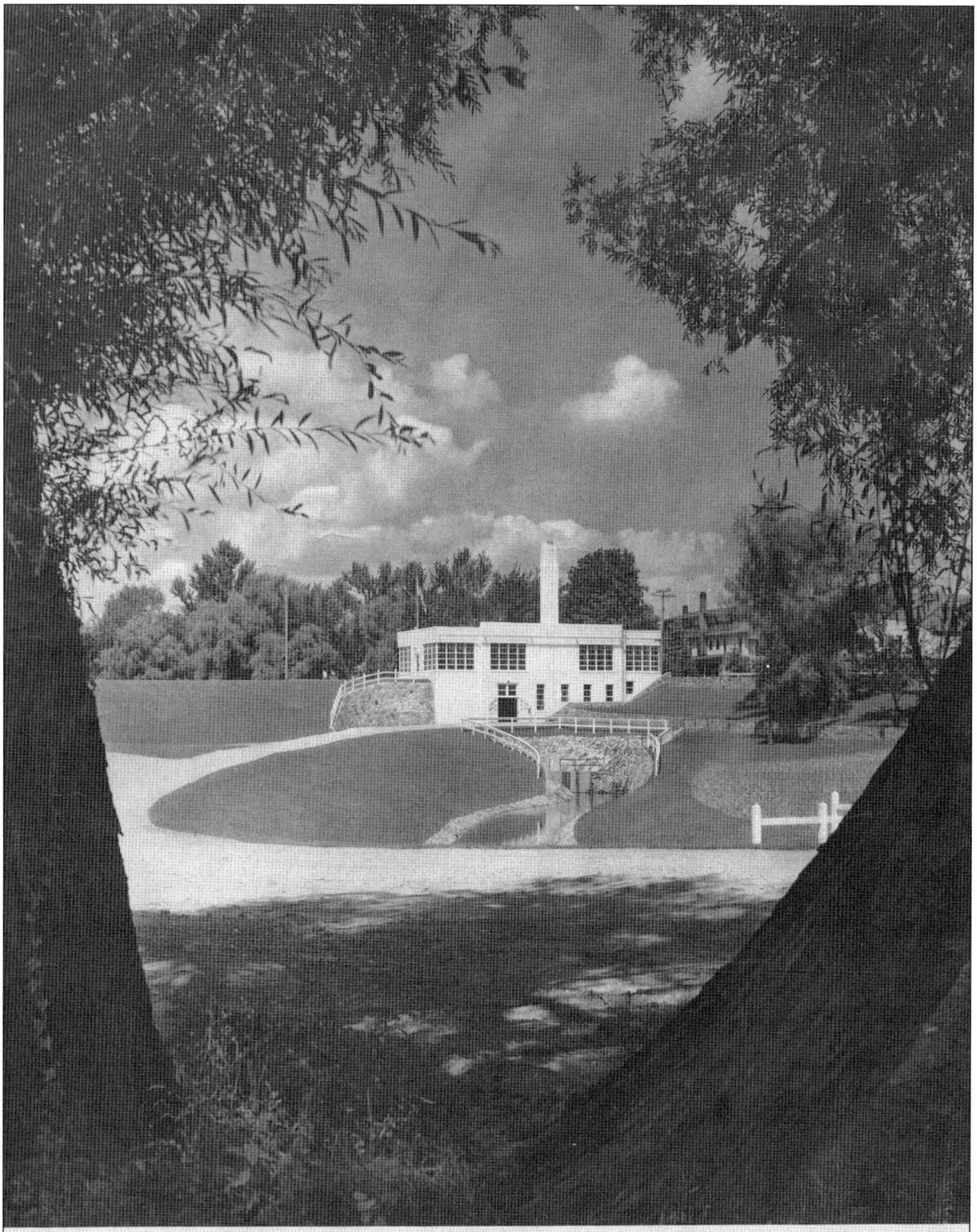

The Village Industries program, begun 25 years ago by Henry Ford, is typified by this plant at Clarkston, Michigan. Most employees of the 18 Ford Village Industries live on small farms. Thus the Ford philosophy—"One foot on the soil and the other in industry," becomes an actuality.

FORD'S VILLAGE INDUSTRIES PROGRAM. Henry Ford saw in Clarkston an opportunity to expand his Village Industries program. With the philosophy "one foot on the soil and the other in industry," Ford envisioned opportunities to gain a workforce without causing people to resettle in the city, far from the countryside, their farms, homes, and families.

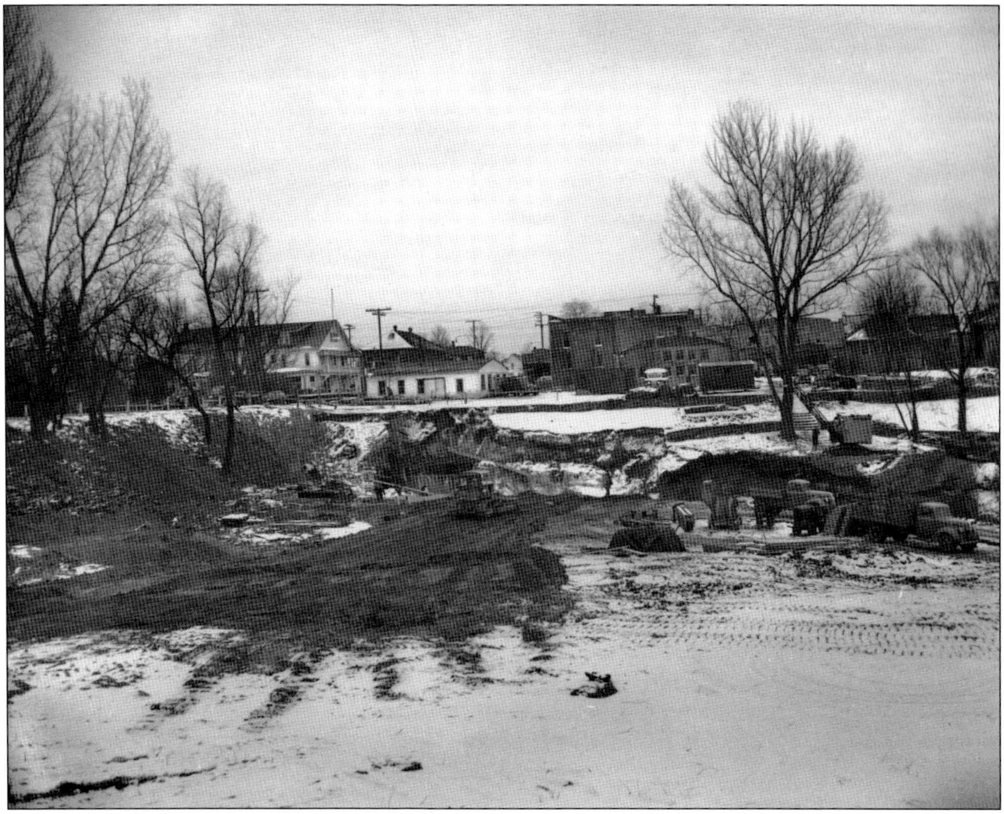

Building the Hydropower Plant. Clarkston offered ample opportunity for Ford to explore hydroelectric power on the former property of the Clarkston Mills, demolished in 1917. The empty lot provided a blank canvas for Ford to build his factory on Washington Street in 1941. (Courtesy of the Collections of The Henry Ford.)

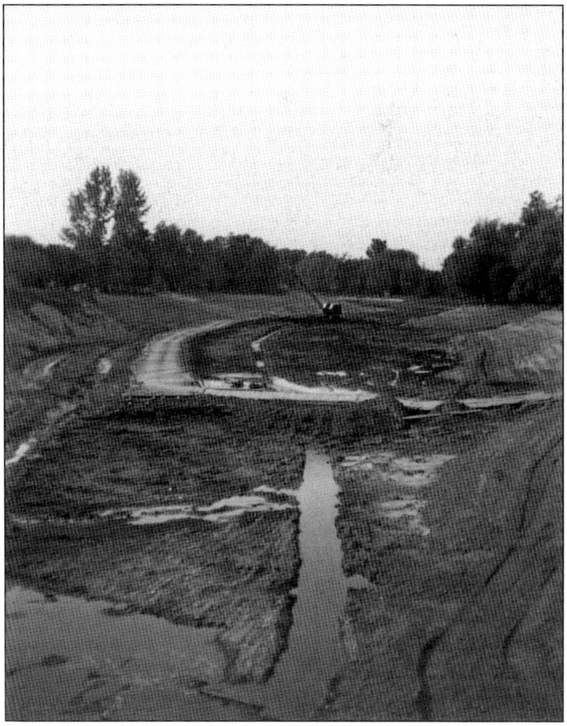

The Dam Break. Residents opposed Henry Ford's request to empty the Mill Pond in order to more efficiently rebuild a modernized dam, so instead he resorted to building a cofferdam. Heavy rains on April 20, 1941, proved too much for the temporary dam, and a 60-foot-wide break caused the Mill Pond to burst through, washing out the cofferdam's construction and draining the pond onto Depot Road. Some locals suspected the dam break was anything but accidental, and that Ford emptied the pond intentionally.

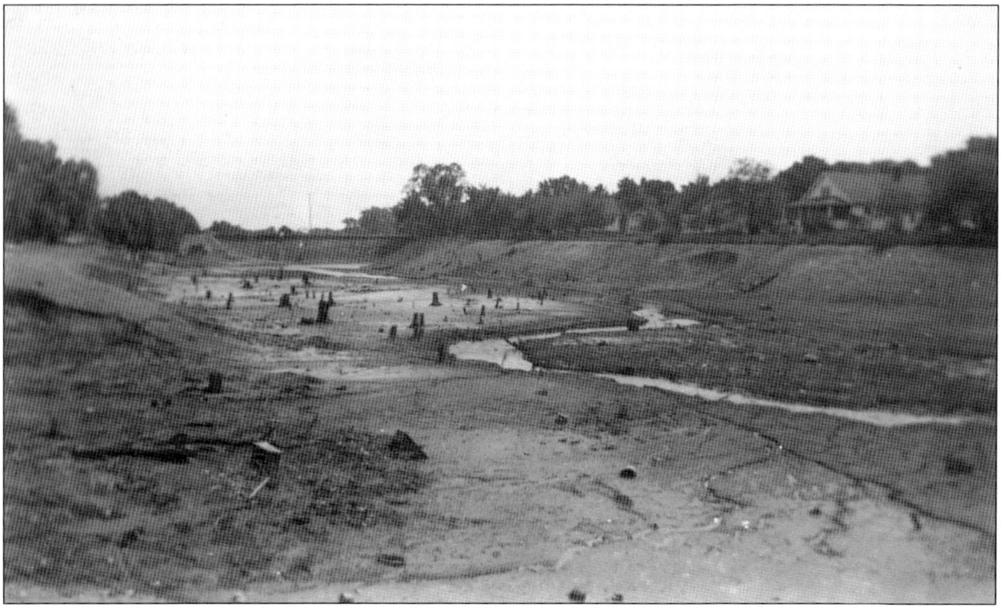

The Empty Mill Pond. Once the pond emptied, locals crowded the shoreline to see what the Mill Pond collected through the years—a buggy, old sleighs, a coal stove, and wagon wheels. Ford brought in 20 new Ford trucks to remove loads of dirt and stumps from the bottom of the pond, offering the nutrient-rich silt to feed local gardens and lawns. Then, Ford was able to rebuild the dam to his specifications, and it was up and running by mid-summer, allowing the pond to refill. Rain that autumn completed the job quicker than anyone imagined. The bungalow-style cottage visible on the shore at right is 22 North Holcomb Road.

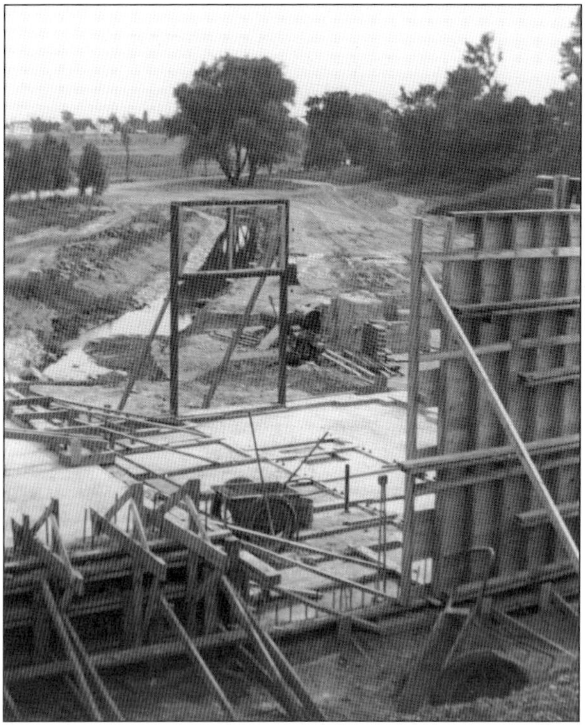

The Factory Grows. Ford's factory begins to take shape on West Washington Street. Depot Road is in the distance, near the trees. (Courtesy of the Collections of The Henry Ford.)

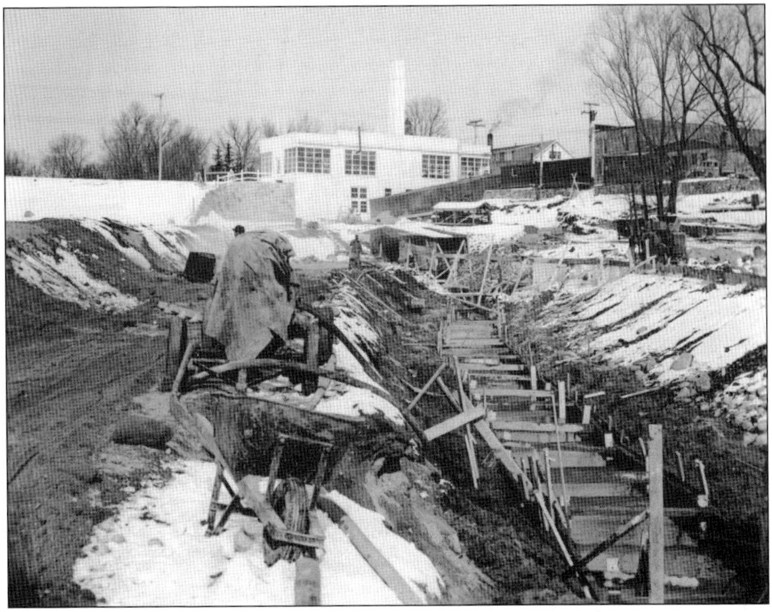

Dredging a Raceway. While the factory waits patiently, workers dredge a raceway to enable water to flow under the building, continuing toward and then beyond Depot Road. (Courtesy of the Collections of The Henry Ford.)

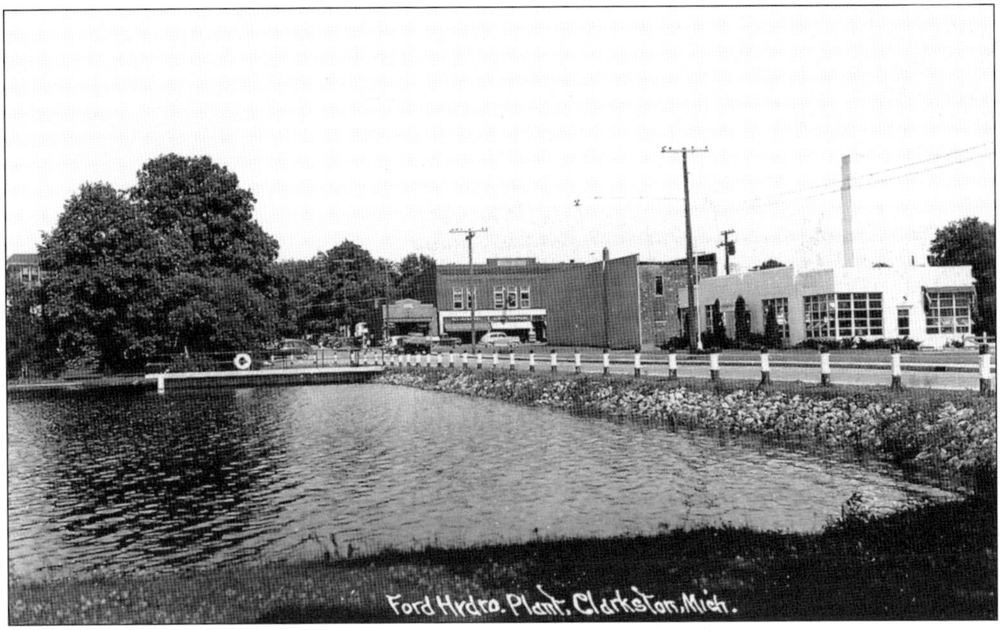

Ford Hydroelectric Plant. The plant only operated for a decade. Its waterpower was not as abundant as Ford had hoped, relying on electricity most of the time. Legend has it that the factory manager would turn the power from electric to hydro whenever Ford was in town, so Ford could see the moving wheel through the factory's large windows if he happened to drive by, ensuring job security for the factory's workers. After Ford, the building underwent extensive renovations and additions, first to become Hawke Tool Company, and then in the late 1970s to become a 22,000-square-foot retail complex known as the Clarkston Mills mall.

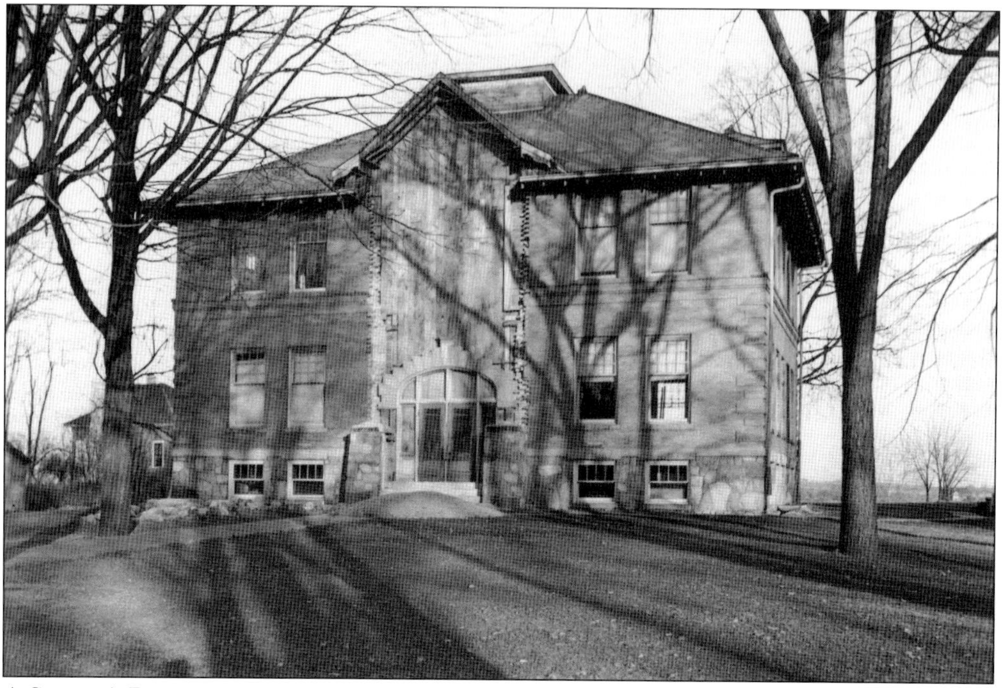

A SCHOOL'S REUSE, 90 NORTH MAIN STREET RENOVATIONS. After standing vacant for years, the old Clarkston School became available for purchase in 1938. Several locals bid on the boxy brick structure, including a local doctor who hoped to reuse it as a hospital and home, and someone who wanted to convert it into a private residence. Washington "Wash" Irish, former 26-year Independence Township supervisor who happened to live across the street in the Clark House, made the winning bid. Irish planned to convert the building into apartments, but he died the next year at age 83 before seeing the work completed. In 1940, Henry Ford purchased the property from Irish's estate with the mind to transform it into a manufacturing plant. Ford opted to simplify and modernize the building by removing its domed belvedere and decorative frontispiece and adding a vestibule. (Courtesy of the Collections of The Henry Ford.)

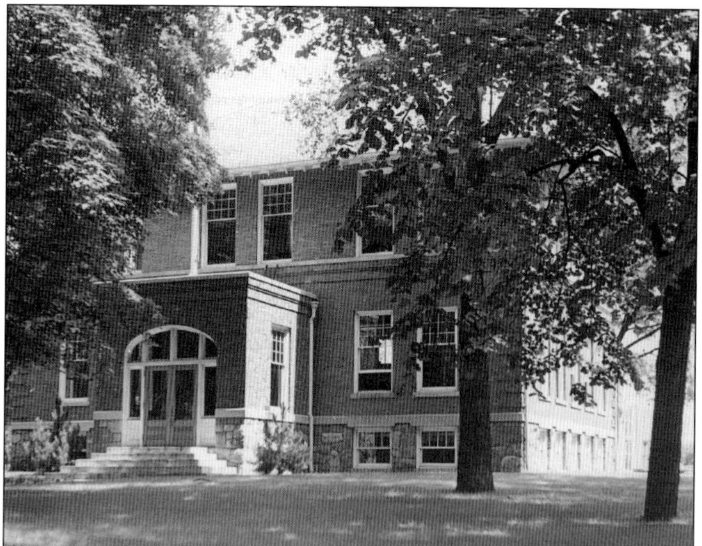

Men at Work. Although Ford initially planned 90 North Main Street to be a trade school, when the war broke out, he opted to use it as a factory that could help the war effort, possibly by sewing parachutes. Ford's manufacturing plant there primarily sewed upholstered seat cushions and straps for both military and civilian vehicles. (Courtesy of the Collections of The Henry Ford.)

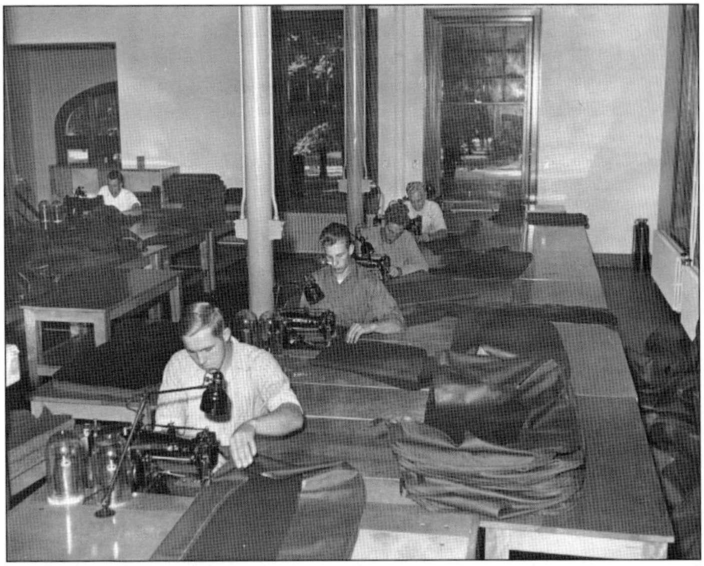

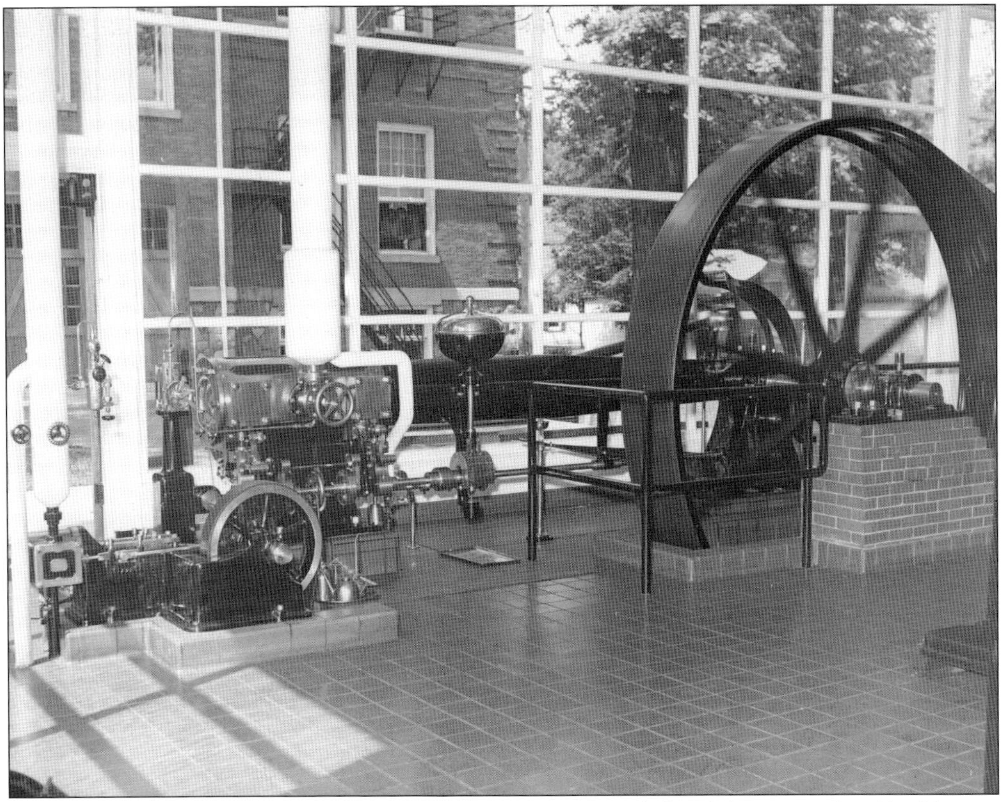

The Power Building. Ford Motor Company built the annex behind the main school building to house a power plant, helping to produce valuable waterpower from Parke Lake. The plant's wall of windows offered a view of the steam engine that powered the small factory, which only operated for several years. In 1959, the company deeded the property back to Independence Township to use as a community center. After many years as township hall, the buildings became headquarters to Union AdWorks advertising agency. (Courtesy of the Collections of The Henry Ford.)

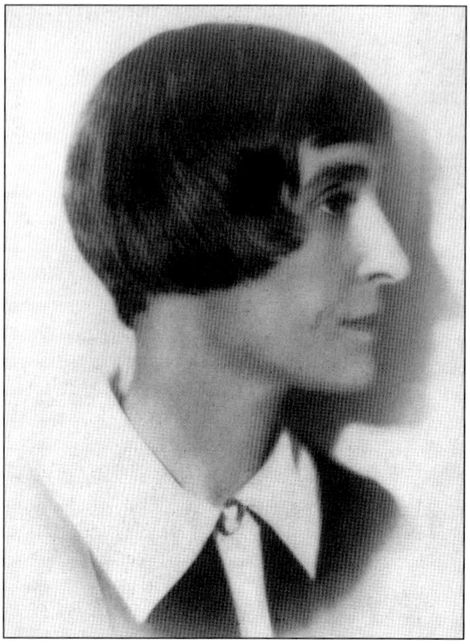

Fanny Irish. On a visit not long after he purchased 90 North Main Street, Henry Ford reportedly found Wash Irish's daughter Fanny on a ladder touching up the paint on the property's small house. When Ford inquired why—as her family did not own it any longer—she responded that she was certain Ford would not want anything associated with his name to look rundown. Ford reportedly appreciated Irish's can-do attitude, so he put her on the payroll as caretaker of the property with the condition that she hired jobs out. He also allowed her to stay on in the small building, sparing it from demolition. When Ford asked if she would have any use for a car, Irish explained that the only car she had ever driven was a Model A, which Ford Motor Company no longer made. It took six months, but under direct orders from Ford himself, an employee was able to gather enough parts to build a 1930 Ford, especially for Fanny Irish, in 1942.

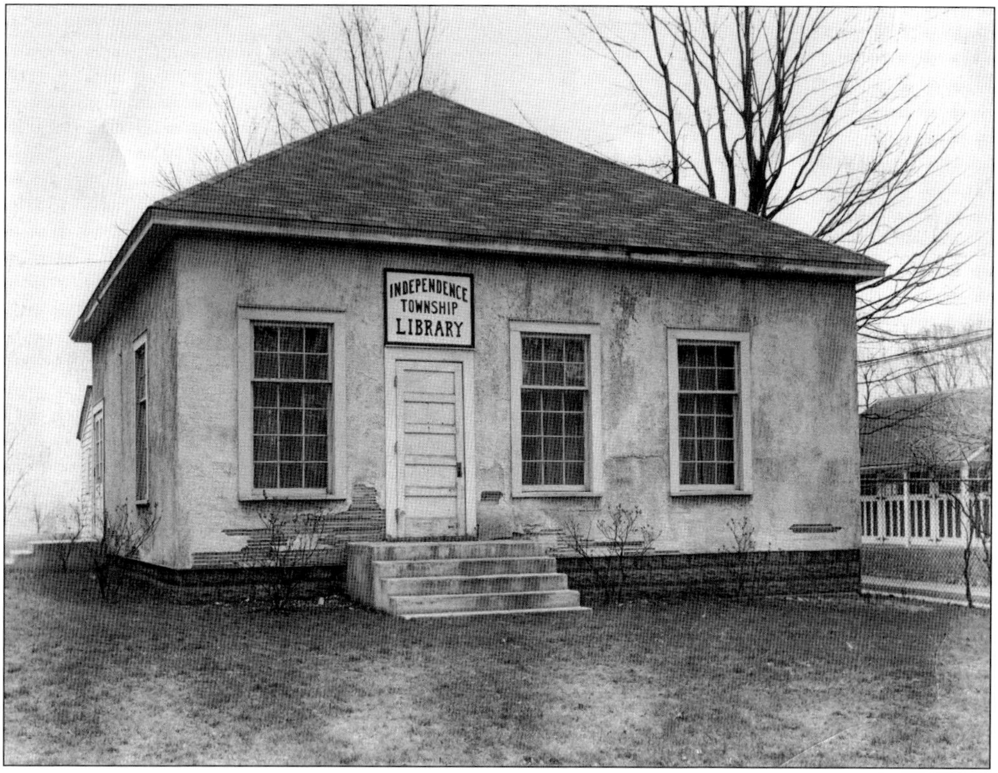

The Library, c. 1955. Built in 1925, the small squarish structure next to 90 North Main Street housed school directors before the Irish family. In 1955, it became Clarkston's first library, with a collection of 500 books. Esther Smith was the librarian, and the institution boasted 3,000 books by 1957. It later served as an Oakland County sheriff substation before undergoing renovations to serve as headquarters for Union Joints, a local independent restaurant group. (Courtesy of the Clarkston Independence District Library.)

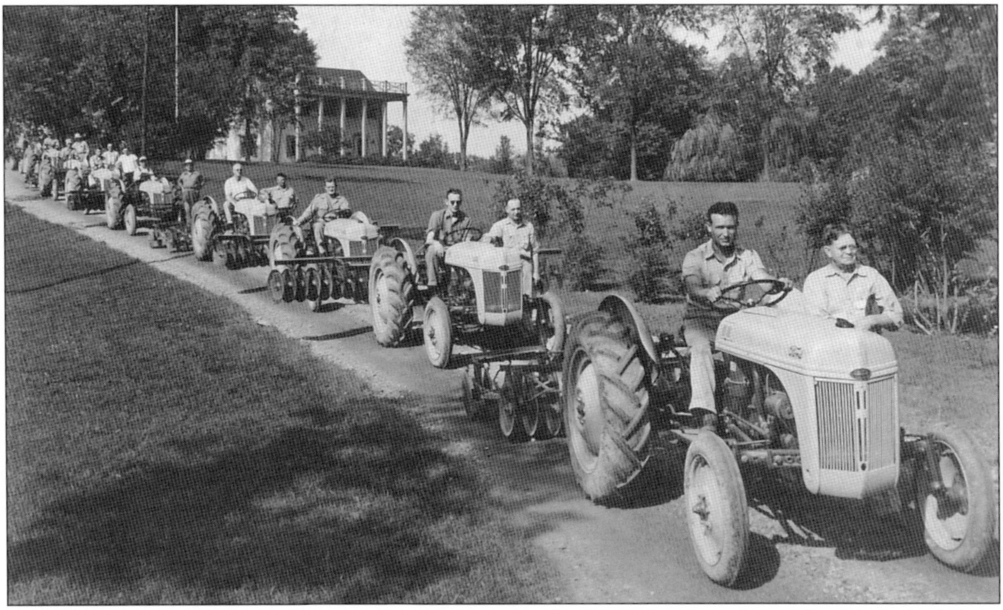

Deer Lake Hills Farm. In 1935, Henry Ford purchased a 500-acre farm that stretched from Holcomb Road to Deer Lake to use as a summer residence. Many say that Ford bought the house around the time of the Lindbergh kidnapping because he felt protected on the secluded property. Ford's wife, Clara, supposedly was less enamored with the farm, so the property became a training facility for Dearborn Motors, the company that ran Ford Tractor and Dearborn Farm Equipment.

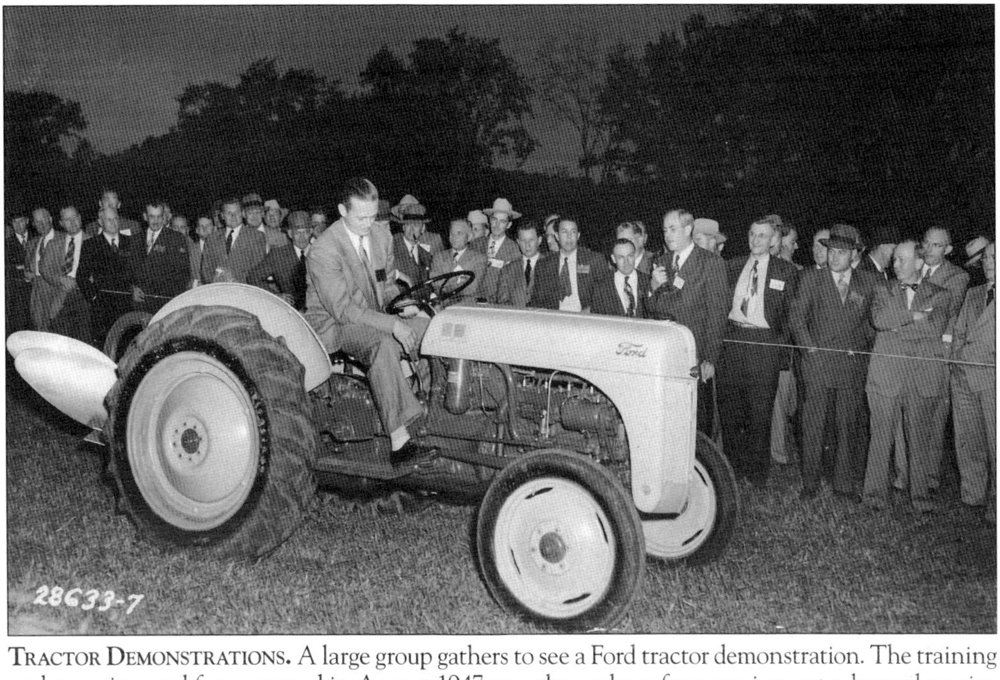

Tractor Demonstrations. A large group gathers to see a Ford tractor demonstration. The training and experimental farm opened in August 1947 as a place where farm equipment sales and service personnel could learn about, test, and demonstrate the latest in tractors and farm implements. During its run, Deer Lake Hills Farm hosted thousands of people from around the world.

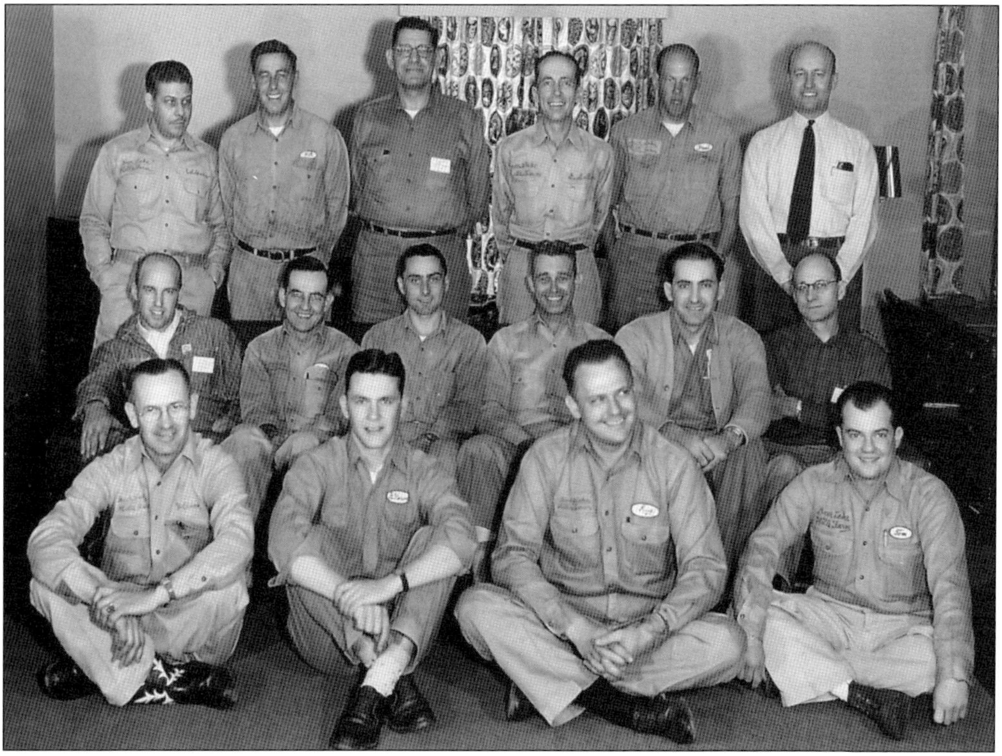

The Facilitators. Staff took care of visitors who came to Deer Lake Hills Farm, housing them semi-dormitory style in what was called the manor house and serving large homemade meals on-site three times a day. In 1962, the tractor division relocated to Georgia for year-round training.

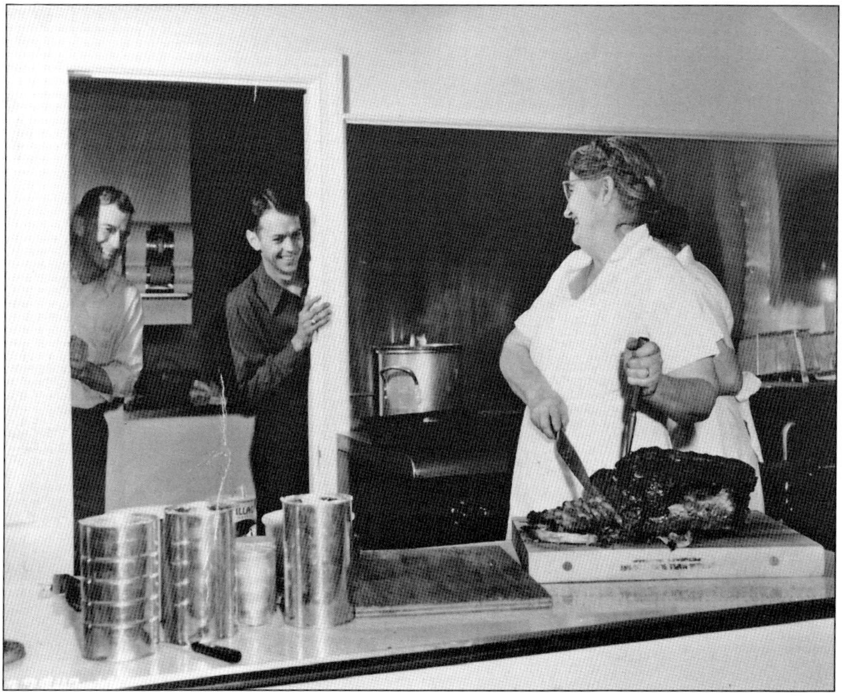

Four

Greater Clarkston's Farming Roots

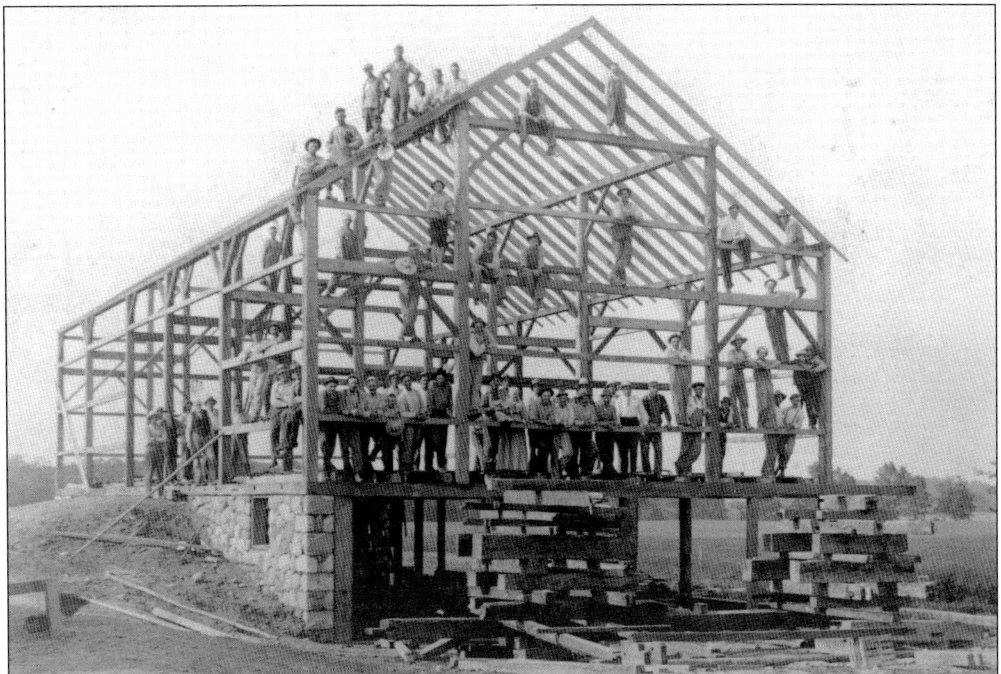

Morgan Barn Raising, June 1915. Though initially considered poor land for farming, the area's soil proved fruitful for many of the early settlers, including Clarkston namesake Jeremiah Clark III, who settled on a farm just outside of town. This image captures the community coming together to build a barn, in this case one belonging to Nelson Morgan.

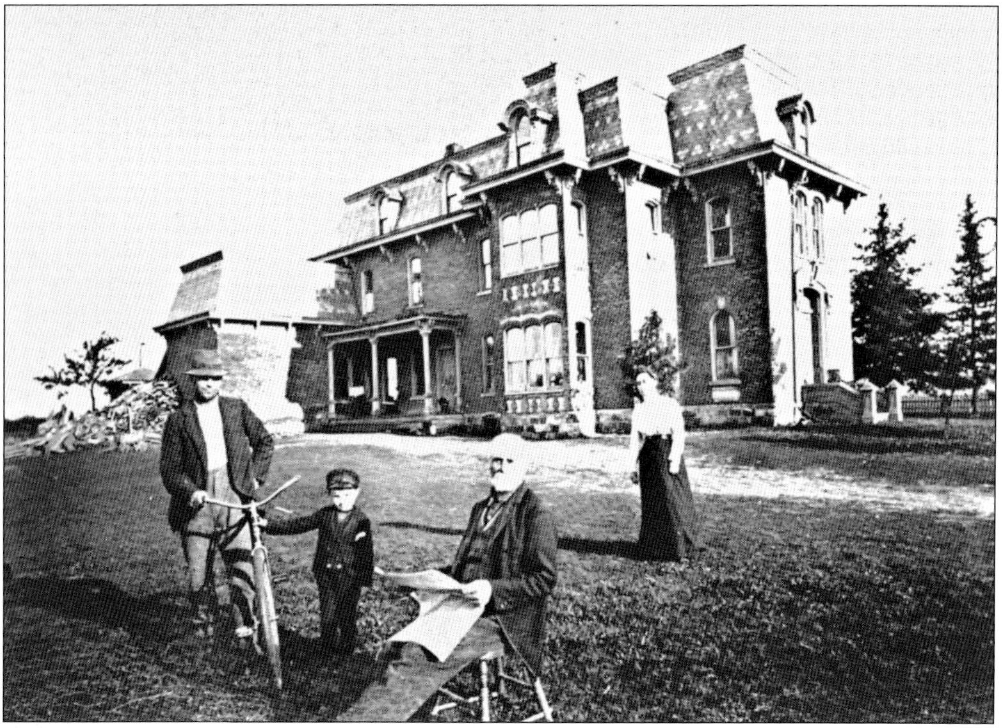

The Miller Farm. Samuel Miller came to Michigan from New York as a boy with his family in 1835. He long recalled the hub-deep mud making the trek north of Pontiac so challenging that they had to do much of it on foot. In 1877, Miller (seated) built this 19-room brick house on the corner of Davisburg and Bridge Lake Roads for $6,500. There he raised wheat and other crops, as well as sheep and hogs, though the 650-acre farm's main focus was as a dairy. (Courtesy of Sharlene Miller.)

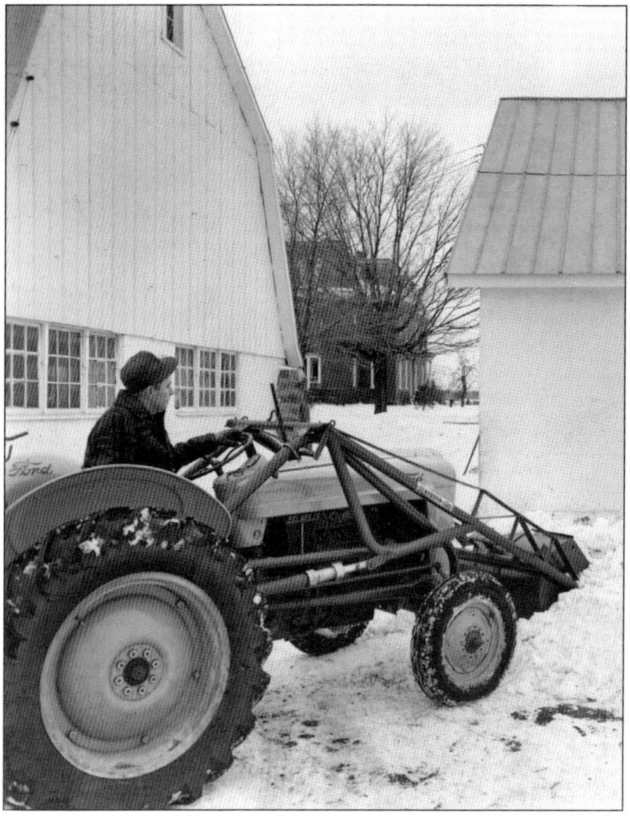

Sam Miller, c. 1955. Farmer Sam Miller, grandson of Samuel Miller, uses a tractor and power loader to clear snow from the Miller property. This image and several others ran in *Better Farming* magazine in February 1955. (Courtesy of Sharlene Miller.)

STORING HAY AT THE MAYBEE FARM. John and Malinda Maybee came to Independence Township in 1828, establishing their 240-acre family farm that would continue on through several generations, including their son Jesse and his wife, Martha; their grandson John Maybee, who grew beans and potatoes; and finally James Russell Maybee and his family.

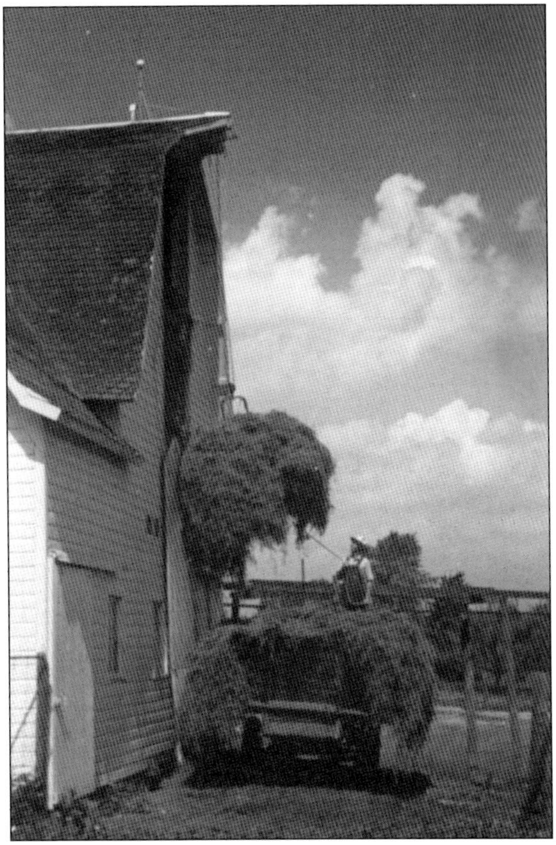

ICE CUTTERS, JANUARY 1911. Two men cut ice on the Maybee family farm on what is now Maybee Road.

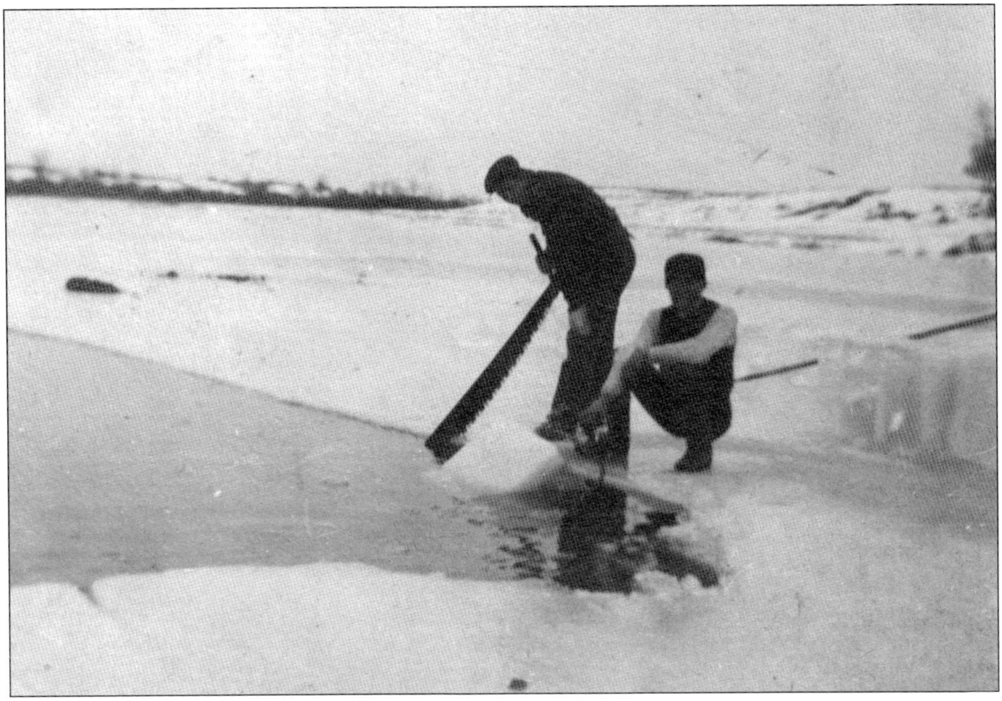

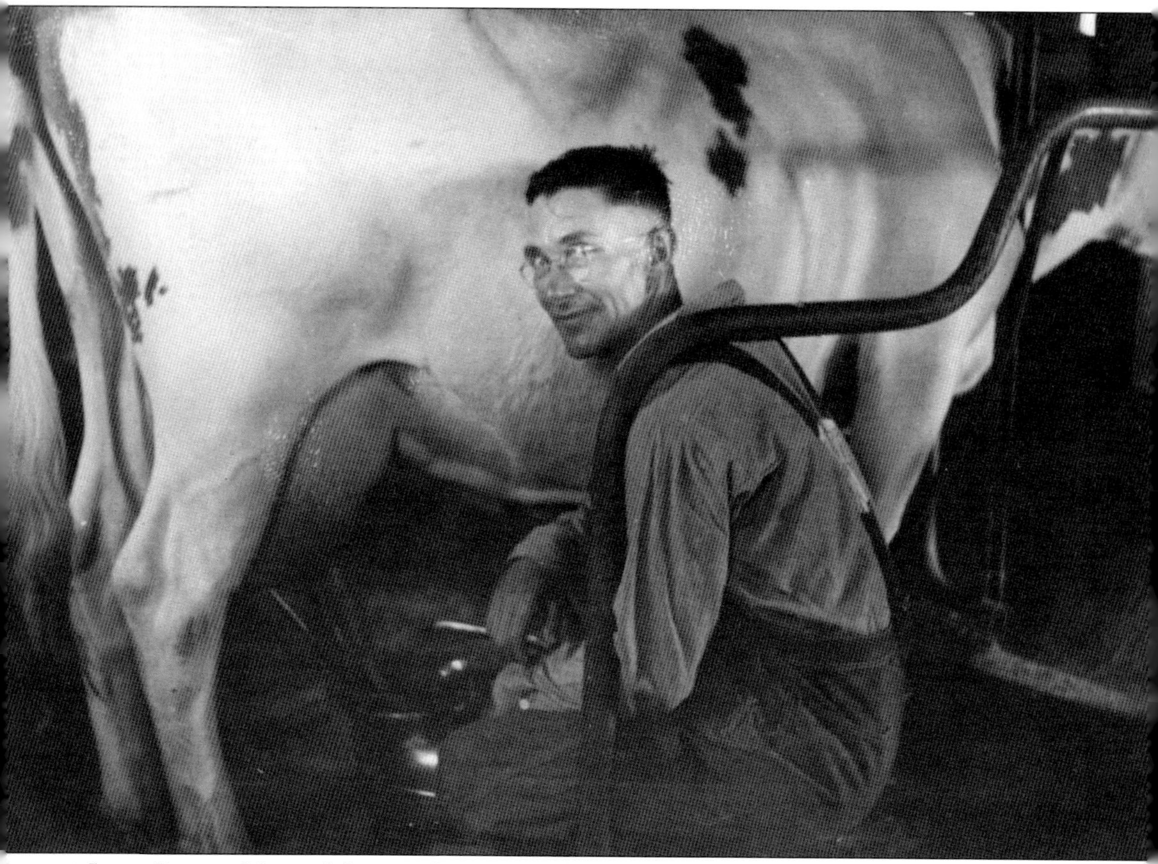

JAMES RUSSELL MAYBEE MILKING. Carrying on the Maybee farming tradition, James Russell Maybee milks cows at the family farm. He is listed on the 1933 National Dairy Association Honor Roll for his herd of 11 cows yielding a yearly production average of 316 pounds of butterfat.

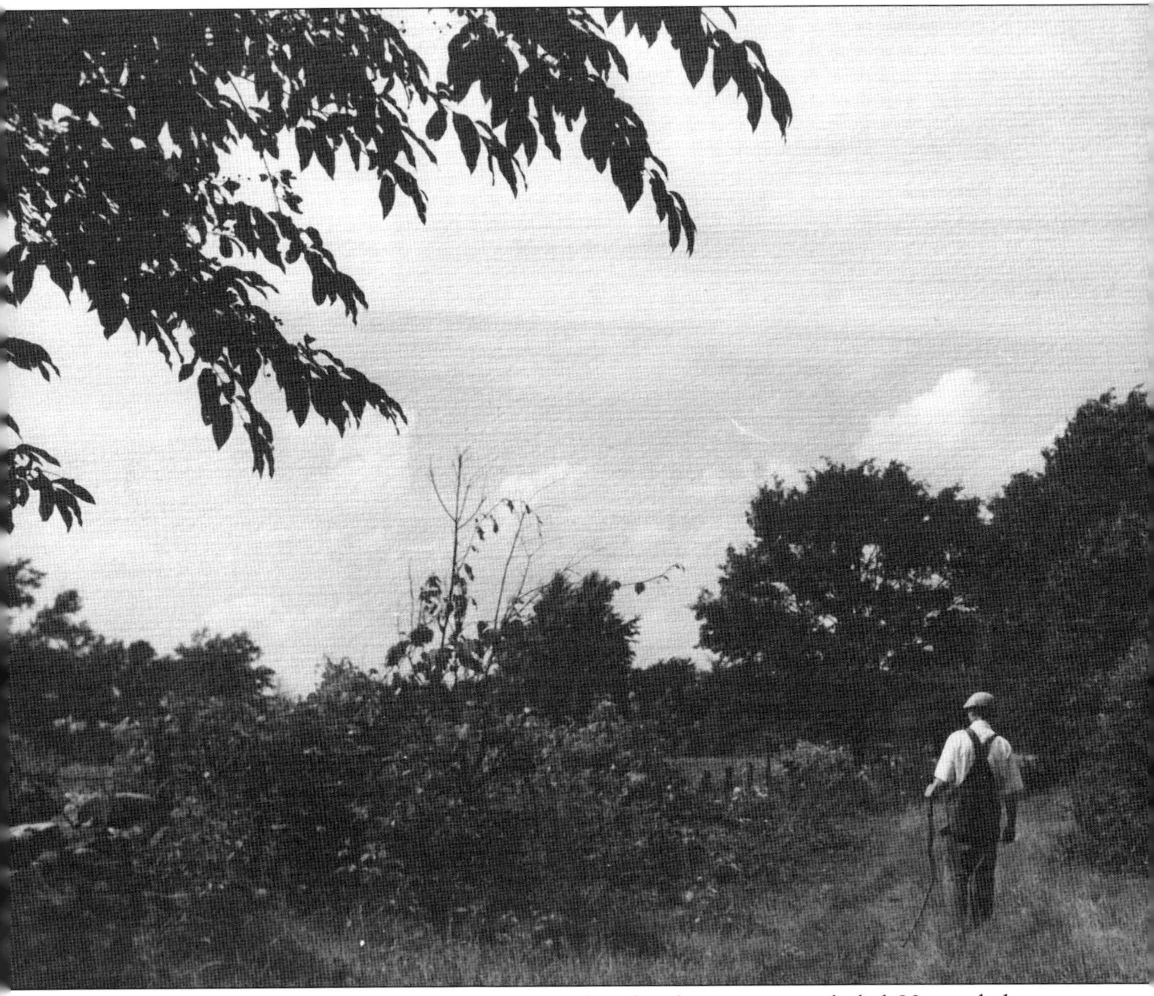

James Russell Maybee, Late 1940s. The Maybee family property included 80 wooded acres that later became the Birdland Subdivision, on the road that bears the family's name.

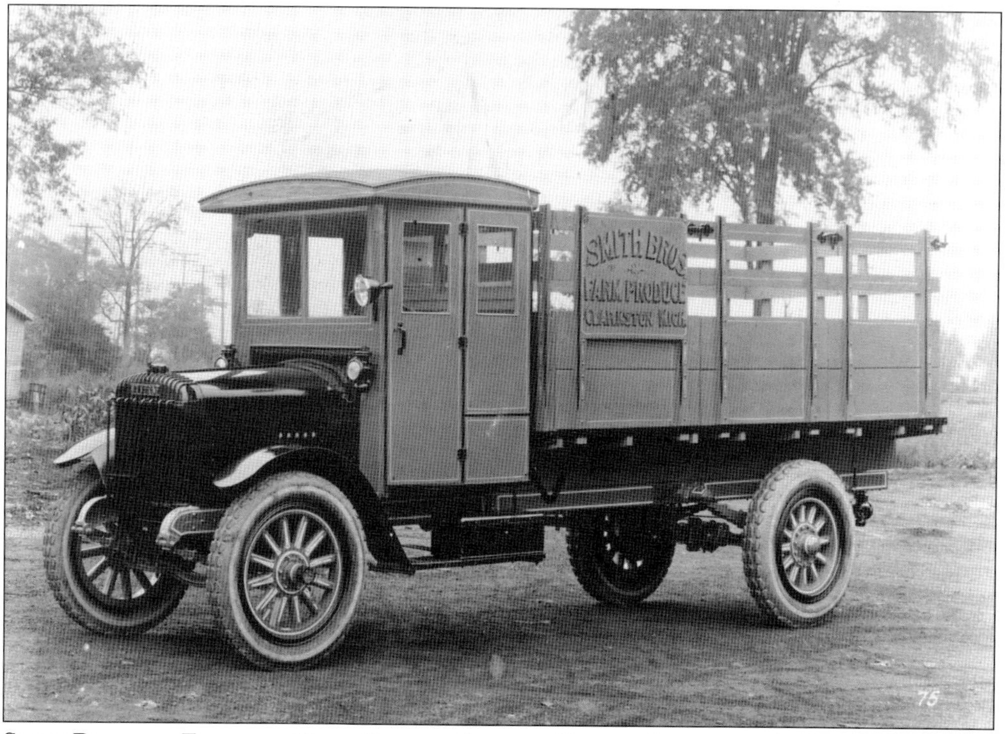

SMITH BROTHERS FARM AND WARD ROBBINS CARTAGE TRUCKS. Cartage trucks like these delivered freight such as grain and produce from local farms to and from Clarkston Station and markets in Pontiac, Detroit, and elsewhere.

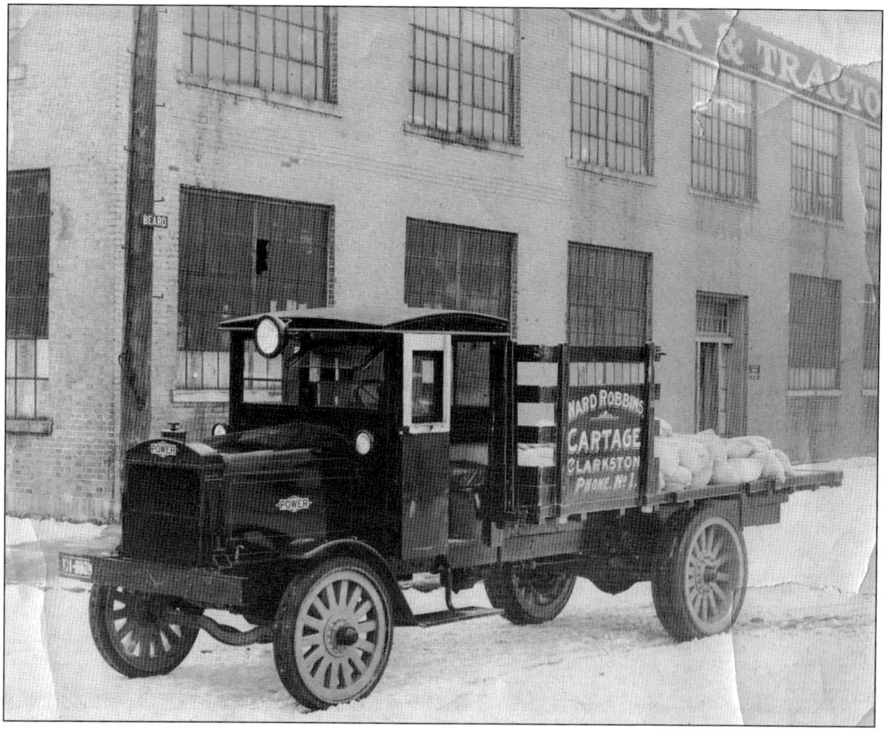

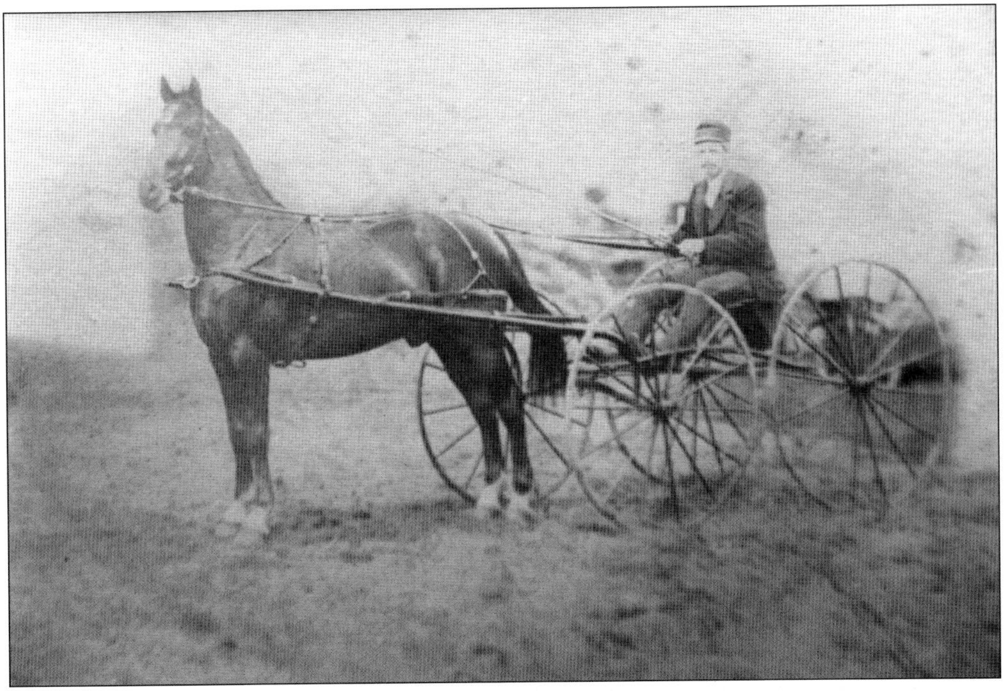

Norman Ellis and the Ellis Farmhouse. After Norman (above) and Esther Ellis's first house burned down in the early 1880s, Norman recalled a house that caught his eye in his native New York. So, he and a carpenter went to New York to visit that house, drawing up plans to rebuild a similar one, seen below on the Ellis's Springfield Township property.

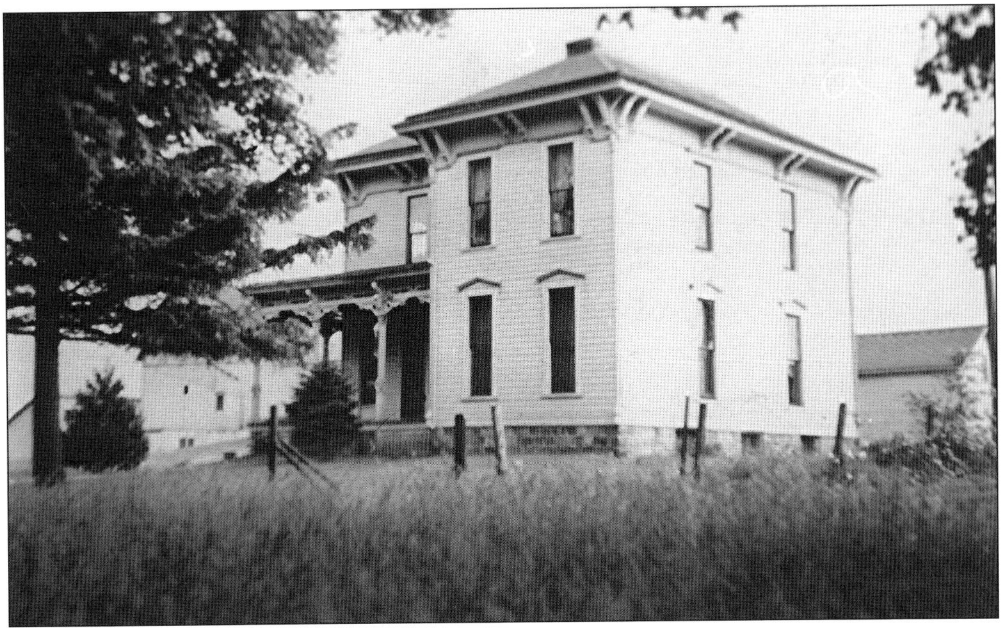

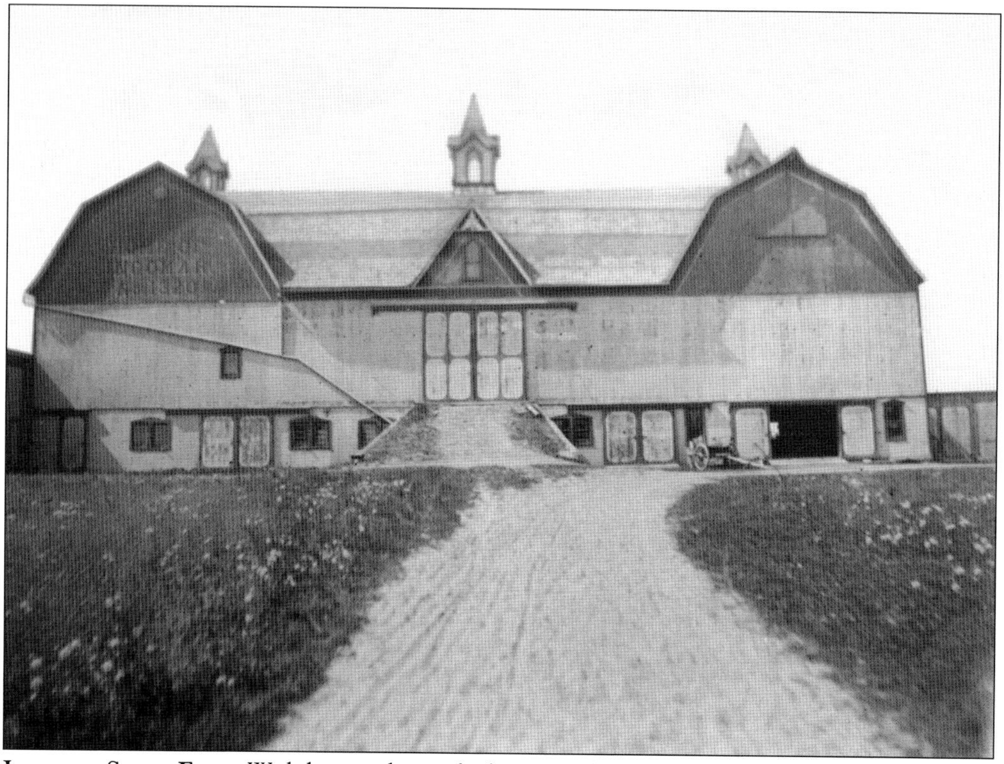

INGOMAR STOCK FARM. With his purchase of a five-year-old Percheron draft horse stallion named Ingomar, Norman Ellis started a stock farm and raised enough money to eventually purchase 750 acres of land where he bred, raised, and trained show horses. Ellis's horse stock thrived, and for more than 20 years he sold and shipped horses. When workhorses became a less desirable commodity, the family evolved its equestrian focus to Tennessee Walking horses. Norman Ellis died in 1923 and Esther in 1918. Their son Glen Ellis and his wife, Mabel Green Ellis, continued the farm. In 2005, after great community-wide effort, the huge white barn that could house as many as 50 horses was moved to Springfield Oaks County Park. (Courtesy of Oakland County Parks.)

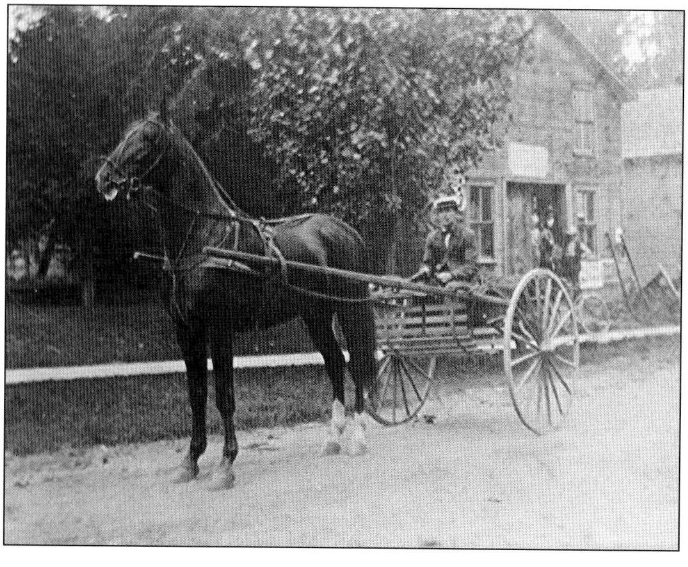

GLEN ELLIS DRIVING HIGH BALL. Glen Ellis, adopted son of Norman and Esther Ellis, poses with his horse High Ball as onlookers watch from the front of Wiltsie Vliet's cabinet shop. On a cold February night, the Ellises discovered a willow market basket at their door. Inside they found a baby boy, near death. For six weeks, Esther Ellis nursed the baby back to health. They soon adopted the boy, naming him Glen.

Five

DESTINATION CLARKSTON

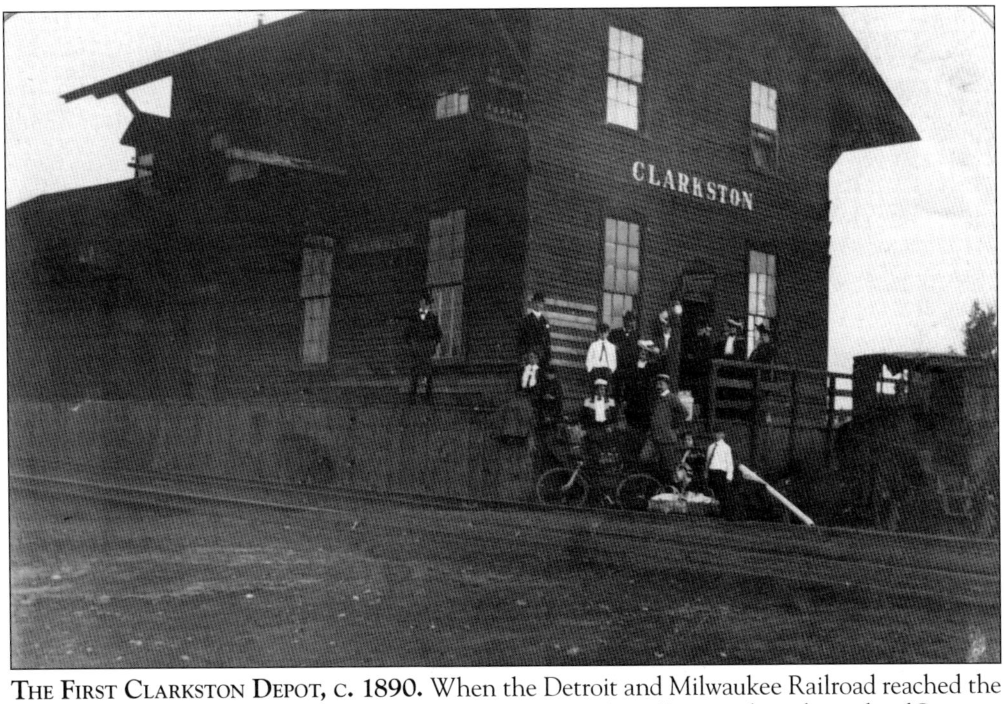

THE FIRST CLARKSTON DEPOT, C. 1890. When the Detroit and Milwaukee Railroad reached the Clarkston area in 1851, the community debated moving the village to the other side of Saginaw Trail (now Dixie Highway), closer to the railway line. But the village's mills and waterpower won out. To make travel easier to the original wooden depot and main shipping point, the road needed upgrades. Someone recalled that a route created to transport grist becomes a public road. Soon a pair of oxen pulled a sled between Deer and Cemetery Lakes en route to the mill and back again, thus establishing Depot Road, a plank road that occasionally disappeared when the lake's water levels peaked in the springtime. The road enabled exports to leave the village more easily and tourists to enter. The bus from Clarkston came twice daily, carrying anything from passengers to mail. Sadly, a spark from a passing train led to this station burning down in the early 1900s.

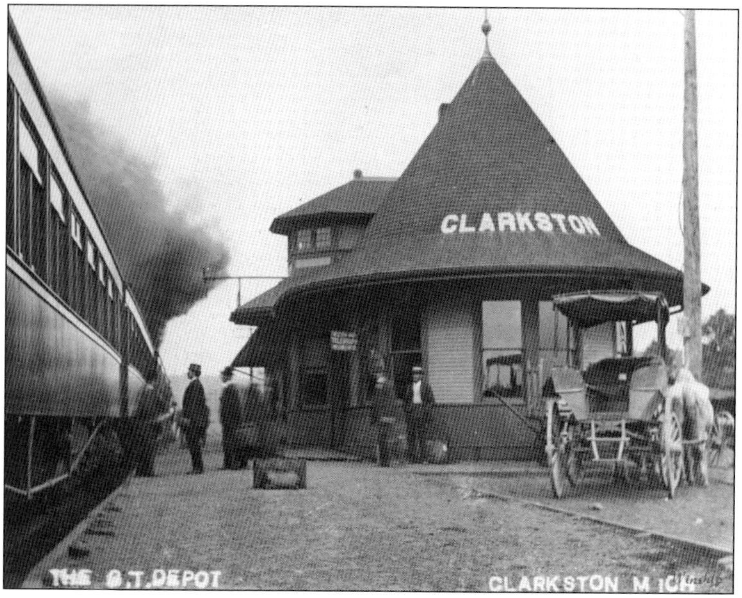

The Witch's Hat Depot, Early 1900s. A conductor guides passengers onto the train at Clarkston's second depot, built early in the new century and featuring the distinctive witch's hat roofline design. Summer months were busy times at the depot, as tourists poured into the local resorts. At one point, the railroad put on 12 coaches to deliver summer visitors to Clarkston.

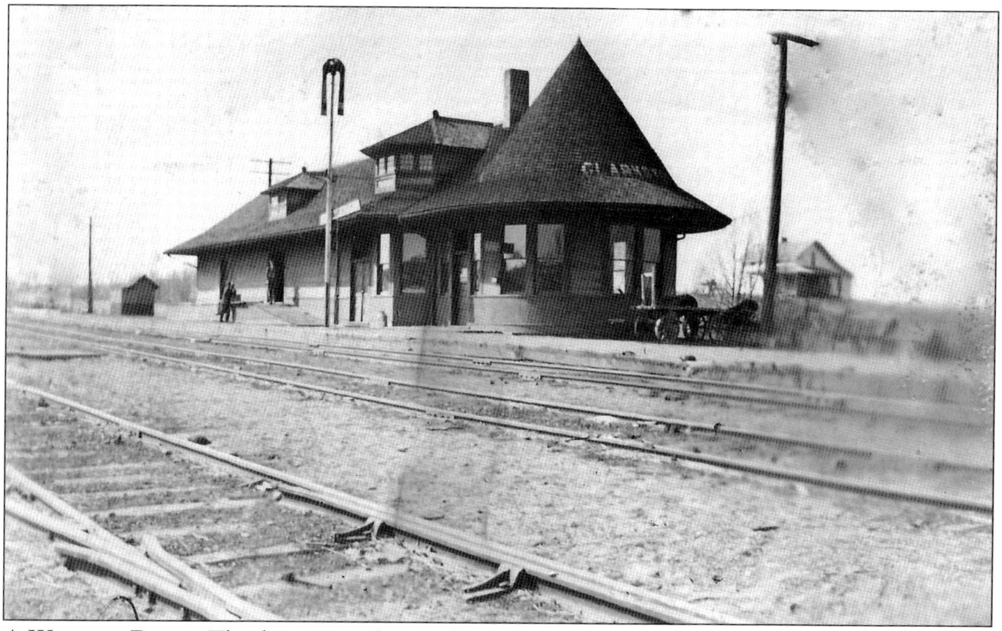

A Working Depot. The depot served more than tourists. It also was the area's main shipping point, including taking Clarkston-area sheep to market in Detroit. The train also became responsible for mail delivery and pickup. Accounts say that the 5:00 p.m. train stretched out an iron arm to snatch the mailbag from a pole as the train zipped by the station. Sometimes it would miss, or grab the mail pouch only to accidentally drop it, scattering mail on and near the tracks, where someone would gather up the pieces and hope for a better result with the next train.

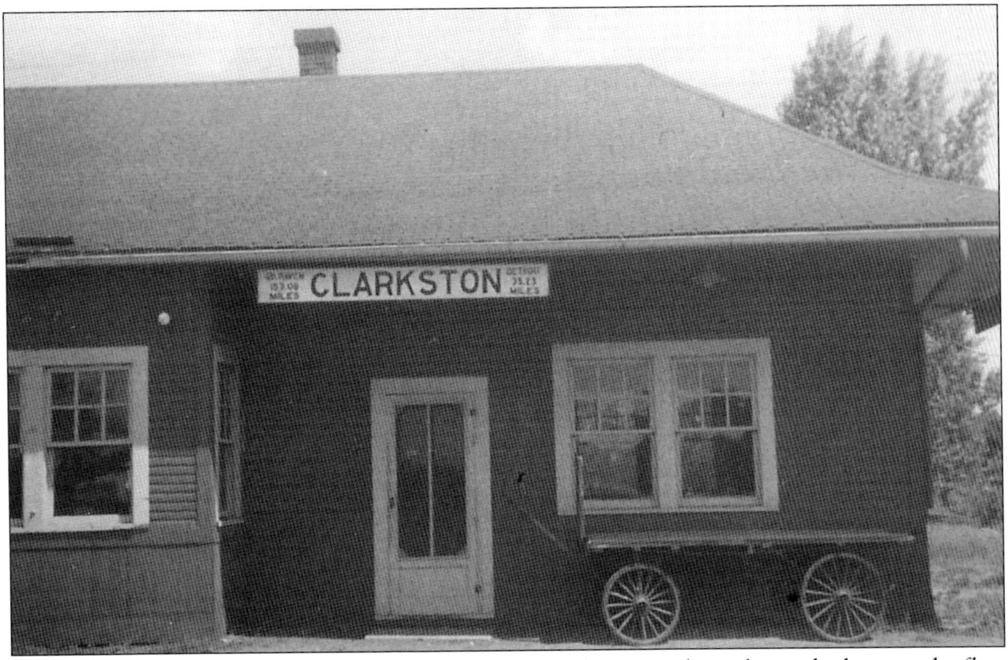

The Depot's Last Call and Rollin Clark. More than one depot burned when sparks flew off a coal-fired locomotive. So was the fate of Clarkston's witch's hat depot, which burned in the early 1920s. With no fire station nearby, the stationmaster could do little more than watch the depot burn. This final, simpler depot served the community until 1959, when stops to Clarkston ceased and the depot closed. The Clarkston Village Players purchased the station from Grand Trunk for $150 for rehearsal and performance space. Below, Rollin Clark, a descendant of the village founders, poses on the tracks during the heyday of Clarkston railroading.

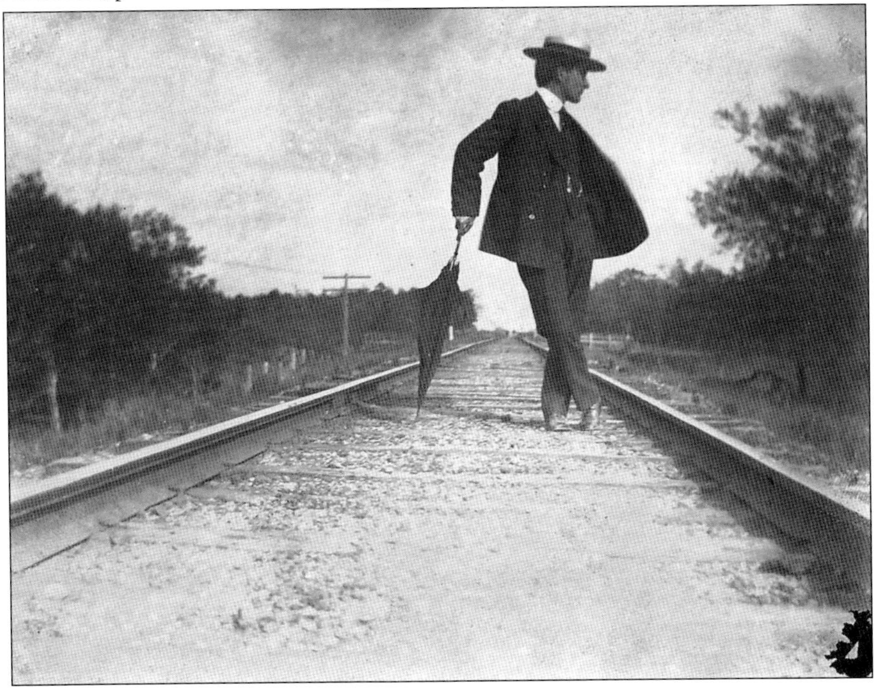

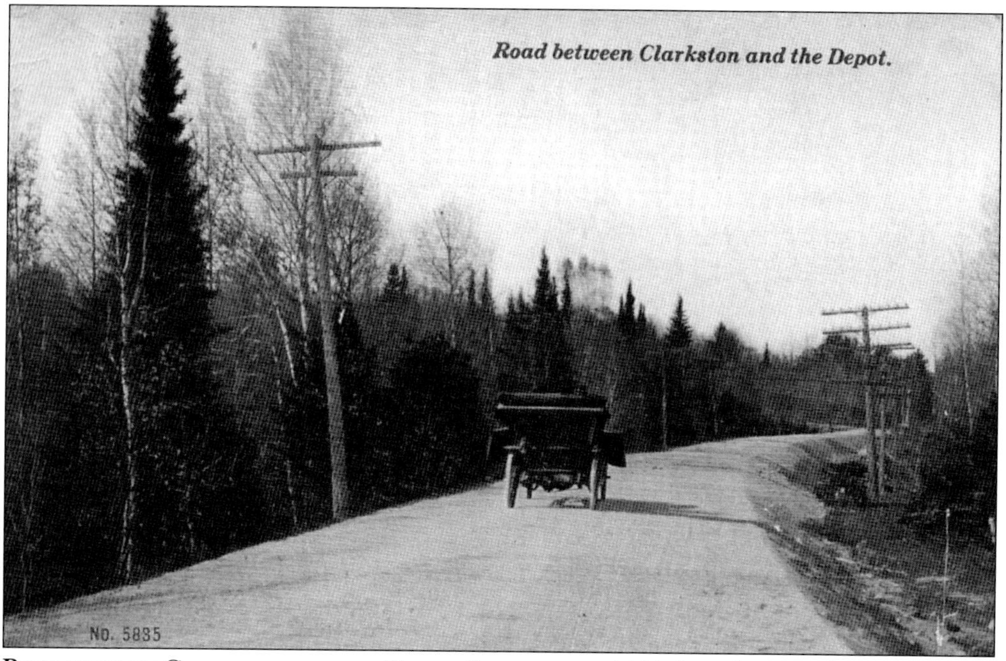

Road between Clarkston and the Depot, Postmarked 1901. Just where on the two-mile trek between the depot and the village this early automobile happens to be is hard to determine, but it is likely White Lake Road before reaching Saginaw Trail, later known as Dixie Highway, headed towards town. Because the depot was not within the village limits, buses—first horse-drawn and later motorized—traveled back and forth from the depot to greet trains.

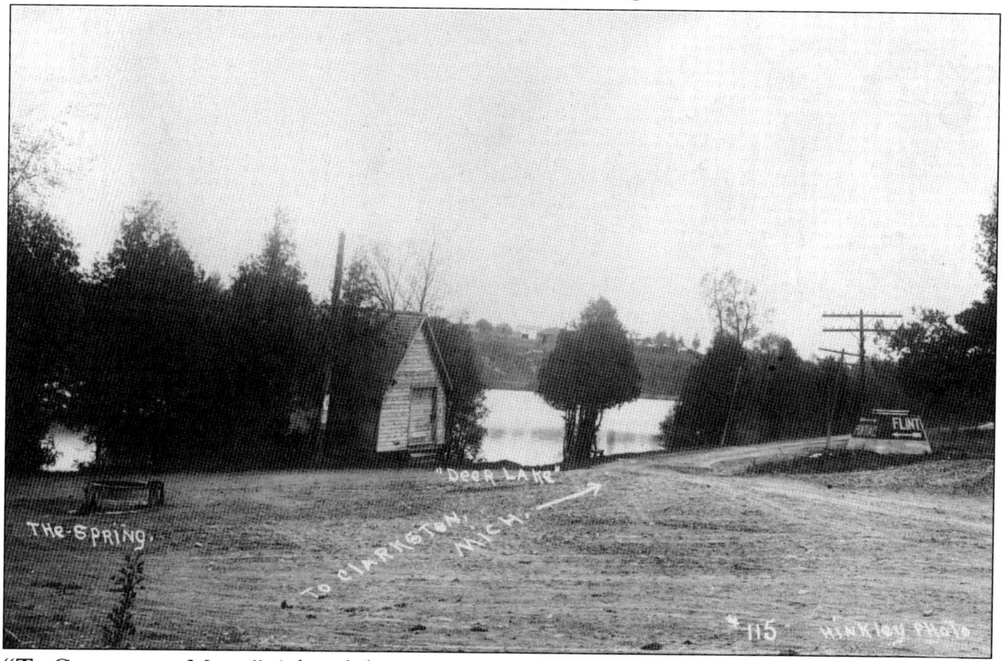

"To Clarkston, Mich." A hand-drawn arrow points the way to the village, while other labels mark the location of Deer Lake and the nearby spring. Actual signs show the opposing routes to Flint and Pontiac.

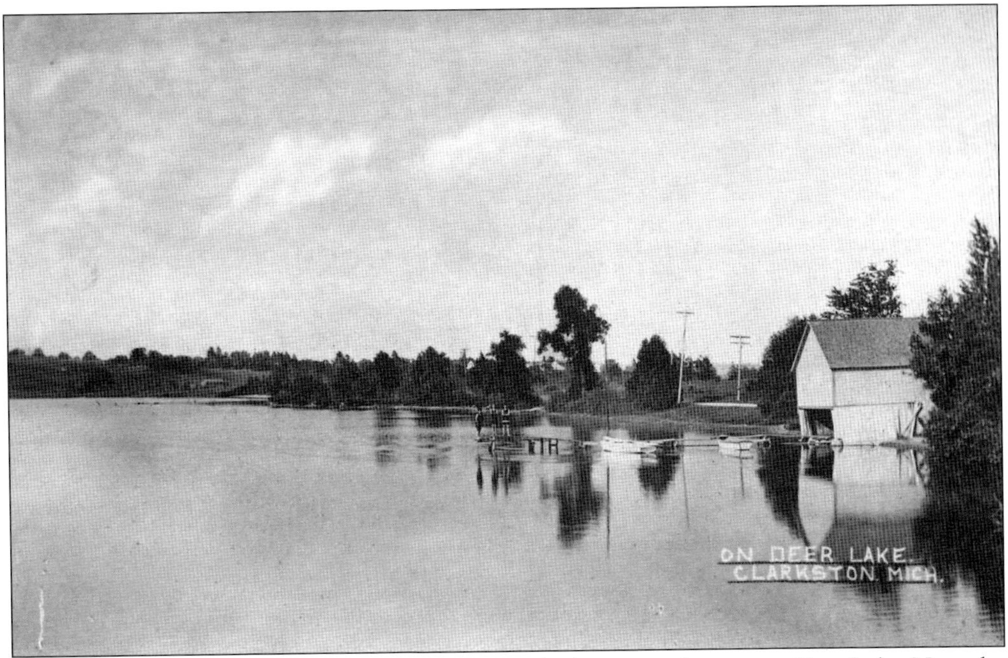

On Deer Lake. Swimmers prepare to leap from a dock into a calm, serene Deer Lake. Note the boathouse in the foreground, which is also visible on the previous page.

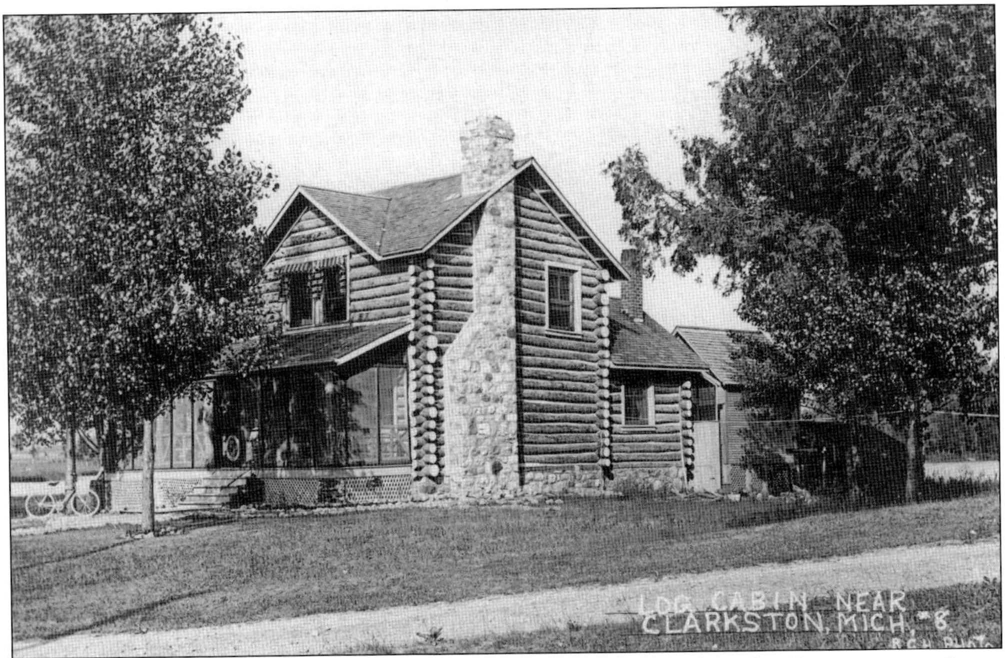

Log Cabin Near Clarkston. This postcard highlights the Lambert family summer residence on the banks of Cemetery (Middle) Lake, just across the street from Deer Lake. In 1925, when the Lamberts decided to use another summer home on the Mill Pond, they deeded the log cabin's beach land to the village to ensure the scenic spot would not fall into commercial hands.

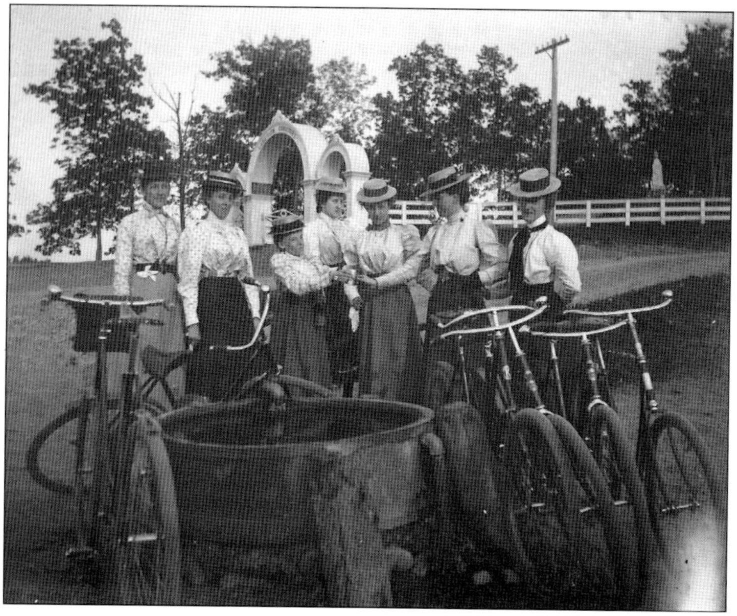

Bicycling Ladies at the Spring, c. 1900. These ladies out for a bicycle ride stop at the spring, a natural drinking hole near where Deer Lake Road meets White Lake Road at the north entrance of Lakeview Cemetery. From left to right are two unidentified, Nellie Smith, Eleanor Garter, Zoa Smith, unidentified, and Esther Walter. Notice the arched cemetery entrance behind them.

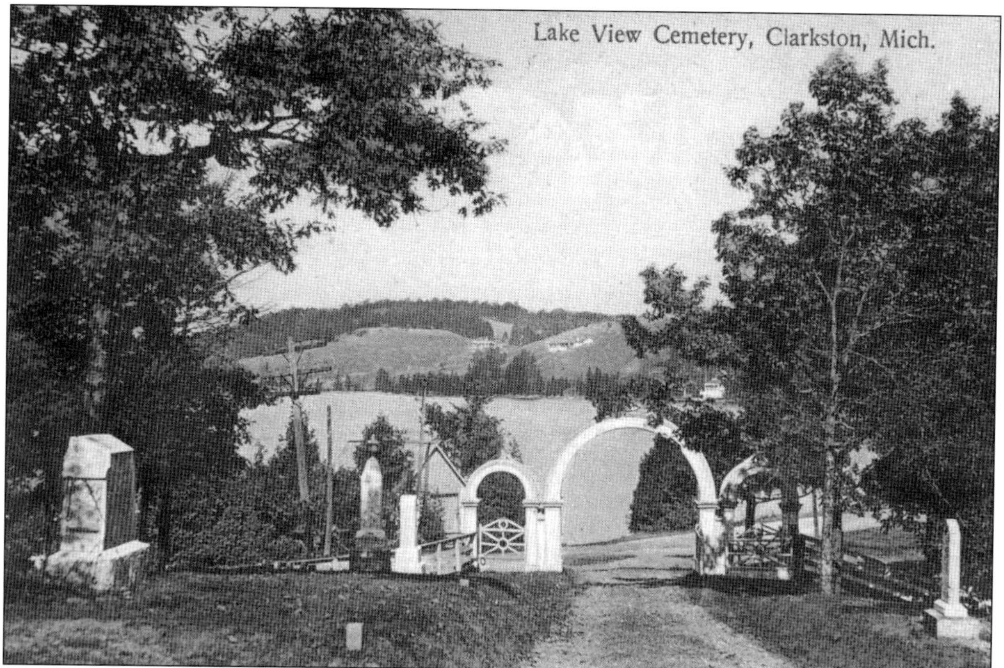

Lakeview Cemetery. Named for its views of both Deer Lake (pictured) and Cemetery Lake (also known as Middle Lake), hilly and tranquil Lakeview Cemetery, established in 1850, is the final resting place of many of Clarkston's pioneers and esteemed citizens.

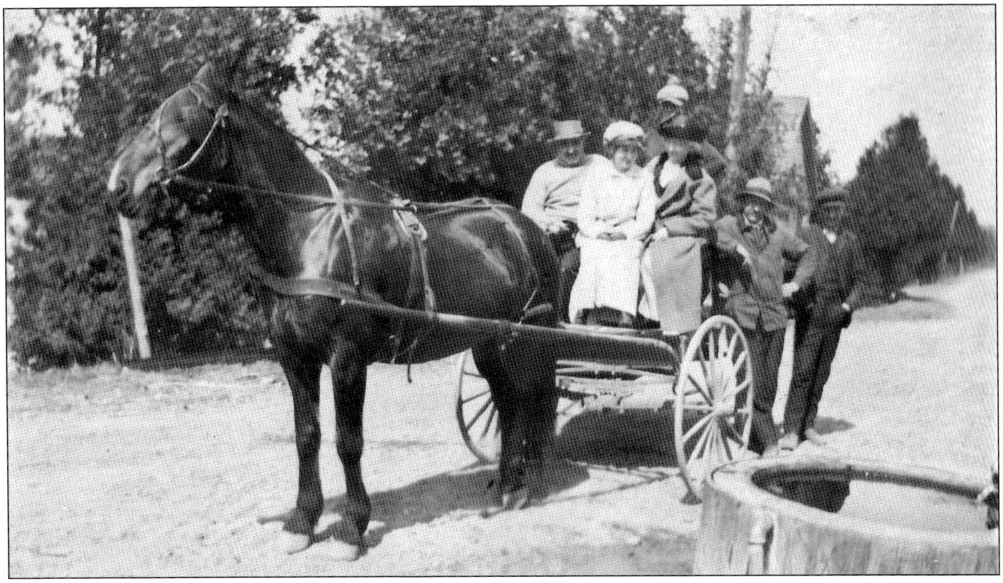

HORSE CARRIAGE AT SPRING, 1914. Traveling to the depot or Saginaw Trail from the village, travelers passed the spring and could stop to quench their thirst and rest their horses.

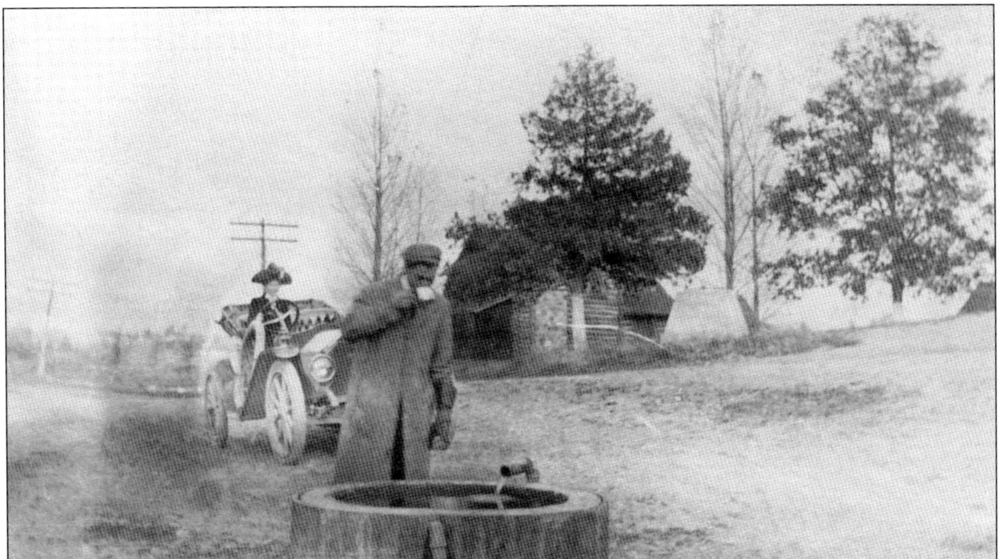

A CAR AT THE SPRING. Even once cars hit the road, the spring was popular. Though the year is not identified, the back of this image reads, "A Snap, 4th July" and "Ready for Camp, the Starting." The Lambert log cabin is in the background.

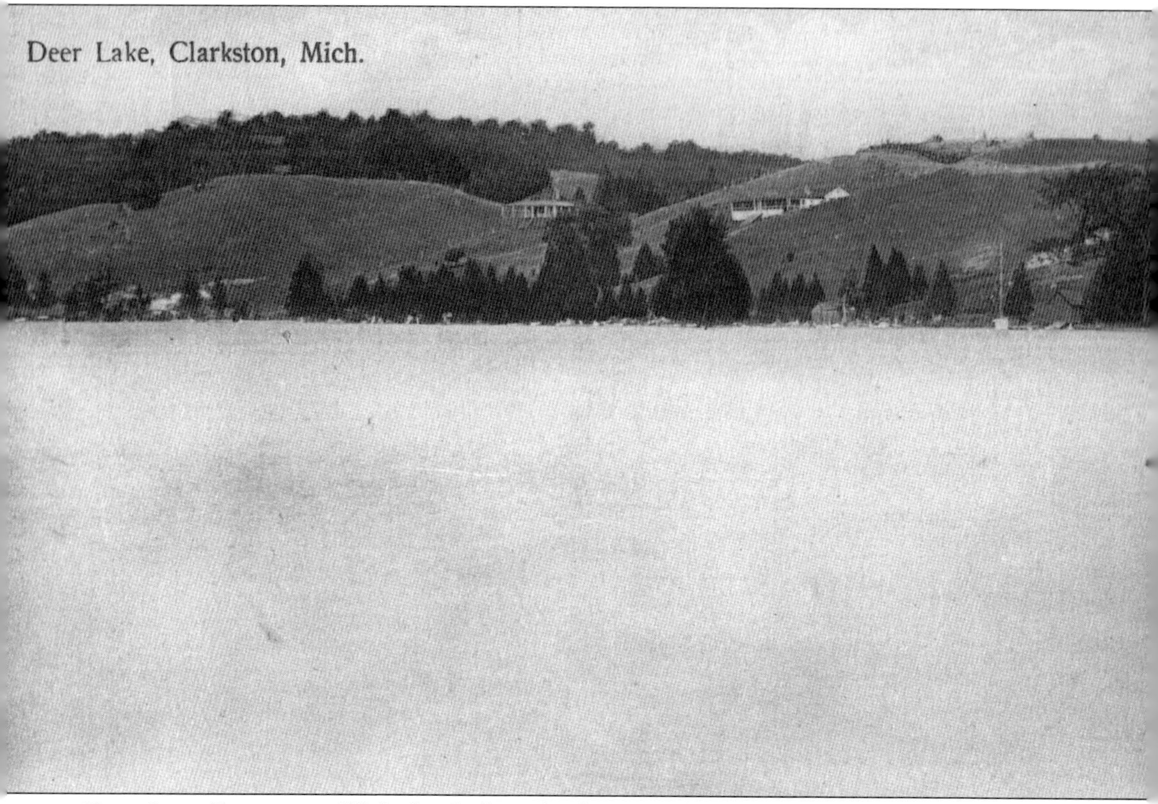

DEER LAKE PANORAMA. With the dock in the foreground and Vliet's-on-the-Hill a distant dot at far right, this panorama of Deer Lake gave visitors a chance to show faraway friends the lake's beauty. On one postmarked August 28, 1908, the sender told a Detroit friend, "Hello 'Des,'

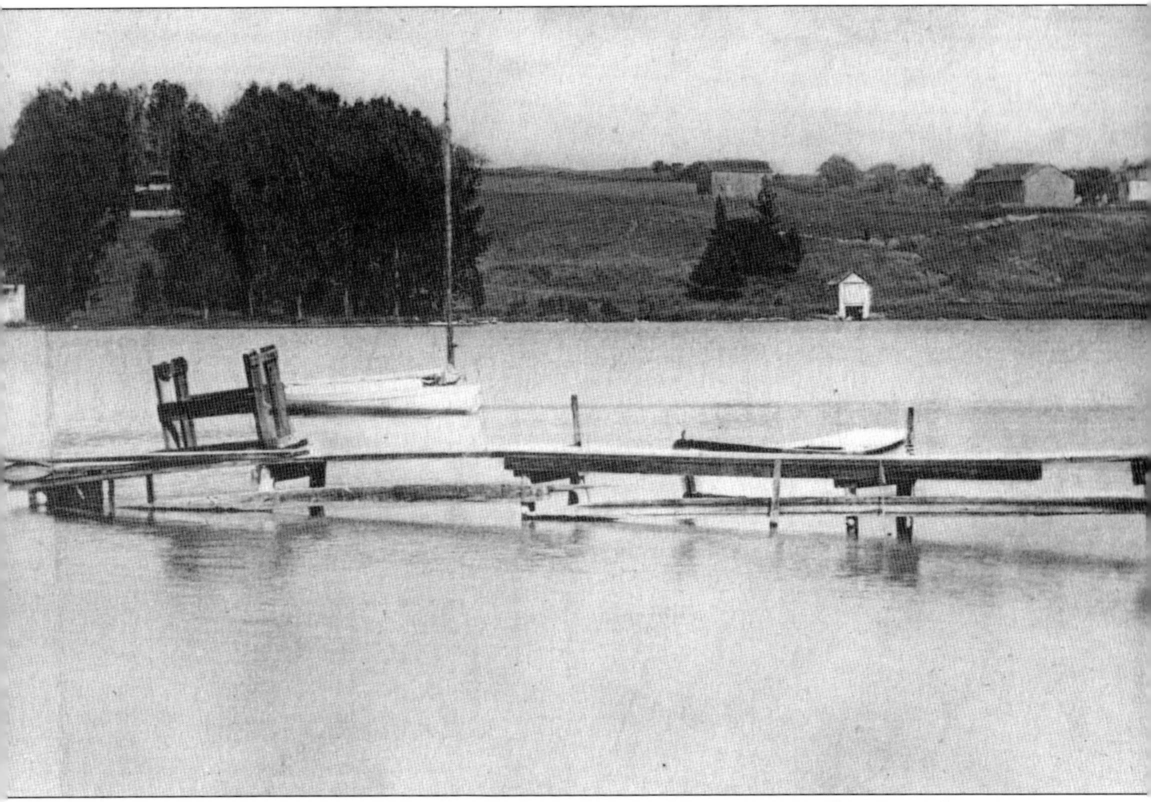

Received your postal. I have been sick all day, caught cold I guess. I am having a glorious time. Here is a picture of the lake. Do you like its looks? Yours as ever, 'Ed.' "

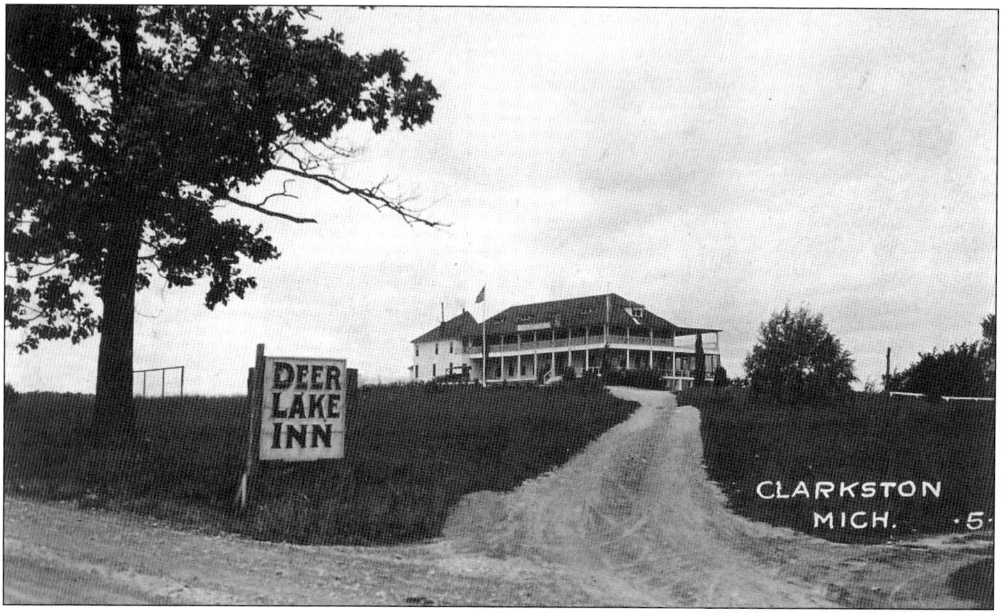

Deer Lake Inn. Clarkston was long a spot for weary travelers to stop for the night or at least a bite to eat when traveling by horse or early car between Detroit, Pontiac, and Flint or points farther north. Once it became known as a summer resort community, Clarkston's inns became so busy that residents even started renting space in their own homes. On July 3, 1912, the Barry family opened Deer Lake Inn and advertised it as a place to enjoy boating, bathing, and fishing. The inn offered 35 guest bedrooms and built about a dozen cottages nearer to the lake.

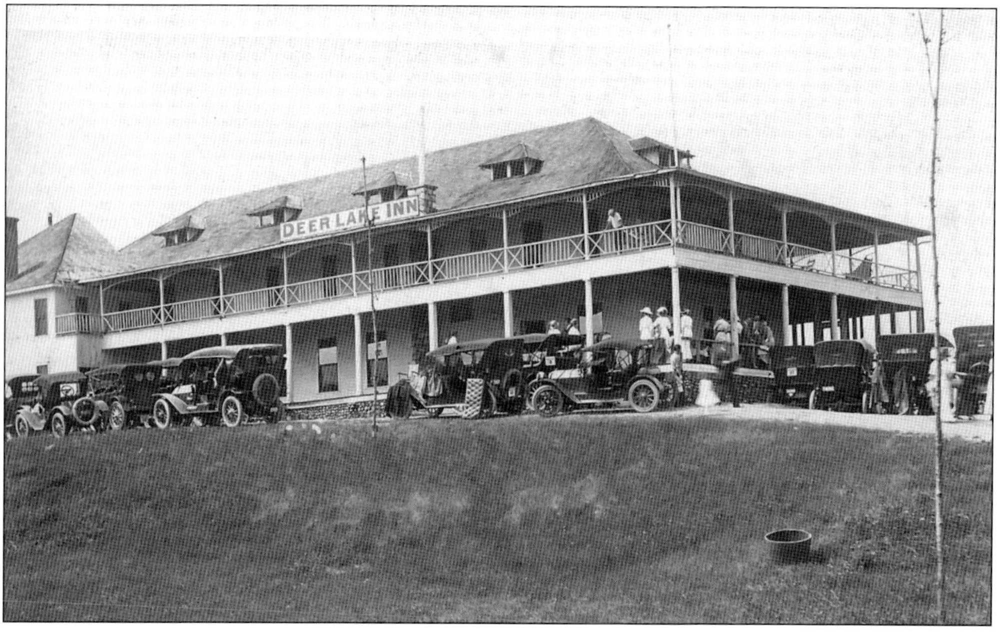

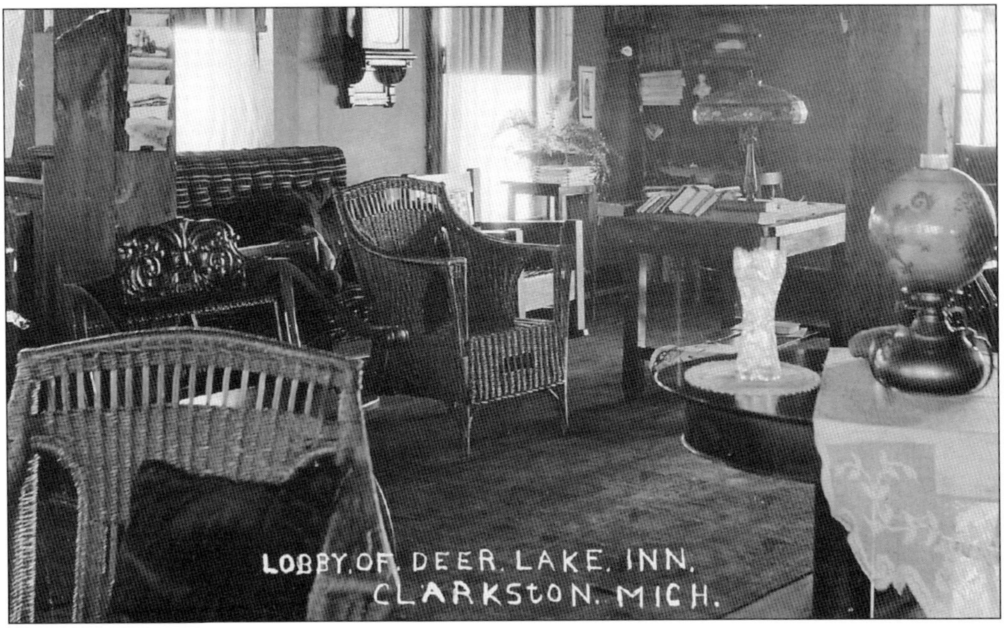

DEER LAKE INN LOBBY, POSTMARKED 1920. The guest register at the Deer Lake Inn regularly boasted a list of prominent people. Guests who came to stay or dine signed it, reportedly including Louis Chevrolet, A. Champion, Walter Chrysler, C.W. Nash, and Henry Ford, among others.

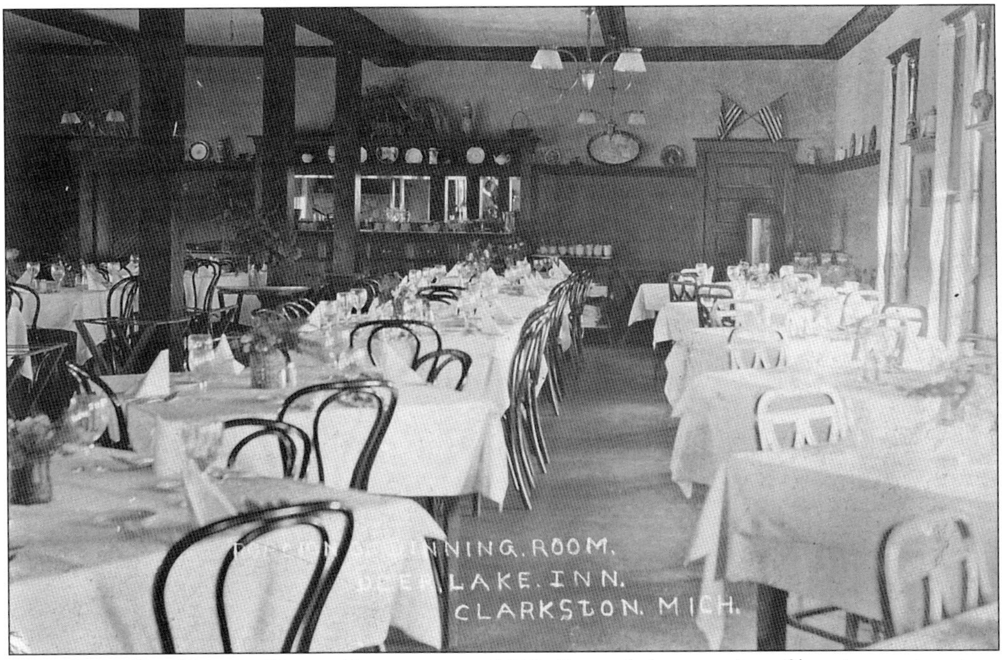

DEER LAKE INN DINING ROOM, POSTMARKED 1921. Beyond the promise of boating, swimming, and fishing, Deer Lake Inn's dining room became a destination itself. This postcard reads, "Dear Robert, We ate our dinner here yesterday. Are having State Fair in Saginaw this week, so there is a great crowd here. Have fine place to stay at private home. Am driving car around myself. I keep off busy streets. With love, Mother." The Barry family sold the inn in 1925, and before long, the building was dismantled, though the name lives on in an area restaurant.

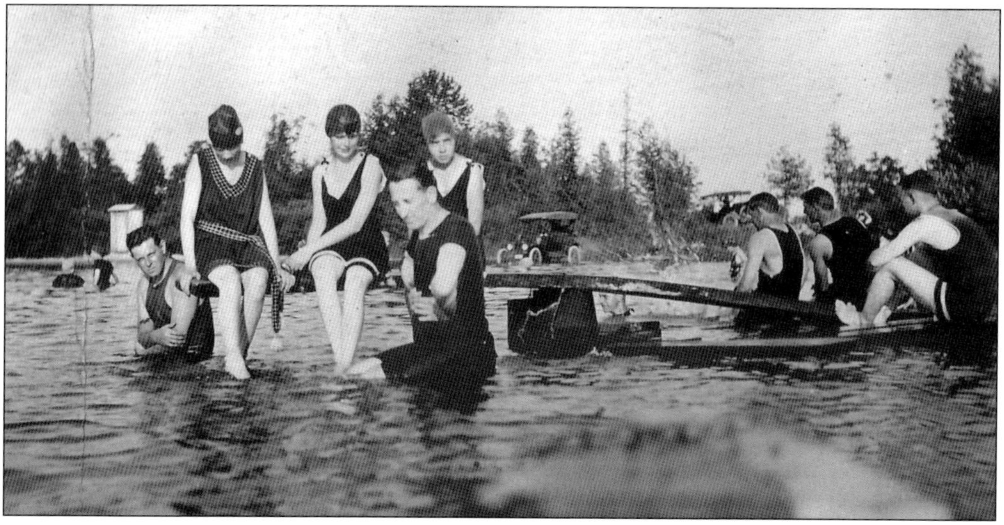

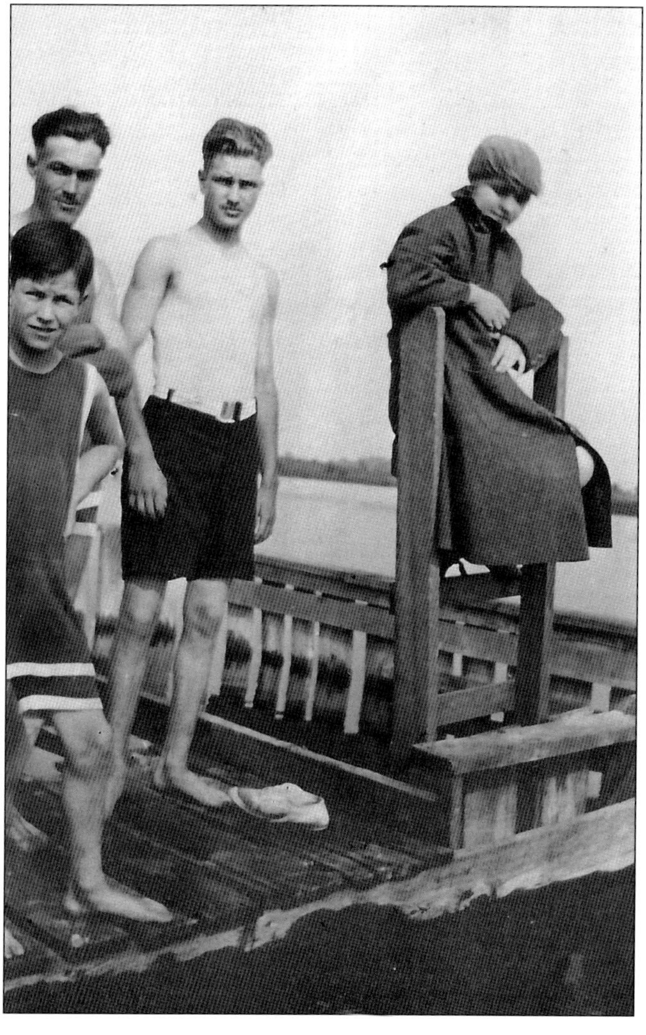

Swimmers at Deer Lake. Above, while several young women contemplate a swim in Deer Lake, their friends already wade in the water. At left, a group of boys stand on a dock, waiting to take the plunge. Summer resort community or not, Clarkston had rules about swimwear. An early sign in the village warned swimmers they would be fined if they did not wear a long coat to the beach, and at one point, legs needed to be covered with long black hose.

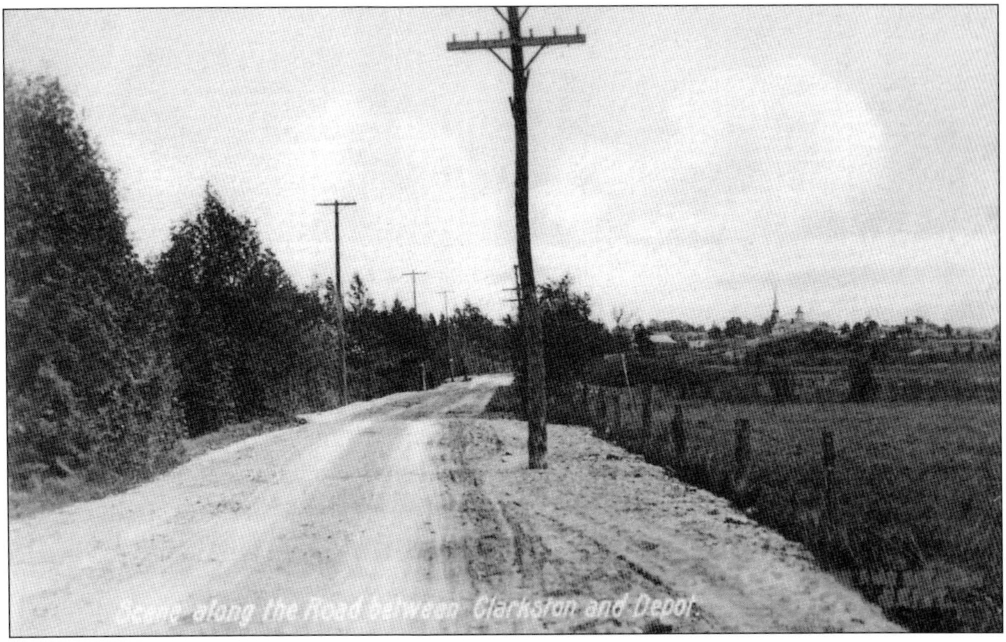

The Road between Clarkston and the Depot, c. 1907. The distant sight of the churches—the First Methodist Episcopal Church of Clarkston (left) and the lower bell tower of the Baptist church (right)—was the first view of the village for people traveling into town by way of White Lake Road from the depot, Saginaw Trail, or the Deer Lake Inn.

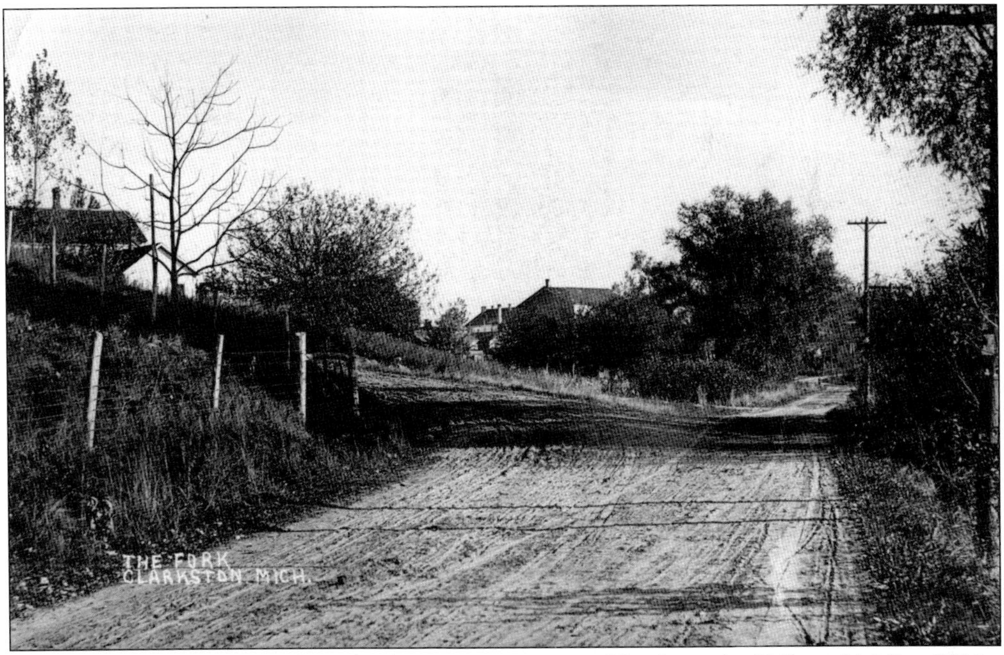

The Fork. Visitors coming from the depot into town or to Vliet's-on-the-Hill would follow White Lake Road and see the village in the distance. They would soon come upon this fork at Depot Road where White Lake Road turns into Holcomb Road. Clarkston Mill is visible in the distance, and the house at left is likely 75 South Holcomb Road, built in the late 1850s or early 1860s.

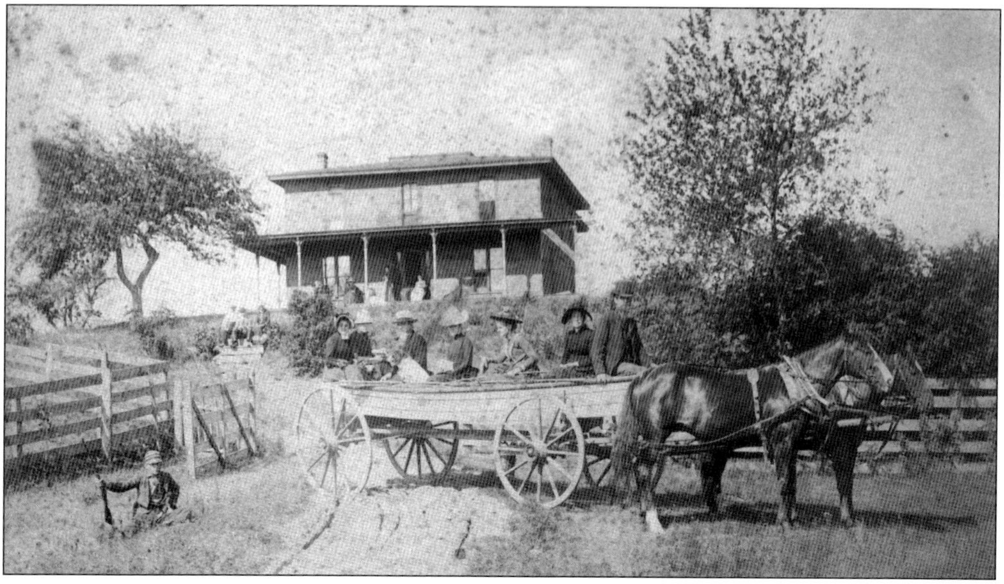

VLIET'S-ON-THE-HILL. A wagon delivers guests to the William V.B. Vliet farm, also known as Vliet's-on-the-Hill, halfway up Church Street almost atop Clarkston, overlooking Deer Lake. Horse-drawn wagons such as Herbert Lewis's Belle of Clarkston and others from the local liveries met guests to take them to the inns. As many families did at the time, the Vliets started offering room and board to those interested in enjoying their lakefront and beaches. Because of the prevalence of Vliet family members throughout Clarkston, it became easiest to describe this particular Vliet home as Vliet's-on-the-Hill if for no other reason than to distinguish it from the others. Note the little boy off to the left above and the guests in the wagon holding fishing poles. Below, the view was so good it even showed a distant Cemetery Lake.

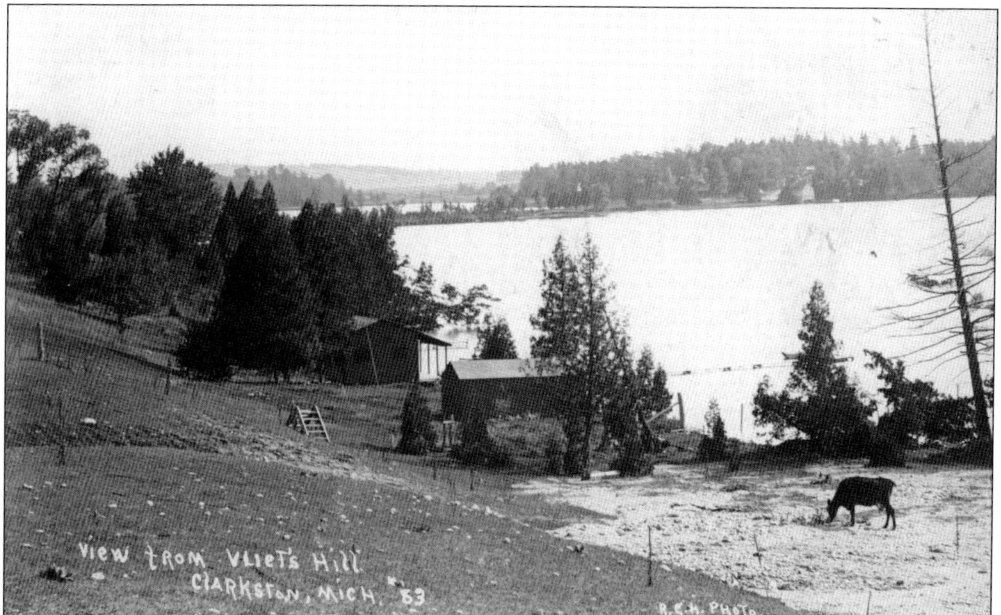

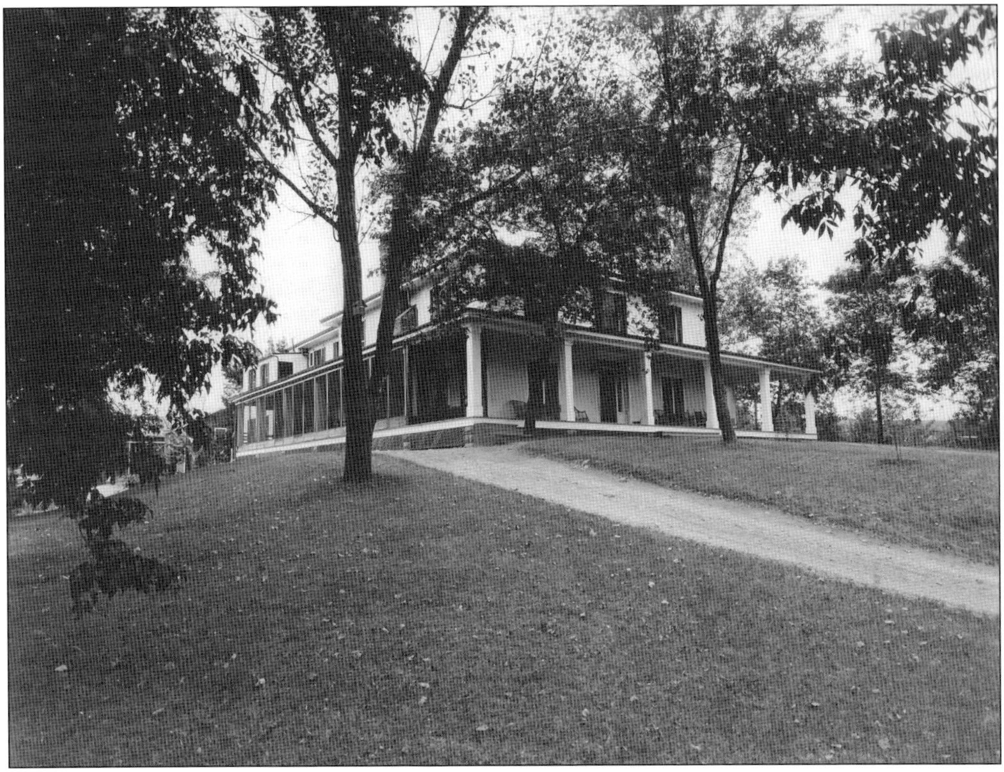

Green Acres Inn. Vliet's later became Green Acres Inn. Families would spend entire summers at inns like these. Often, working family members stayed behind in the city, catching a train to visit each weekend through the summer.

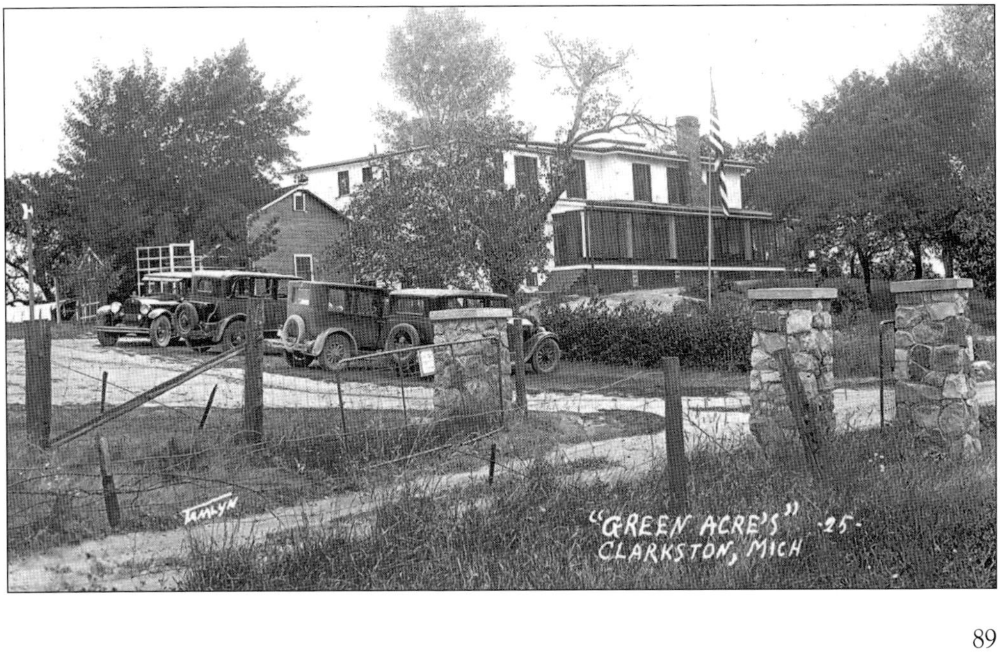

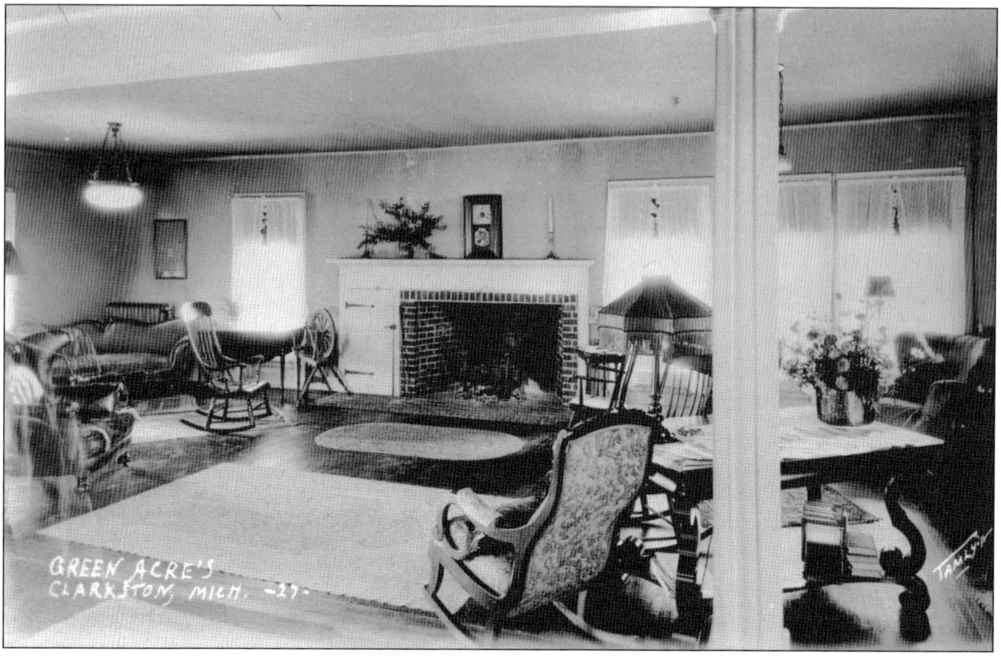

Green Acres Lounge, 1929. Ellen Miller worked at Green Acres and recalled how she and the other young female employees stayed in a room over the kitchen. They accomplished various household chores, including churning butter in the afternoon after skimming the cream from the fresh milk.

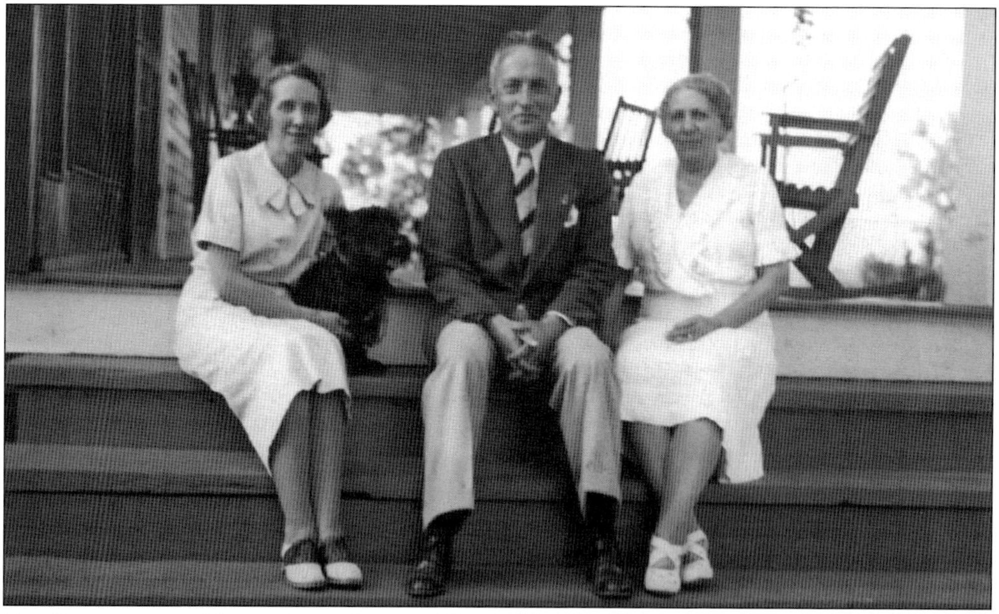

The People behind Green Acres. Jean and Lloyd "Slip" McGee with Jean's mother, Lida Weighell, owner of Green Acres Inn, sit on the steps of the inn.

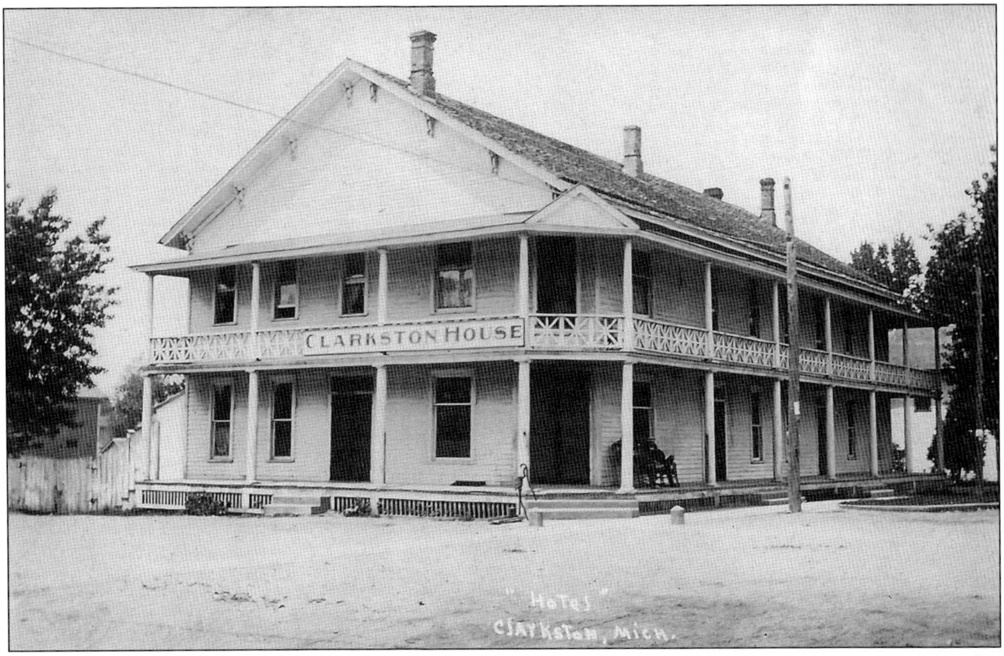

Clarkston House Hotel. In the heart of Clarkston, at Main and Washington Streets where the public parking lot stands now, George Vaughn bought the Demarest Inn, renaming it Clarkston House as the area became an even more booming stop for summer lake resort seekers.

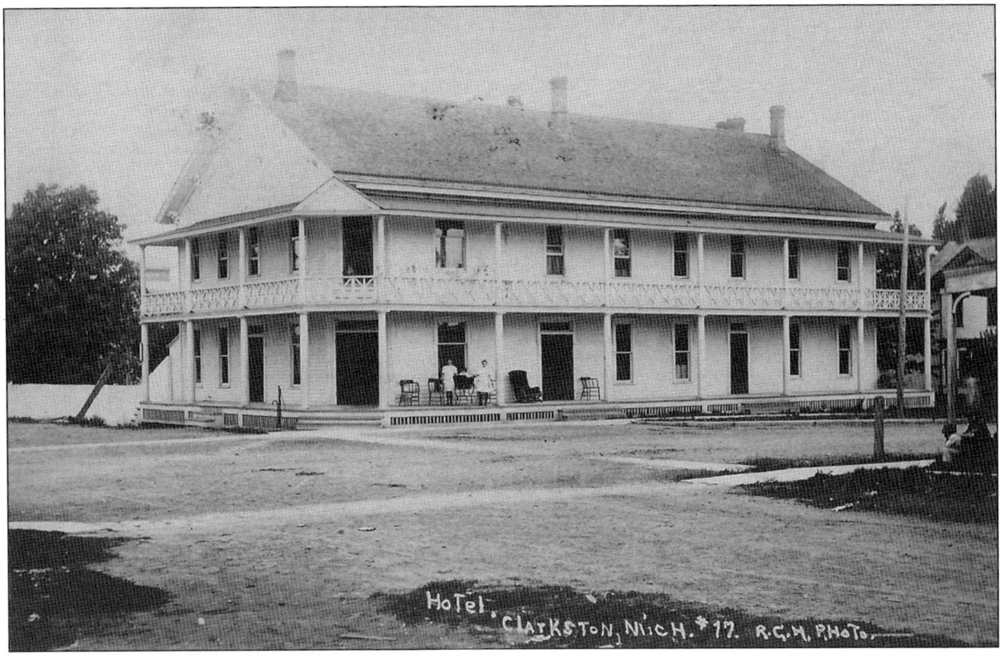

Hotel, Clarkston, Michigan. It is hard to tell which incarnation of the Demarest House this is, as it experienced so many, including Clarkston House, Nelson House, the New Wooster, Wooster, and in the 1920s, the Caribou Inn, among others. Notice the little girls with the baby carriage watching from the side porch.

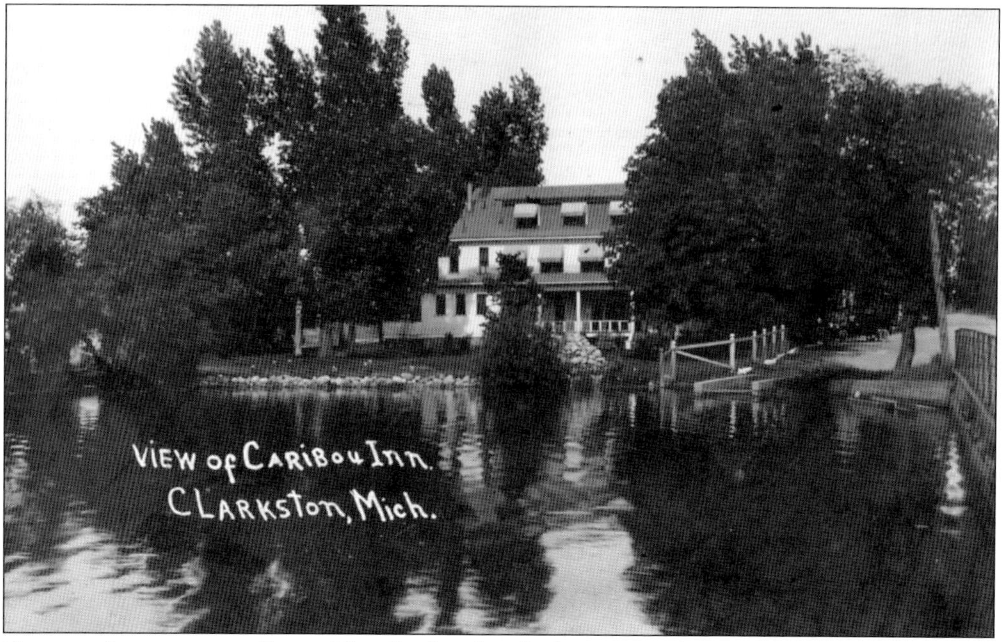

Caribou Inn from the Pond. The Caribou Inn looks inviting from West Washington Street, across the Mill Pond.

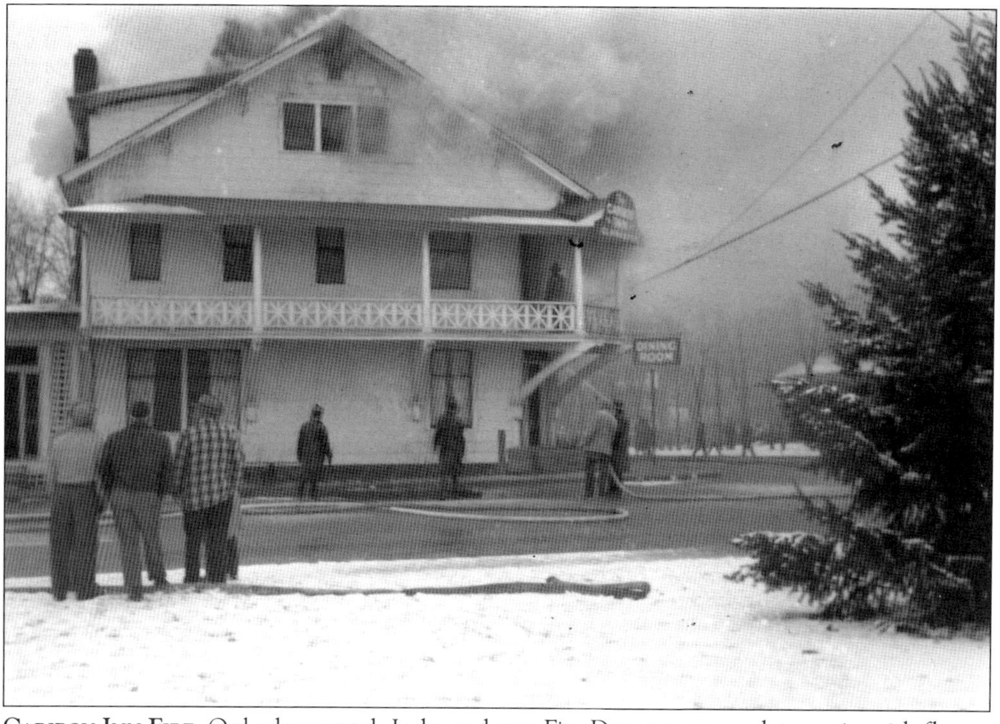

Caribou Inn Fire. Onlookers watch Independence Fire Department work to extinguish flames that all but sealed the Caribou Inn's fate on March 4, 1958. Firefighters broke through Mill Pond ice for water to combat the morning flames that engulfed the roof and third level of the decrepit landmark. It would soon be torn down.

Six

Clarkston Celebrates

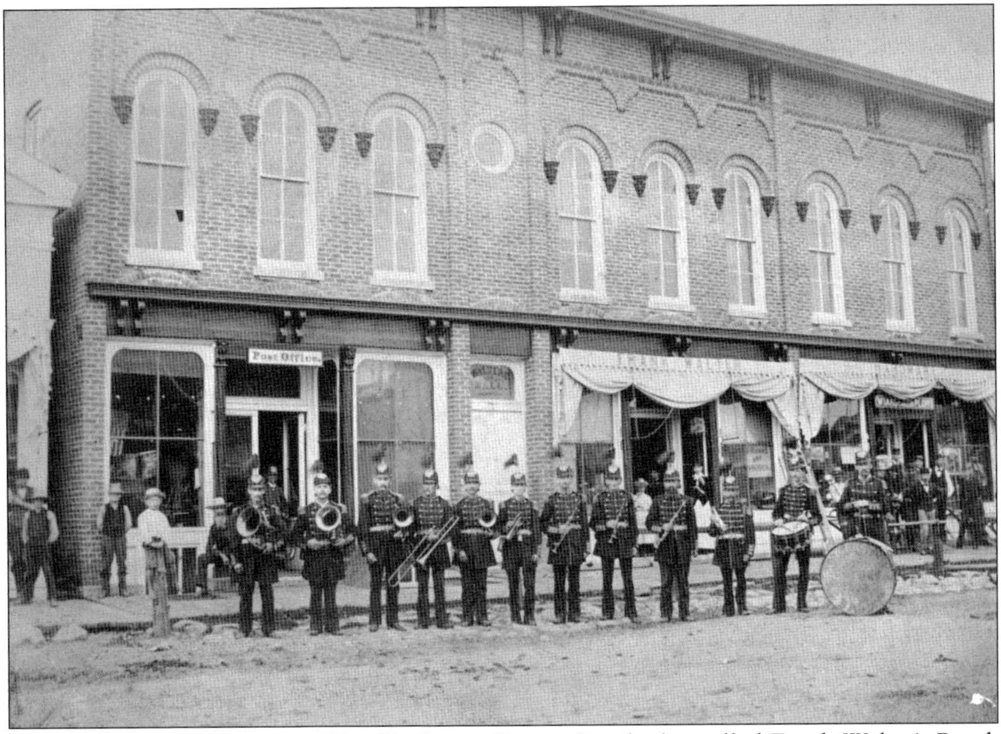

Clarkston Cornet Band. The Clarkston Cornet Band, also called Frank Walter's Band, poses in front of Bingham Hall, which included Walter's Hall upstairs, a 400-seat public space for entertainment, grange meetings, and dances. Built in 1870, this grand brick building stood near the southeast corner of Main and Washington Streets until it burned around 1887. In 1902, the Clarkston Building Association began construction of the Maccabee Temple building in its place. Photographed by W.C. Petty are C. Bird (boy with hat), Wiltsie Vliet (man, seated with hat), and band members J. McKinney, B. Holcomb, J. Carran, C. Dresser, F. Walter, C. Smith, R. Jossman, H. Dresser, L. Allen, A. Carran, ? McKindred, and S. Warren.

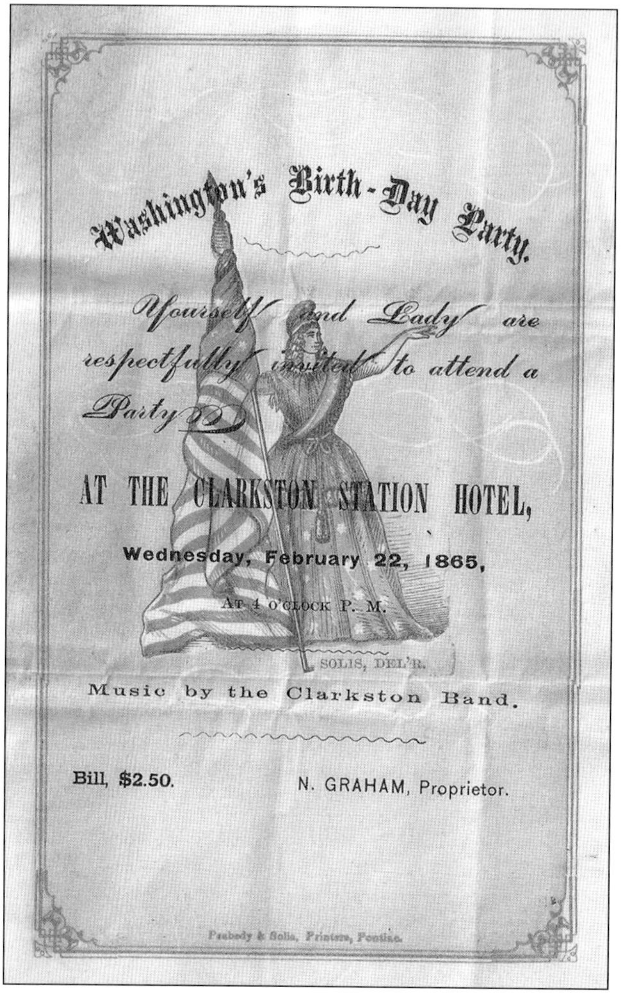

Washington's Birth-Day Party.

Yourself and Lady are respectfully invited to attend a Party

AT THE CLARKSTON STATION HOTEL,

Wednesday, February 22, 1865,

AT 4 O'CLOCK P. M.

SOLIS, DEL'R.

Music by the Clarkston Band.

Bill, $2.50. N. GRAHAM, Proprietor.

Peabody & Solis, Printers, Pontiac.

WASHINGTON'S BIRTHDAY PARTY INVITATION. Not a lot is known about the Clarkston Station Hotel located near the depot, likely an ideal place for visitors and locals alike to celebrate George Washington's birthday with a party February 22, 1865. The cost was $2.50 per couple, which would be about $32 now. The hotel reportedly burned down around the early 1900s, close to when the original train station met a similar demise.

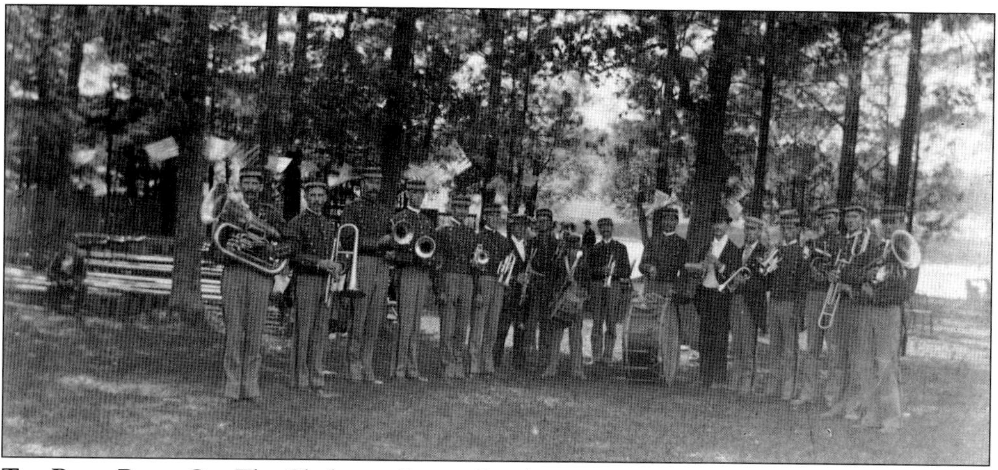

THE BAND PLAYS ON. The Clarkston Cornet Band poses at an outdoor event, possibly a retreat that occurred next to Parke Lake. Like many others, the back of this photograph features the stamp of local photographer W.C. Petty, photographer and crayon artist.

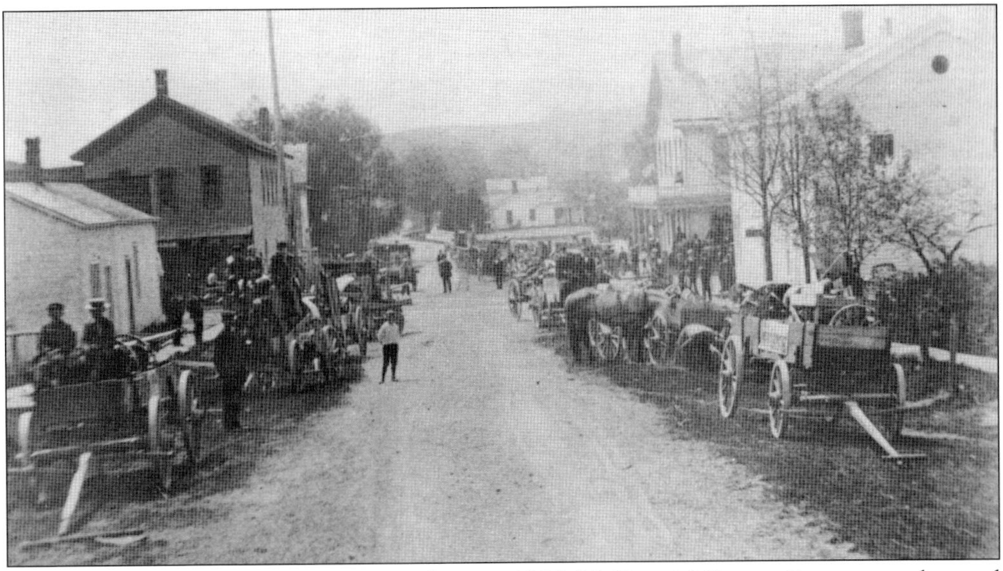

McCormick Day Parade, Washington Street, 1898. McCormick Reaper Company understood that farming families spent Saturdays in town to go to market, run errands, and visit with townspeople, so the company planned Saturday parades featuring its latest equipment draped in bunting—and usually driven by attractive local women—to show off machinery, and, with hope, sell machines. Afterward, local politicians often gave stump speeches before salesmen offered demonstrations. Albert Carran, proprietor of Carran Implements, hosted the McCormick Day parade on May 14, 1898. His shop was in the north half of the Greek Revival building to the right, at Washington and Main Streets. He reportedly delivered 64 machines.

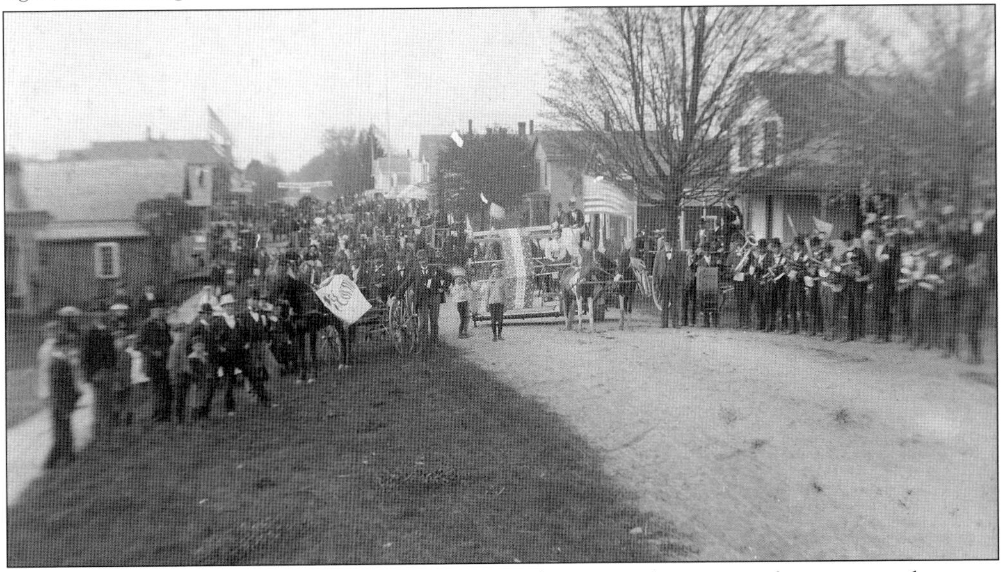

McCormick Day Parade, Main Street, 1898. This unusual image marks a moment between Bingham Hall's demise and the construction of the Maccabee Temple building, which grew in its place in 1902–1903. In the meantime, makeshift structures like a bandstand filled the space. This photograph also shows two houses once on Main Street, now moved. The one directly behind the Clarkston Band on the right relocated farther south on Main Street. The house with parade watchers on its porch is likely now the one at 38 East Washington Street.

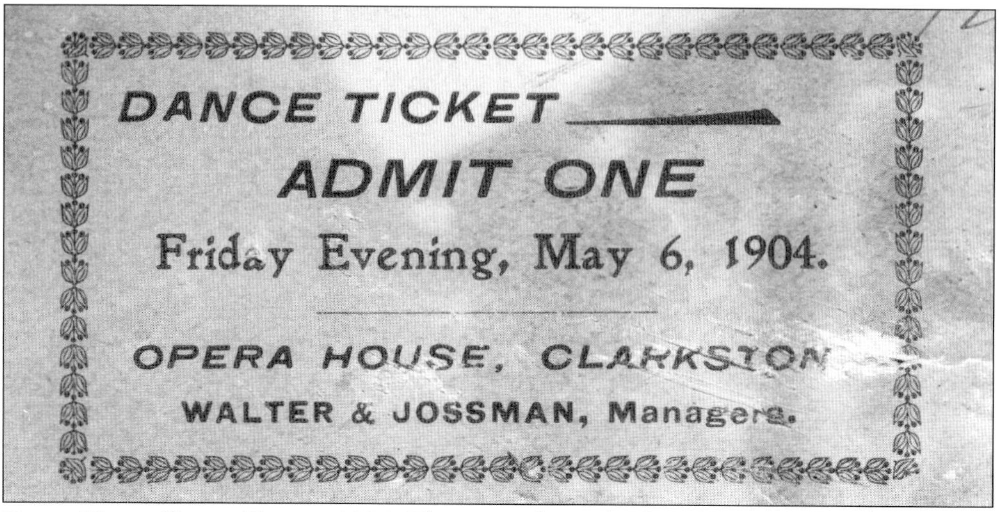
DANCE TICKET

ADMIT ONE

Friday Evening, May 6, 1904.

OPERA HOUSE, CLARKSTON

WALTER & JOSSMAN, Managers.

OPERA HOUSE DANCE TICKET, 1904. The space above the first-floor shops in the Maccabee Temple was an opera house for community activities and performances, even roller-skating parties. In winter, the Redpath Lyceum Bureau of Chicago offered vaudeville medicine shows, plays, and musicals at $3 per ticket. Though many performances sold out, opera house managers Guy Walter and Ralph Jossman made up any difference when necessary, helping to keep the opera house afloat. Eventually deemed unsafe, the space closed to public assembly and later became apartments.

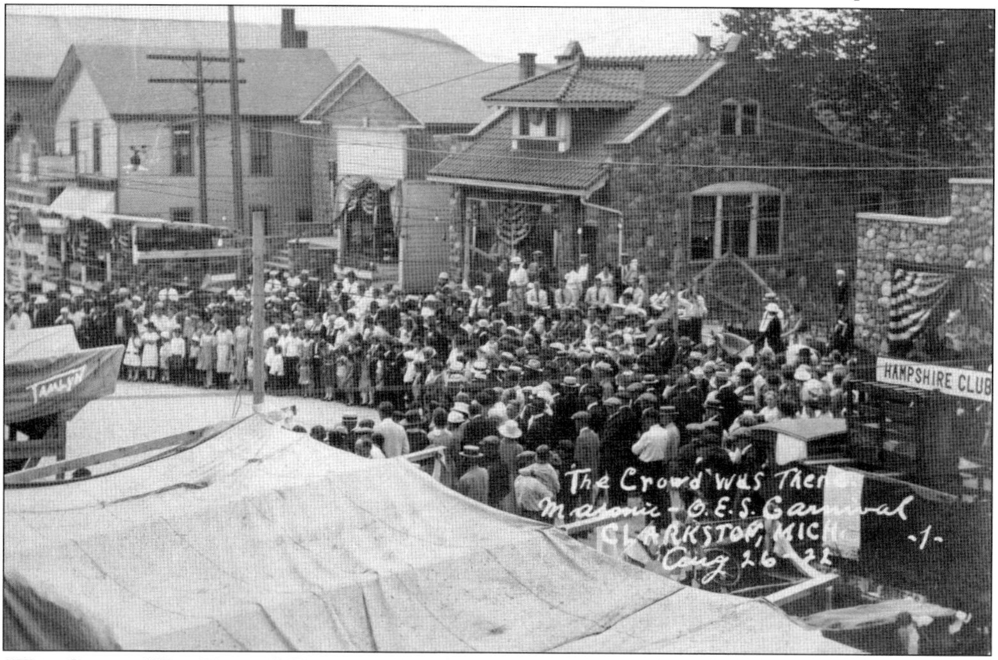

"THE CROWD WAS THERE," THE MASONIC OES CARNIVAL, 1922. Village founders chartered the Masonic Cedar Lodge No. 60 of Free and Accepted Masons on January 13, 1852, originally meeting above Smith's General Store in a Greek Revival building that stood on the corner of East Washington and Main Streets before replacing it with their own commanding brick building in 1916. The Order of the Eastern Star Joseph C. Bird Chapter No. 294 formed April 12, 1901. A fire in the building to its north in 1922 damaged the Masonic lodge, but the community came together for a carnival and parade to raise money for repairs. Scorch marks remain on the building's north wall.

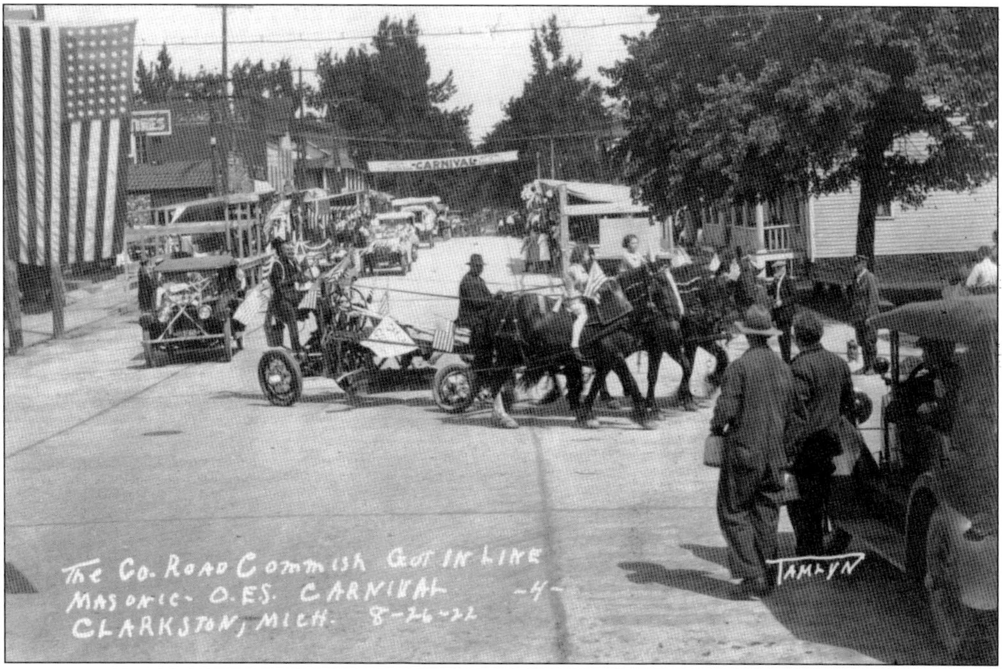

"THE COUNTY ROAD COMMISSION GOT IN LINE" AND "EVERYBODY WAS INTERESTED," 1922. The Masonic parade and carnival also marked a community celebration of the completion of the recent paving of Main Street. The county road commission brought one of its machines to the parade, and the Cedar Lodge paraded its own well-decorated float. Notice the fresh pavement beneath them and the patriotic displays along the Main Street buildings.

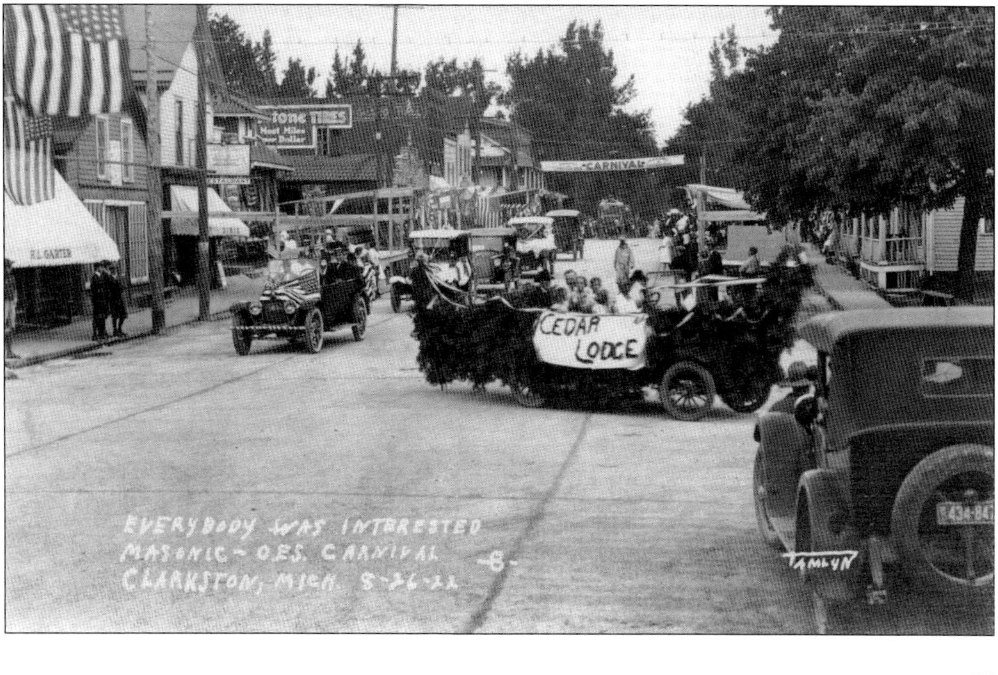

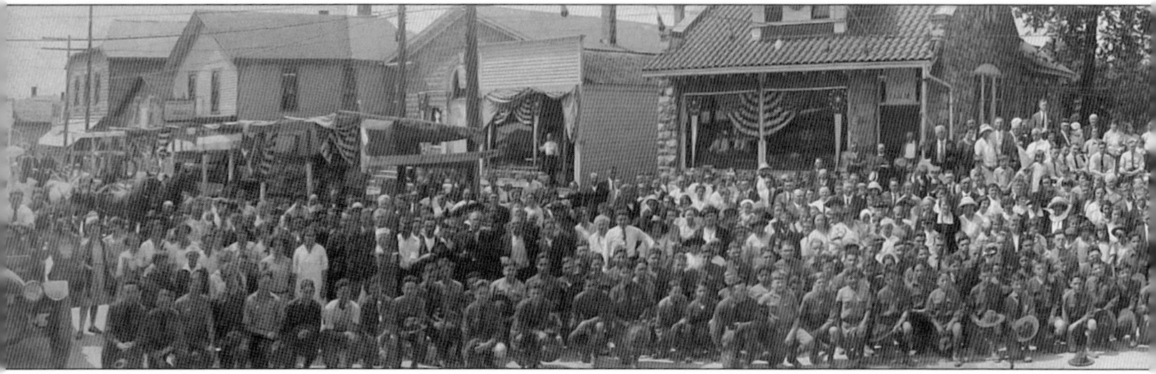

A Clarkston Panorama, 1922. With Clarkston gathered to enjoy the Masonic carnival, it was the perfect opportunity to take a panoramic image of the downtown area. While all of the photographs from the carnival are prized for showing buildings from that era—Voorheis Ford,

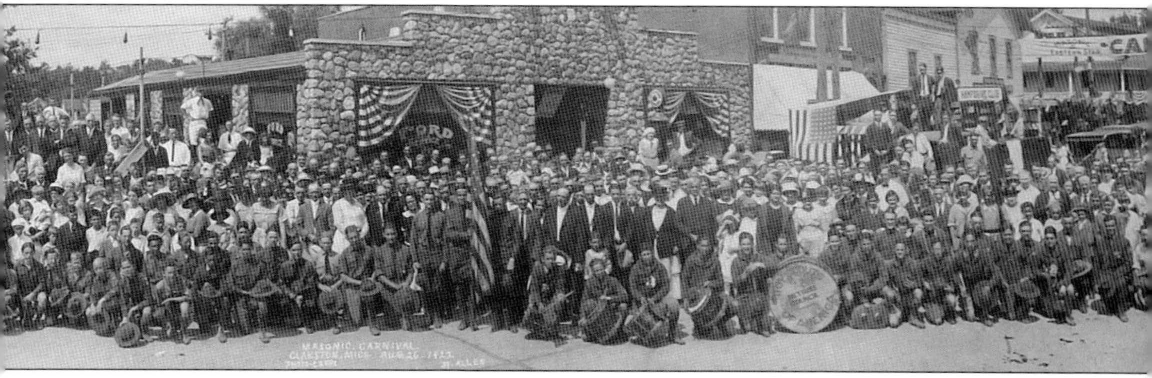

the bank, barbershop, township hall, and the Garter Building—here the townspeople shine, from Scouts to the elderly, captured in time.

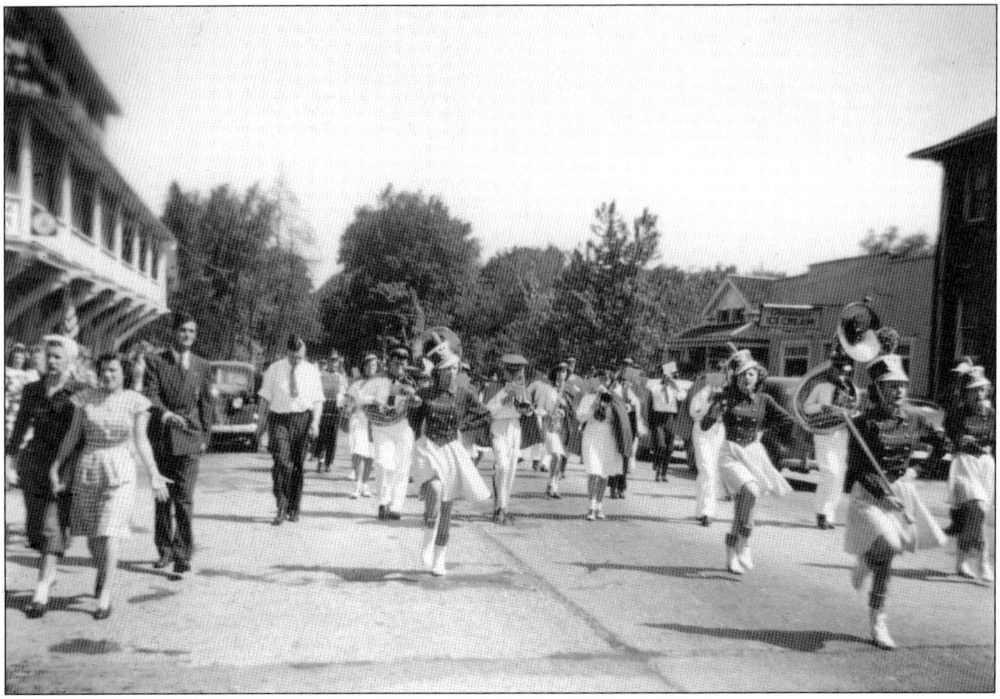

Memorial Day Parade, 1946. A longtime Clarkston tradition, the Clarkston High School Band marches south on Main Street in the 1946 Memorial Day parade.

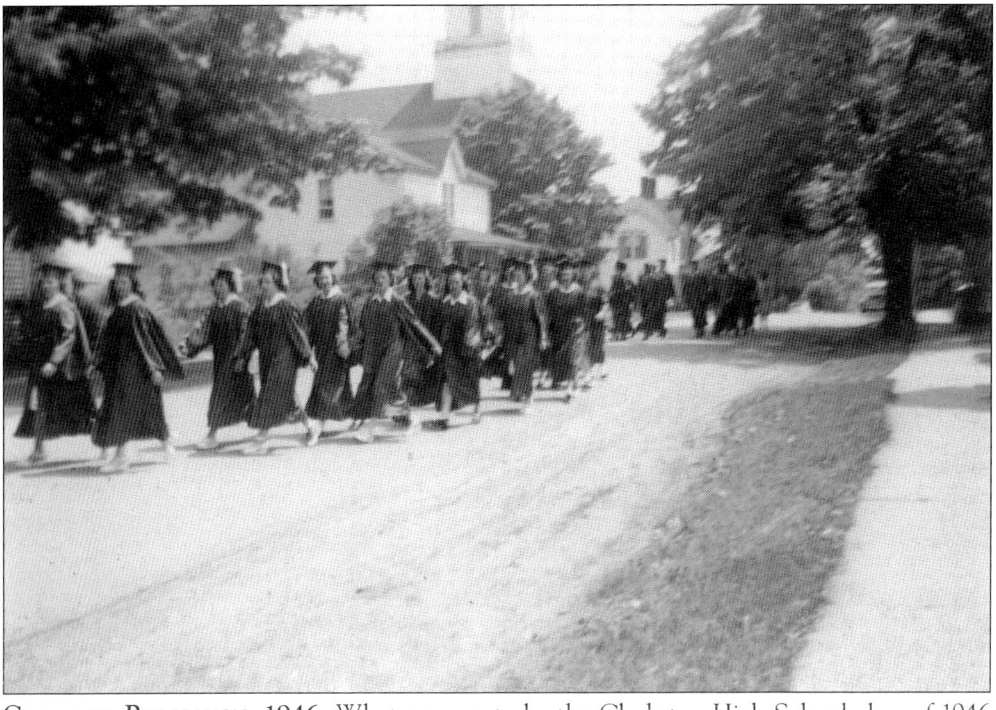

Graduate Procession, 1946. What appears to be the Clarkston High School class of 1946 proudly marches down Buffalo Street in June of that year, likely coming from the school on Church Street.

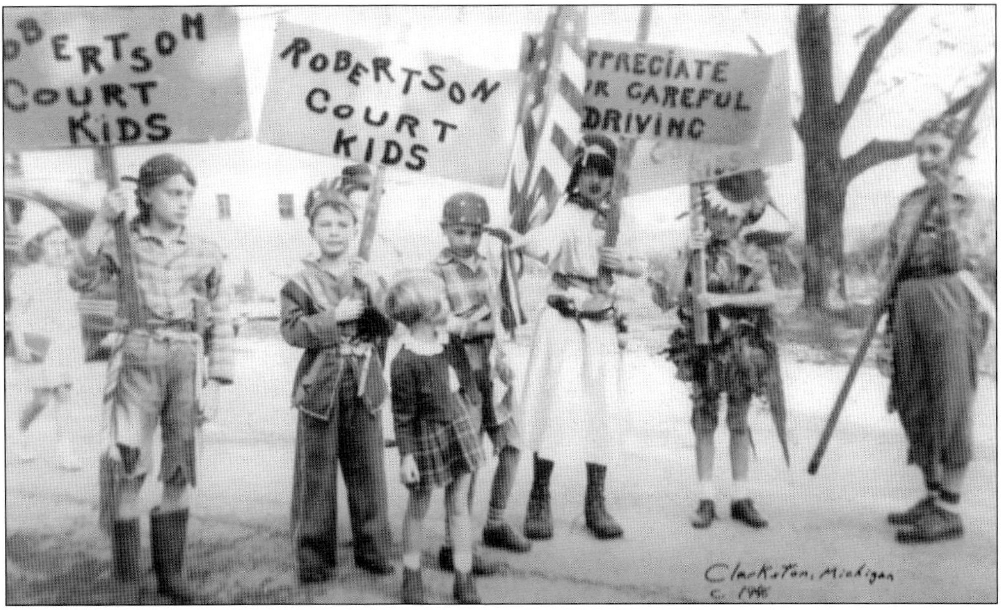

Robertson Court Kids, 1946. The young people of Robertson Court come together to represent their street, and their concerns, in a parade. The "drive slowly" message still resonates today. From left to right, the young man holding a sign and wearing boots is Charles "Chuck" Gray Robertson III, next is his brother Milton Robertson, descendants of local Civil War surgeon Dr. Charles Gray Robertson, the man whose land became the Robertson Court development. The other children are Georgia Robinson, Bobby Jones, Tom Bullen, Kay Robinson, and Don Lord.

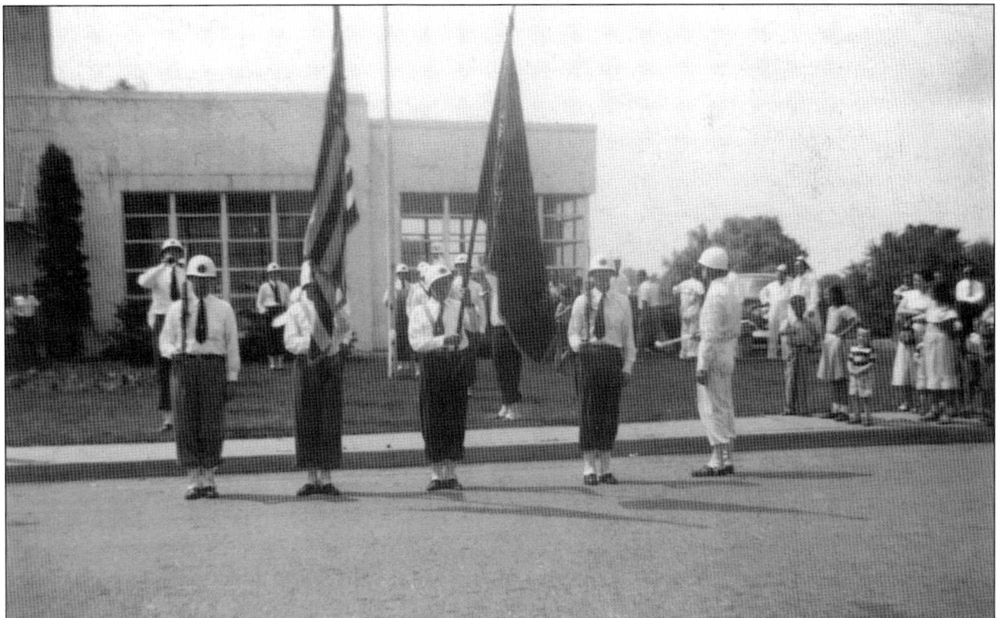

Drum and Bugle Corps, 1950. The drum and bugle corps pauses in front of the Ford facility on Washington Street, July 4, 1950. Five years after Ford closed his factory, the building became the home of the Hawke Tool and Engineering Company.

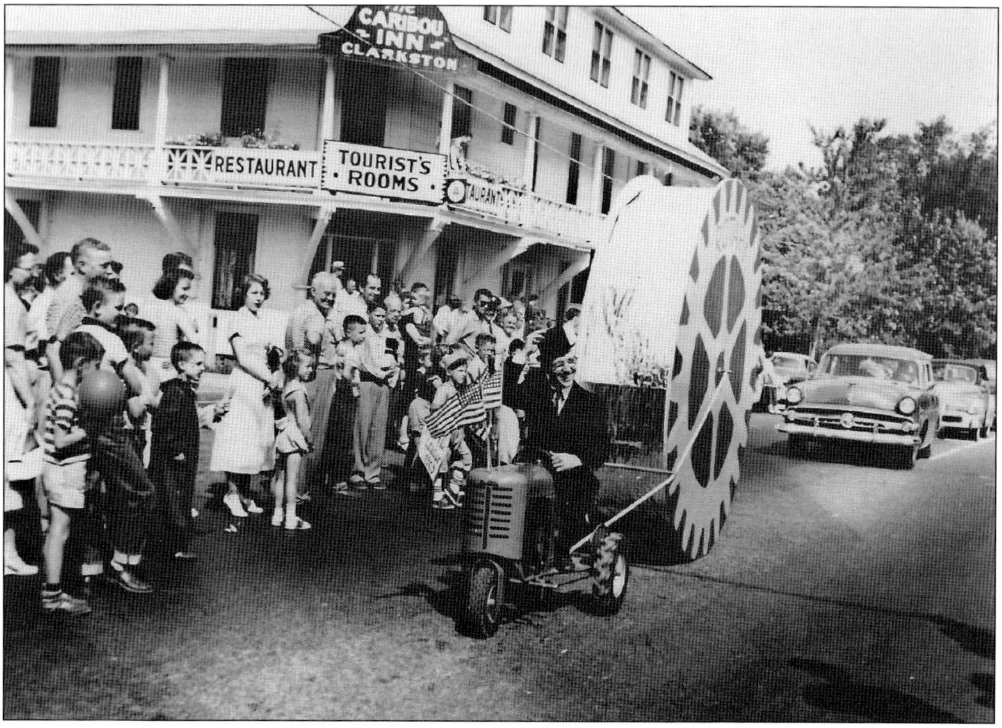

Fourth of July Parades, 1956. Longtime Clarkston resident Virginia Walter once recounted how neighborhoods would get in the spirit of parades by choosing a theme and then creating a float and costumes. Above, a Rotarian pulls the Rotary float, while below, children dressed as Robin Hood and his band of merry men march. From left to right are Dick Spohn, Rocky Bullard, Thayer Wilson, Blair Bullard, Rick Thompson, and Tommy Bullard. Both shots were taken in front of the Caribou Inn, which would be gone within two years.

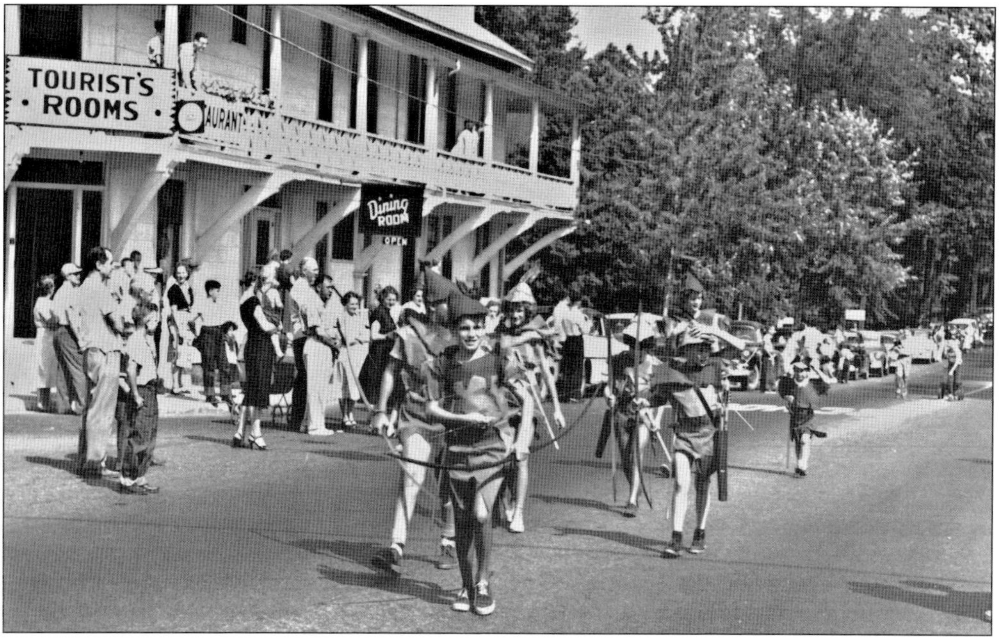

Seven

CLARKSTON LEARNS

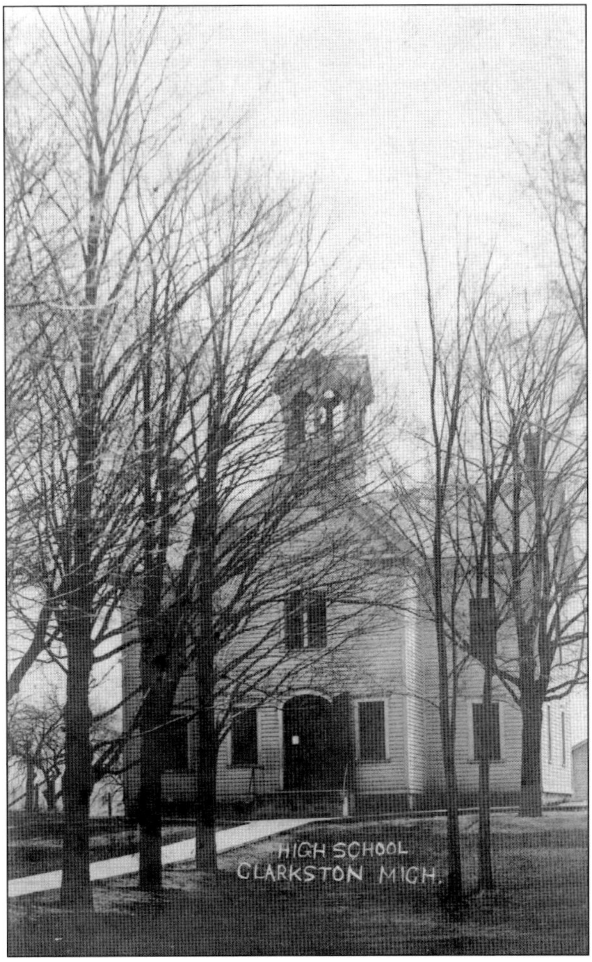

HIGH SCHOOL, POSTMARKED 1908. In 1840, Nelson Washington Clark built this impressive Greek Revival schoolhouse on a lot that stretches down to picturesque Parke Lake. Started as a private academy, Clarkston Union School became a public school in 1862.

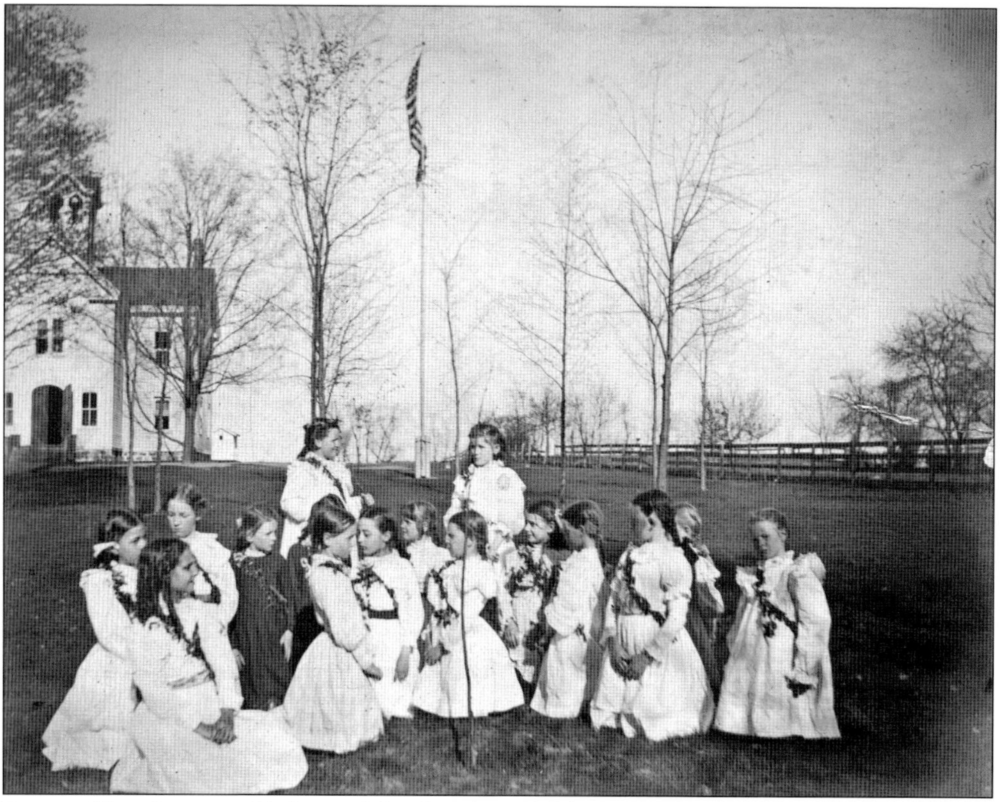

School Kids Gather. Clarkston School students celebrate Flag Day at 90 North Main Street.

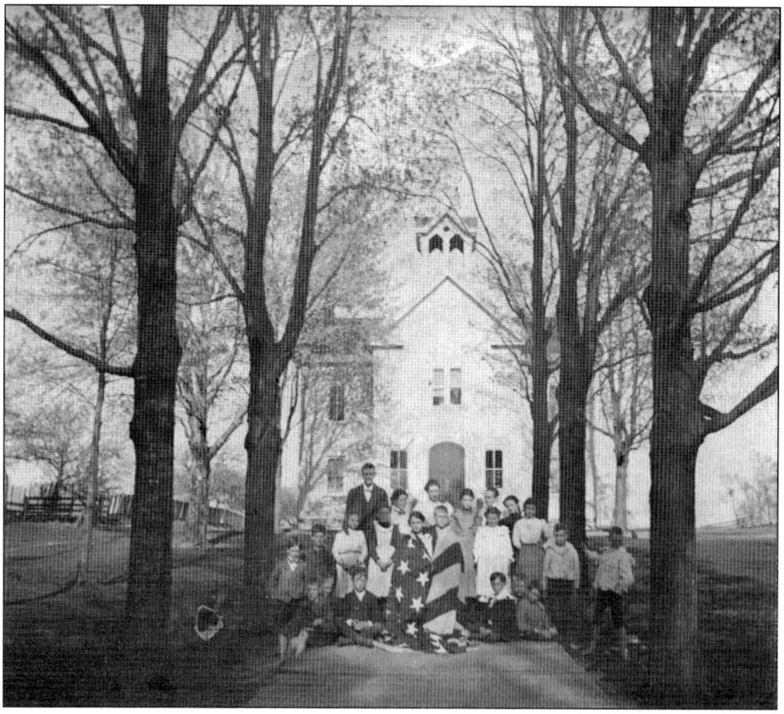

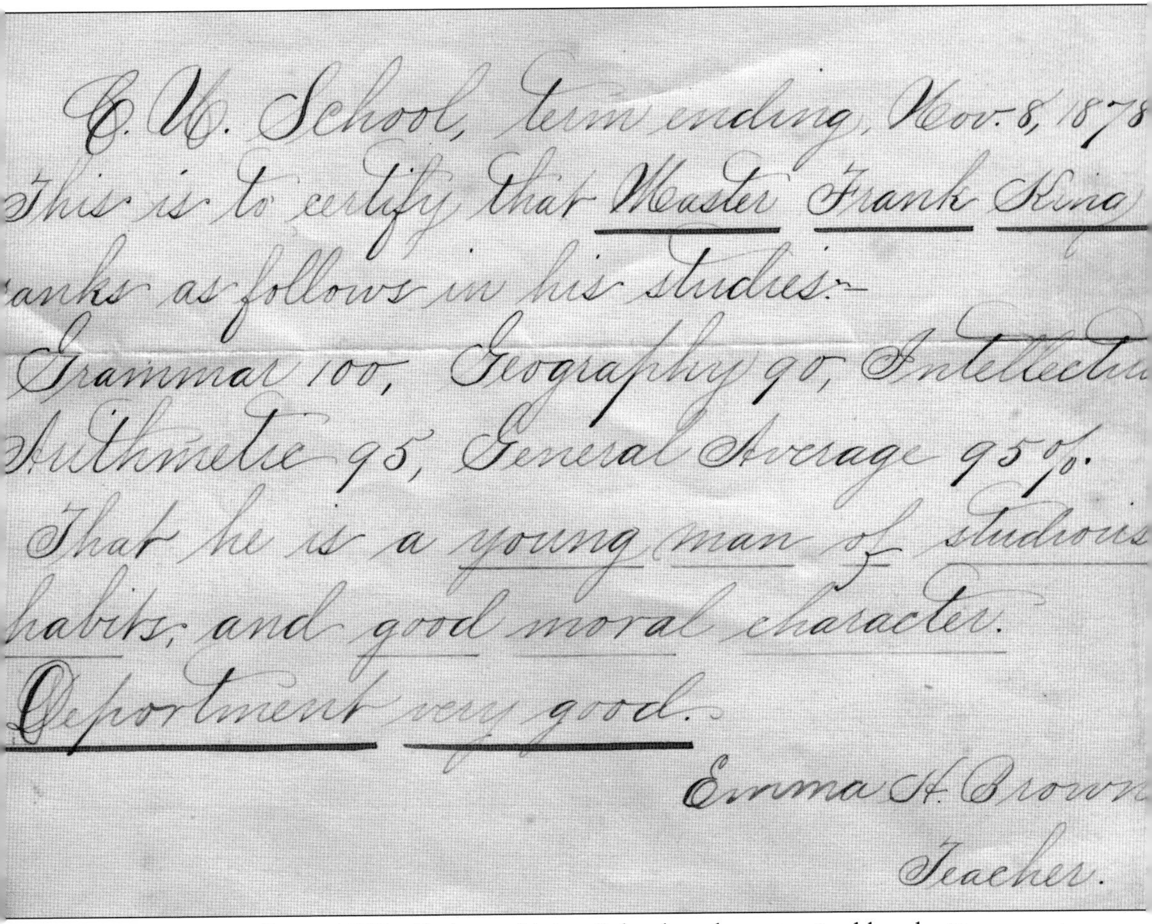
C. U. School, term ending, Nov. 8, 1878
This is to certify that Master Frank King
ranks as follows in his studies:—
Grammar 100, Geography 90, Intellectu
Arithmetic 95, General Average 95%.
That he is a young man of studious
habits, and good moral character.
Deportment very good.
Emma H. Brown
Teacher.

School Report Card, 1878. Clarkston Union School students received handwritten report cards like this one that belonged to Frank King for a term ending November 8, 1878, declaring King "a young man of studious habits, and good moral character."

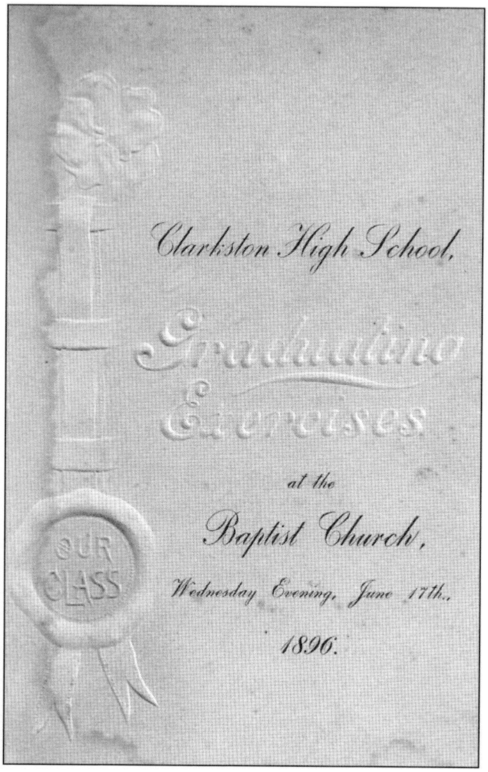

GRADUATION CEREMONY PROGRAM, 1896. Early graduation ceremonies took place in the Baptist church or later at Maccabee Temple's opera house, where graduates often gave a speech or performed a musical interlude.

THE 1896 CLARKSTON HIGH SCHOOL GRADUATING CLASS. The 1896 graduating class of Clarkston High School included, from left to right, (first row) Lulu Hammond and Mary Scrace Hammond; (second row) Durand Ogden, Etta Van Horn, Abraham L. Craft (teacher), Ada Vaughan, and Carleton Bower; (third row) Eliza Shay, Ralph Jossman, Bessie Laurie Beardslee, Ray Addis, Sarah Carran, and Barney Roberts.

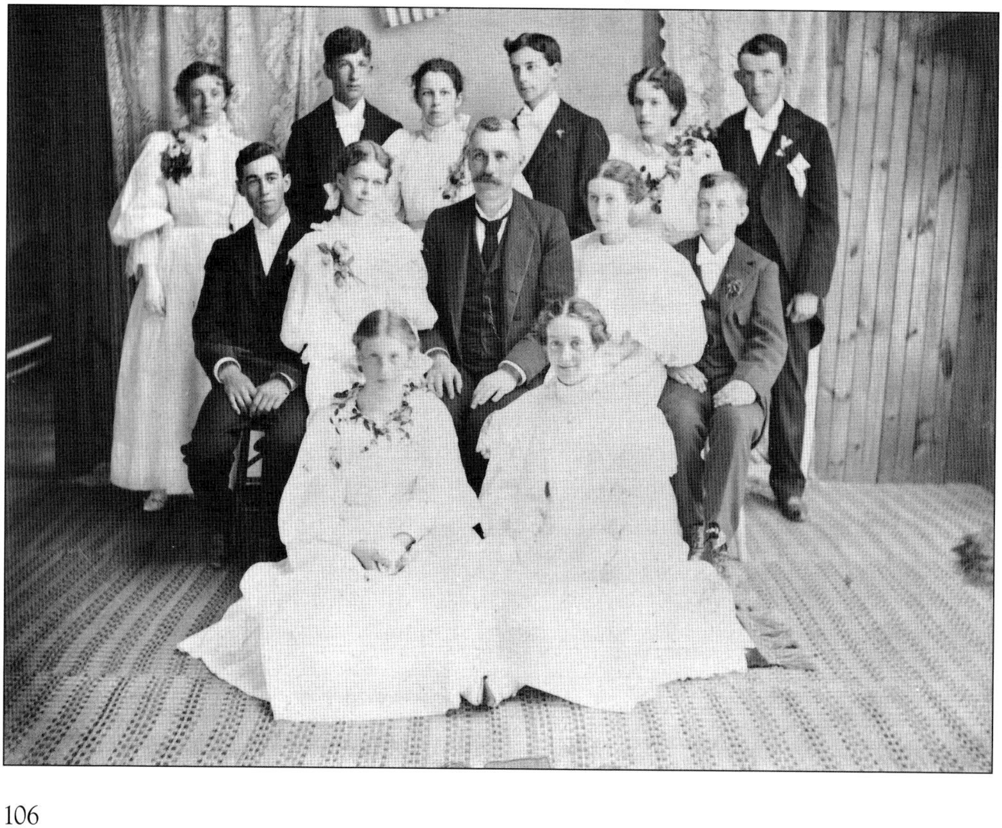

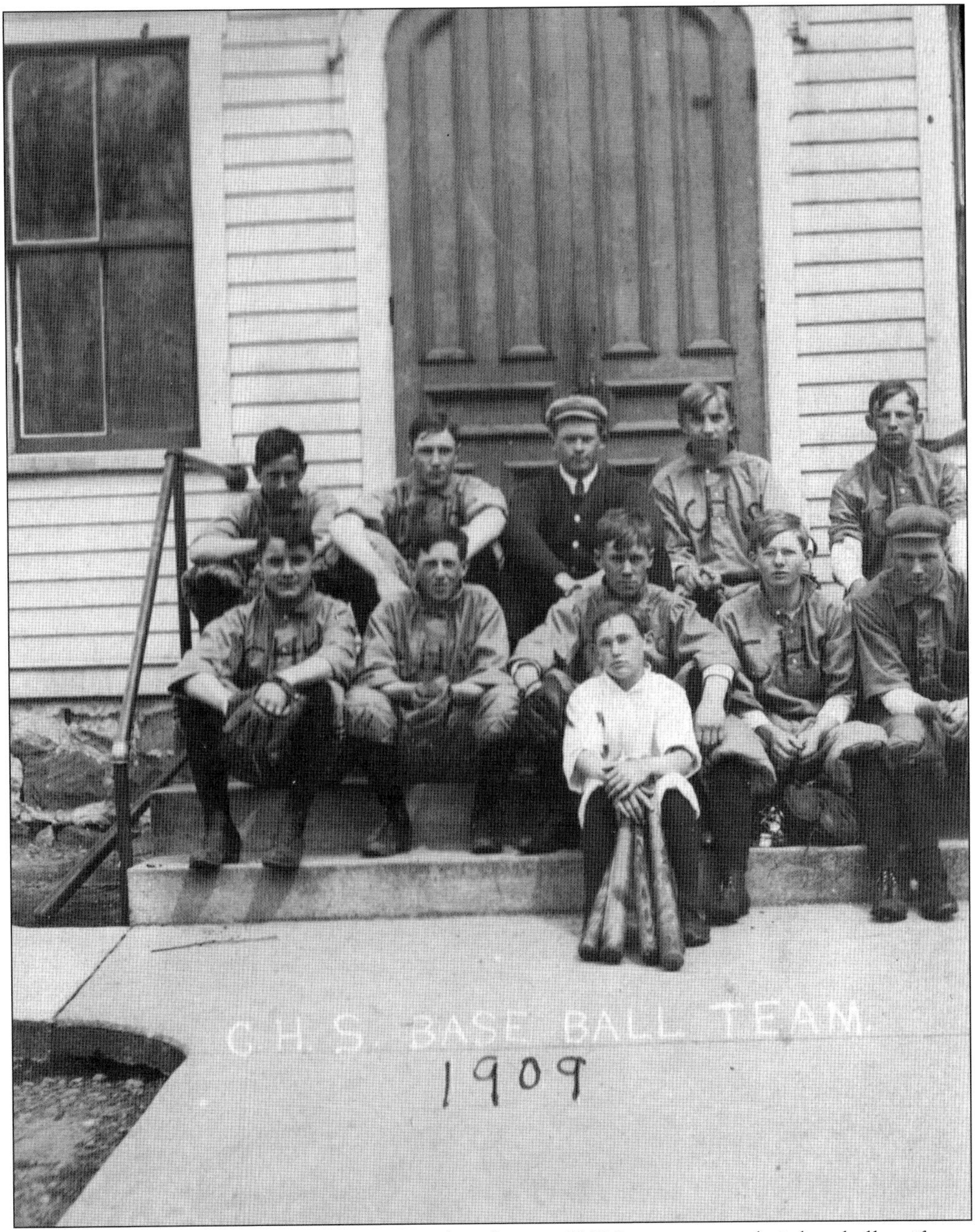

CHS BASEBALL TEAM, 1909. Boys sporting hand-sewn CHS letters across their baseball uniforms pose on the steps of the original white clapboard Clarkston Union School, by then known as Clarkston High School. The postcard explains the lack of smiles: "We got soaked up here. 18 to 6, favor Fenton."

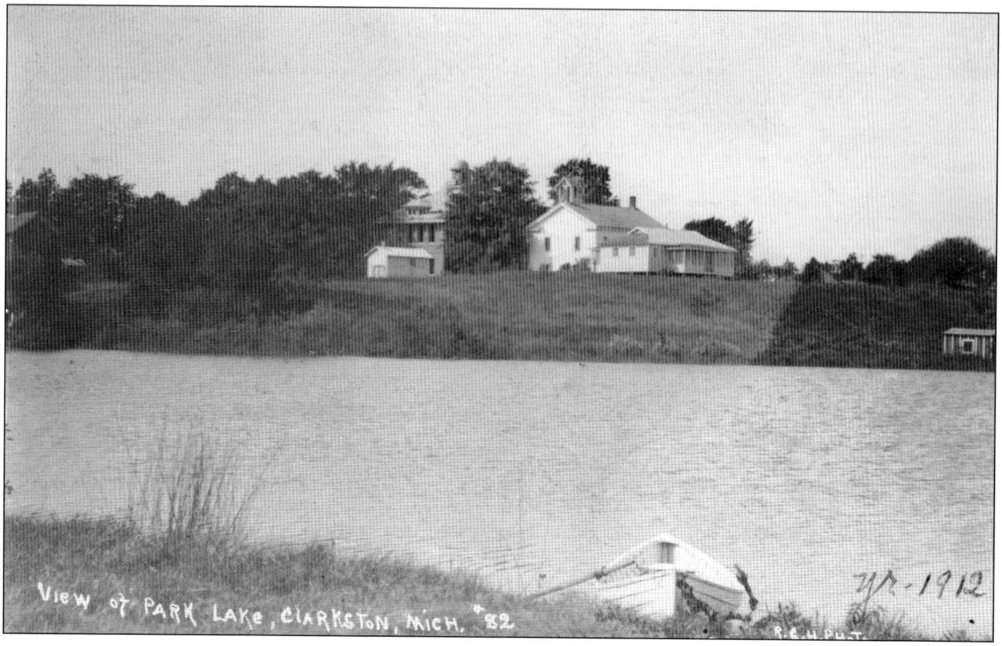

View across Parke Lake, 1912 and Clarkston School, c. 1915–1918. In 1910, the need for more space meant dismantling the wooden structure to make room for a larger school. Pictured above across Parke Lake, the original white school stands near its replacement brick building, still under construction. Below, several years later, students enjoy time outside the new Clarkston School while a few others watch from inside.

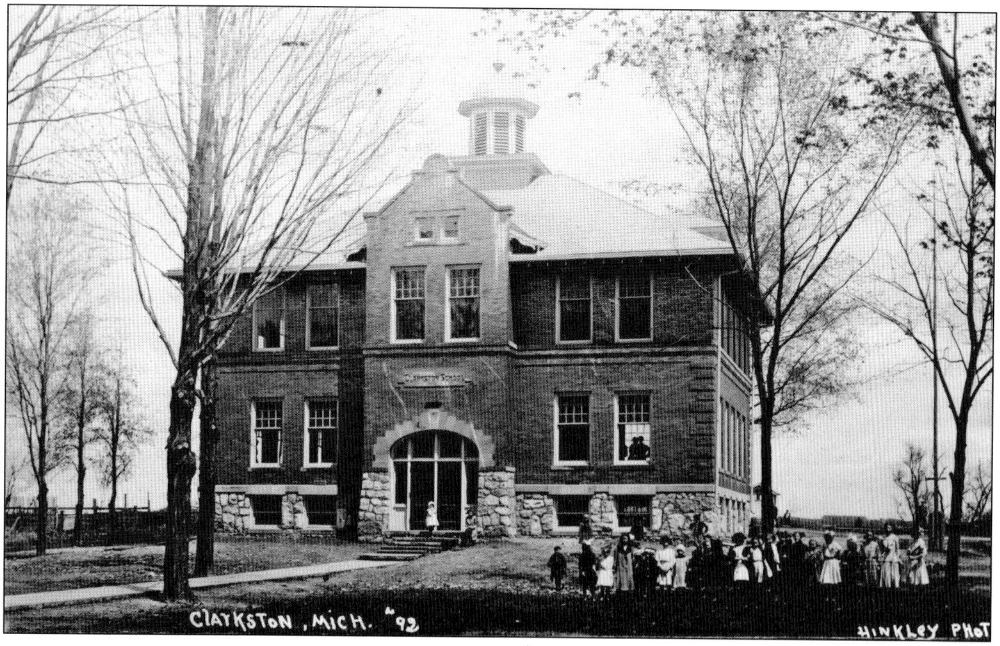

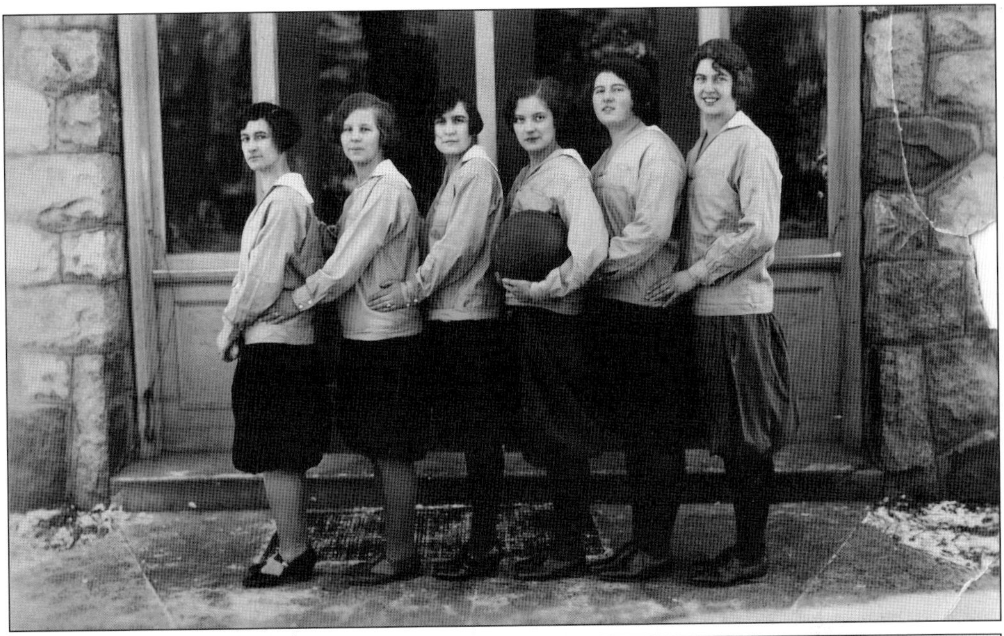

Clarkston School Girls' Basketball Team. Posing in front of Clarkston School from left to right are Blanch Crosby, Bertha Zych, Leola Francis, Evelyn Dunston (holding basketball), Isabella King, and Helen Cheeseman.

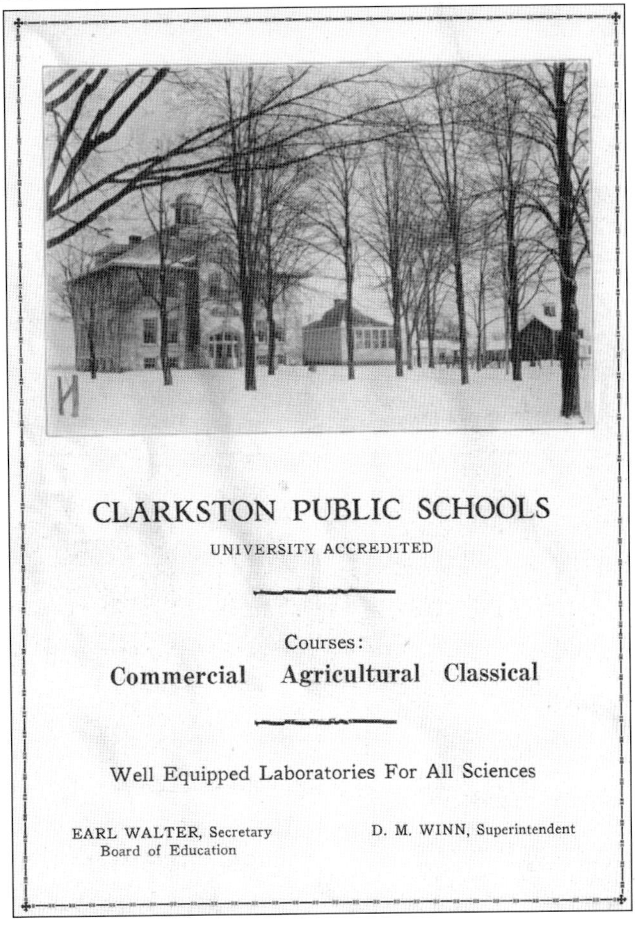

Clarkston Public Schools Advertisement, 1926. An image from the 1926 yearbook, *The Oracle*, touts Clarkston Public Schools' university accreditation, as well as its courses in agriculture and well-equipped science labs. The snow-covered scene also shows the school's small square outbuilding, built in 1925, that in 1955 became Clarkston's first public library.

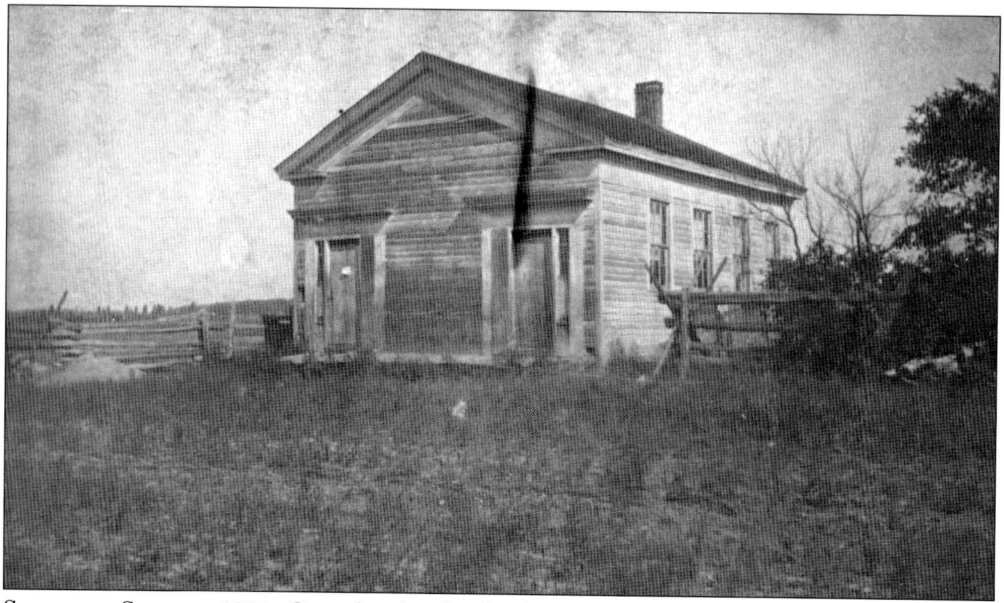

Sashabaw School, 1901. Considered to be the first school in the township, the early school district established Sashabaw School in 1834 and the small Greek Revival building pictured here was built by the late 1830s. The district relocated the building in 1902.

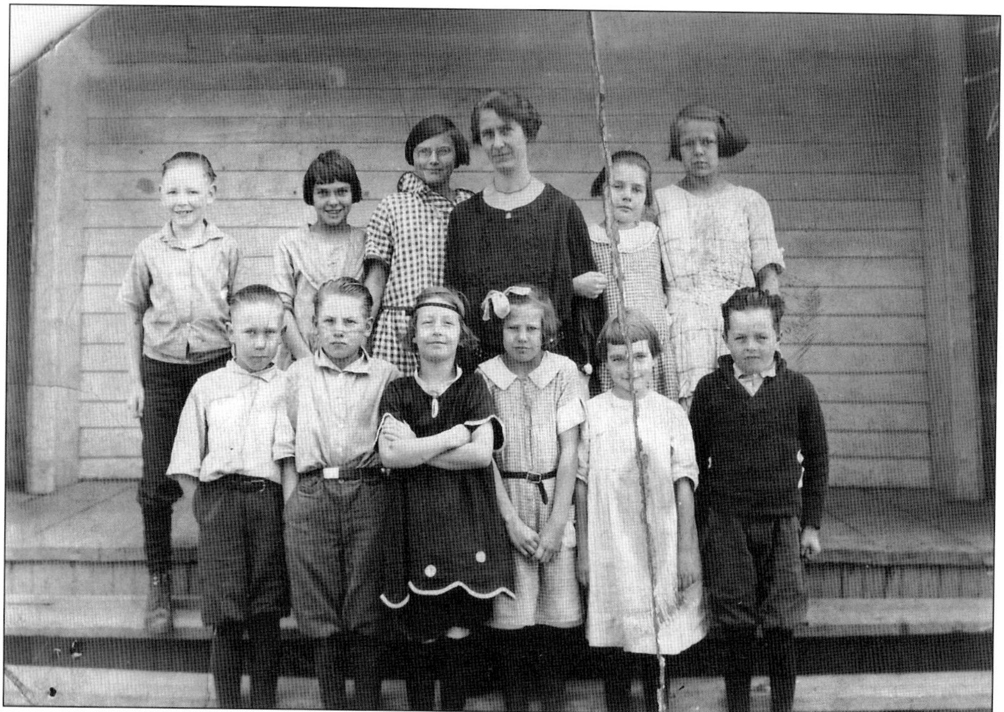

Class at Clarkston Station School, 1923. Teacher Jane Cuthbert poses with her students on September 13, 1923. Named for its proximity to the depot, the Clarkston Station School on White Lake Road near Andersonville Road also stood where four townships basically converge: Waterford, White Lake, Springfield, and Independence.

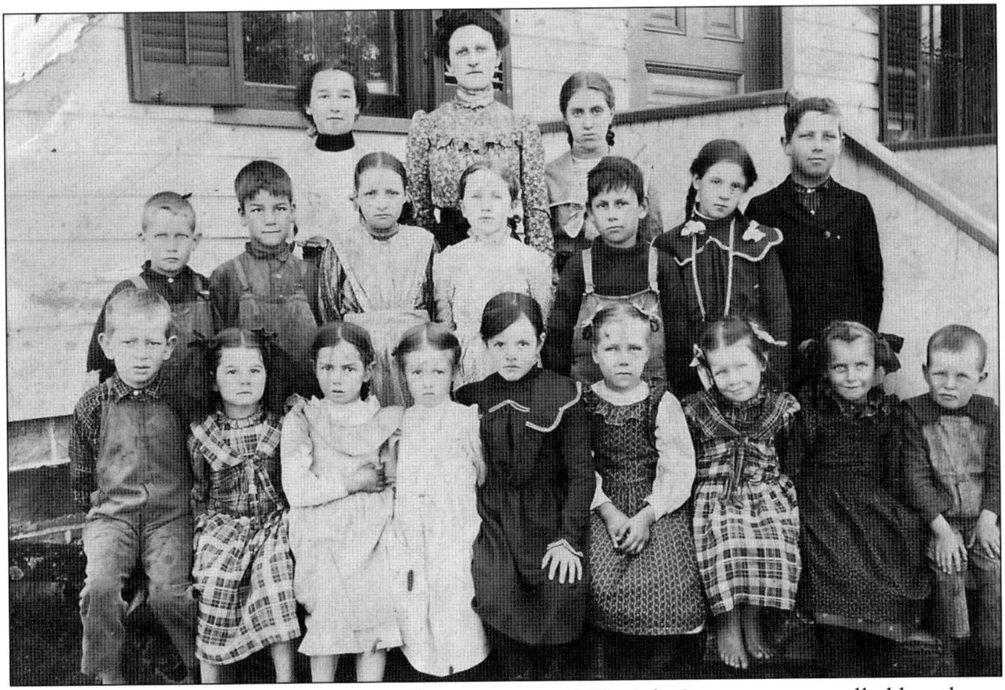

Bailey Lake School Students and Souvenir, c. 1901. Ada Scrace once recalled her three-quarter-mile trek through snow to get to school, trudging a path for the smaller kids to follow. Above, teacher Della Wolfe poses with her students at Bailey Lake School. Pictured are Maude Bailey, Della Wolfe, Olive Scrace, Howard Bailey, Mary Darling, Ada Scrace, Clarence Miller, Winnie Bailey, Bill Hart, Cleve Collins, Alma Bailey, Bessie Bailey, Dorothy Bailey, Mildred Bailey, Jessie Cline, Mabel Klein, Clara Cline, and Elmer Collins.

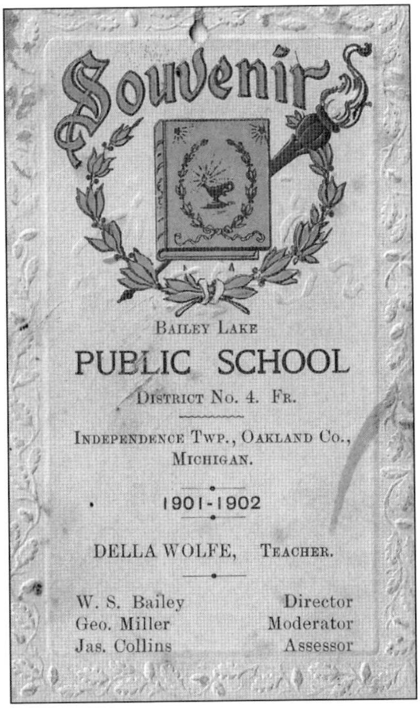

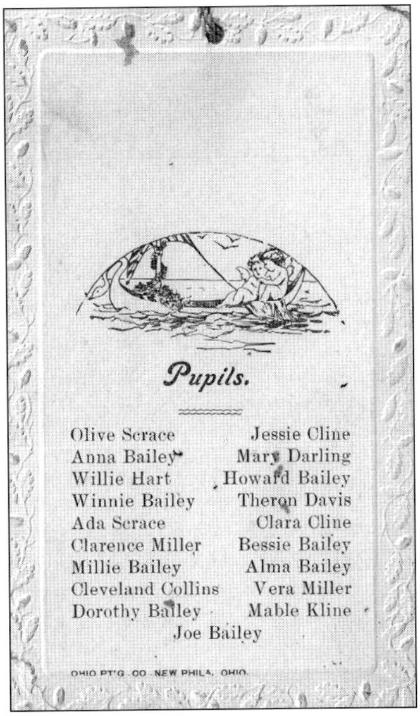

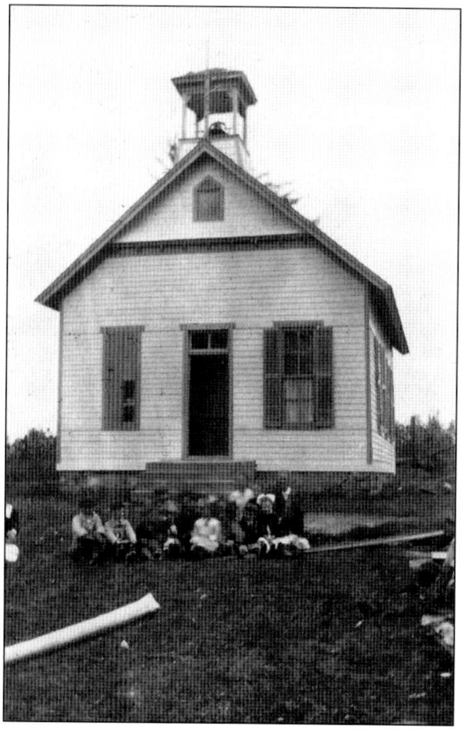

Bailey Lake School, c. 1917. The one-room Bailey Lake School stood at the corner of Stickney and Whipple Lake Roads.

Bailey Lake Students in Water, c. 1917. Teacher Vera Miller's students wade in water.

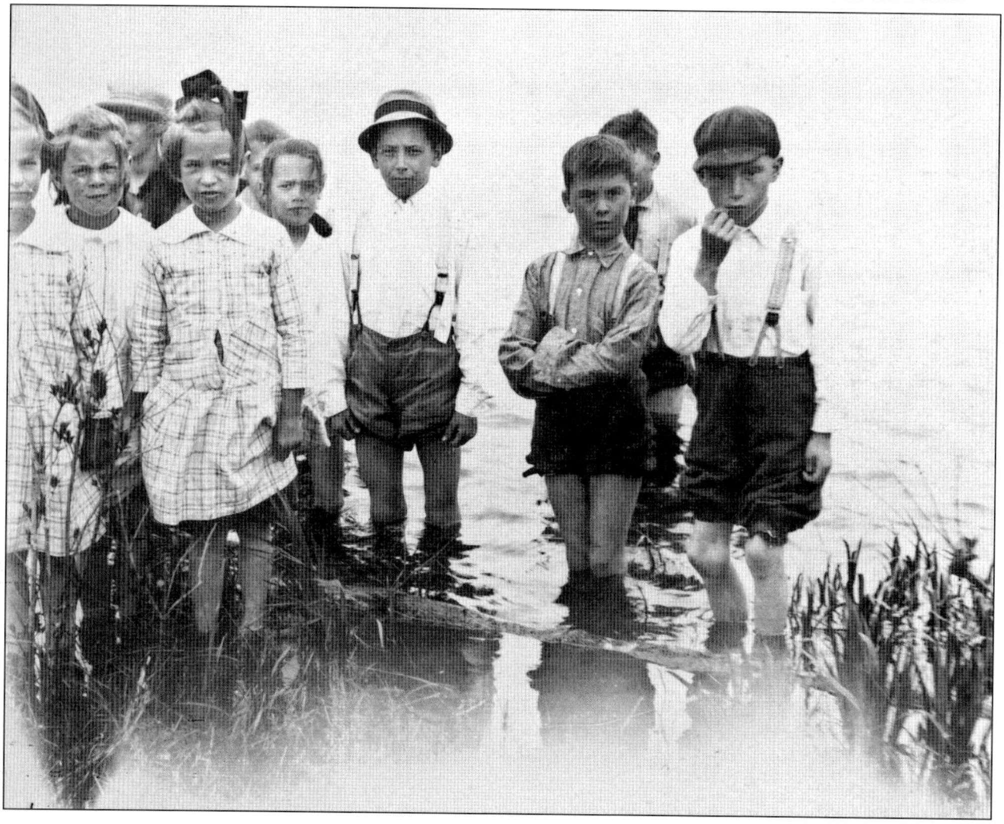

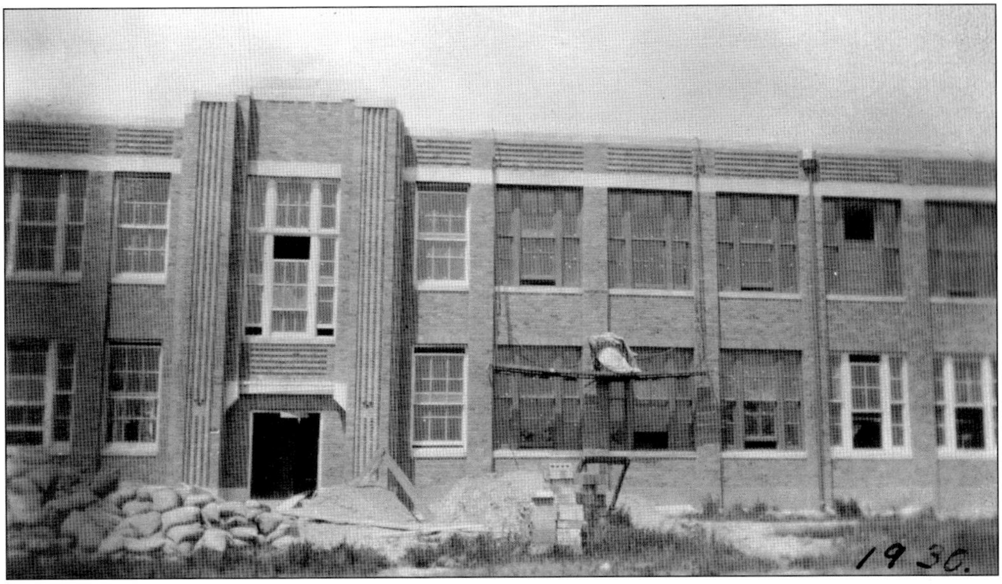

Construction of a New Clarkston High School Building. With more of the rural schools coming together for high school, and the Clarkston School at 90 North Main Street feeling cramped, the district needed a new building. Construction of the new Clarkston High School building between East Church Street and Waldon Road took place in 1930.

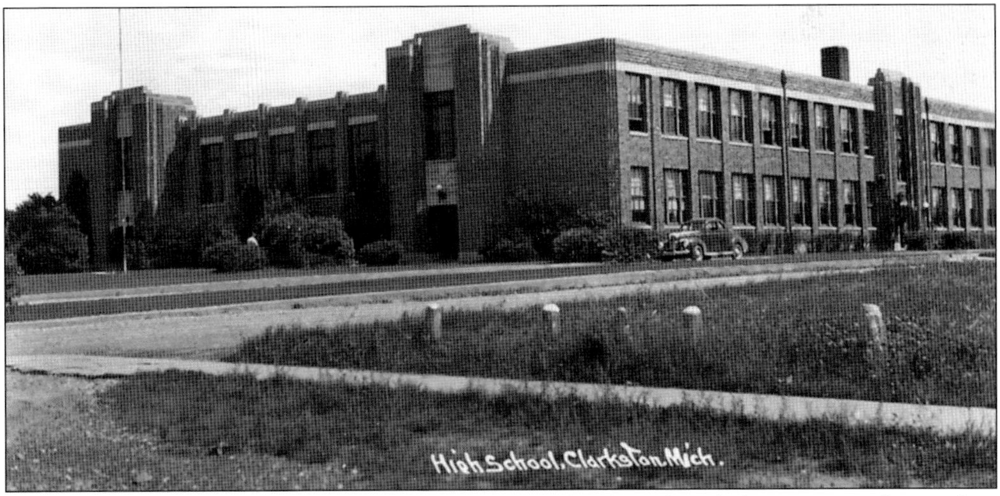

Clarkston High School. The 21-room Clarkston School combined elementary and secondary schools. Its Art Deco design features dual-brick corbels that climbed the two-story brick building's Church Street side, the main entrance at the time. The building cost $140,000 to build.

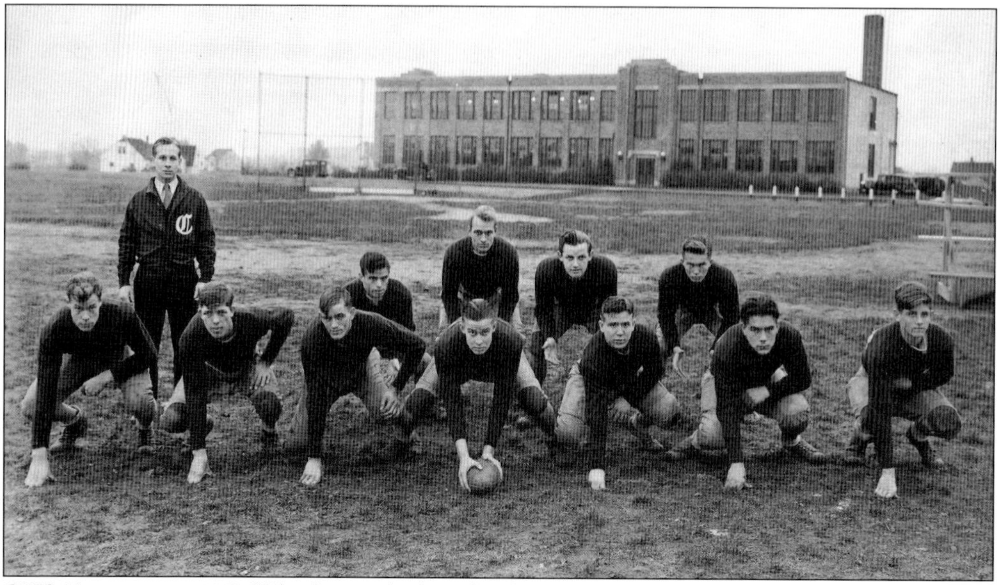

CHS Football, 1935. Whether with the school orchestra or on the football team, the bigger school meant greater extracurricular opportunities inside and out.

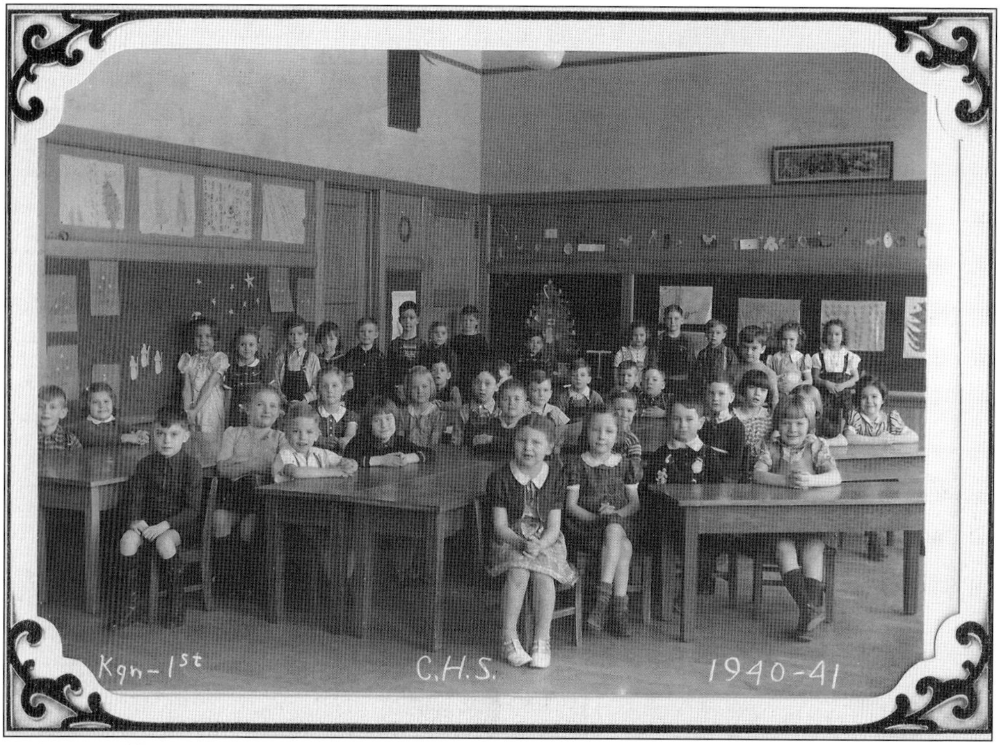

1940–1941 Kindergarten Class. Charles "Chuck" Gray Robertson III (front left) warmly recalls his time in the Art Deco building attending half-day kindergarten straight through to finishing high school in 1958. Robertson's pleasant memories of crawling in through a window with his friends to play basketball in the gym after hours outshine more serious ones, like when school administrators built bomb shelters at the main entrance on Church Street after the start of World War II.

Eight

Clarkston Worships

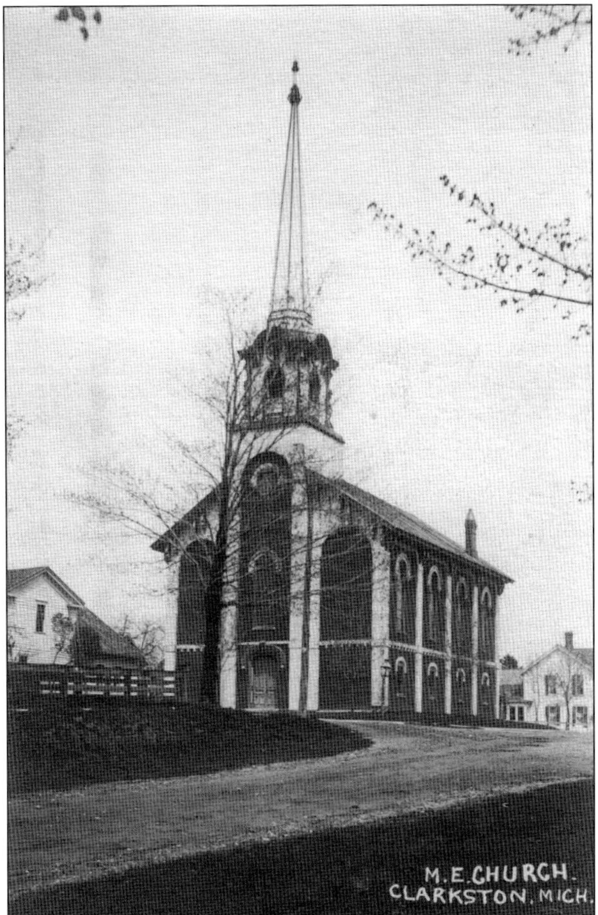

The Methodist Episcopal Church. Although the oval frontispiece reads first M.E. Church Clarkston, parishioners began construction on an earlier wooden-frame church building in 1841. With that original church unfinished until 1847, the 35 members at that time met most often in the schoolhouse. In 1873, parishioners razed the wooden church to build this 40-by-60-foot brick building on its site at Buffalo and Church Streets.

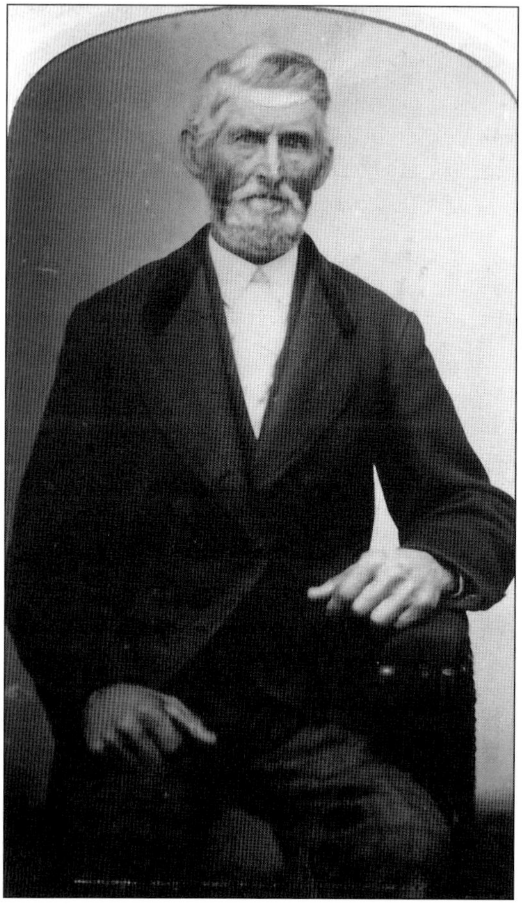

PETER ADDIS. Local farmer and church member Peter Addis used an ox team and a stoneboat to transport rocks from his farm to form the building's foundation. On June 1, 1873, parishioners set in place the cornerstone and six months later dedicated the new building, big enough to hold a 300-person congregation.

METHODIST CHURCH INTERIOR. In 1930, a fire caused extensive damage to the church, destroying much of the interior. And though the parish repaired the building, soon it could no longer accommodate growing membership. In 1961, the parish constructed a new Georgian Colonial–style church on seven nearby acres between Church Street and Waldon Road. The Salvation Army used the old church for a number of years, but later the building became empty and fell into disrepair. In 1980, a family purchased and renovated the structure to use as a private residence.

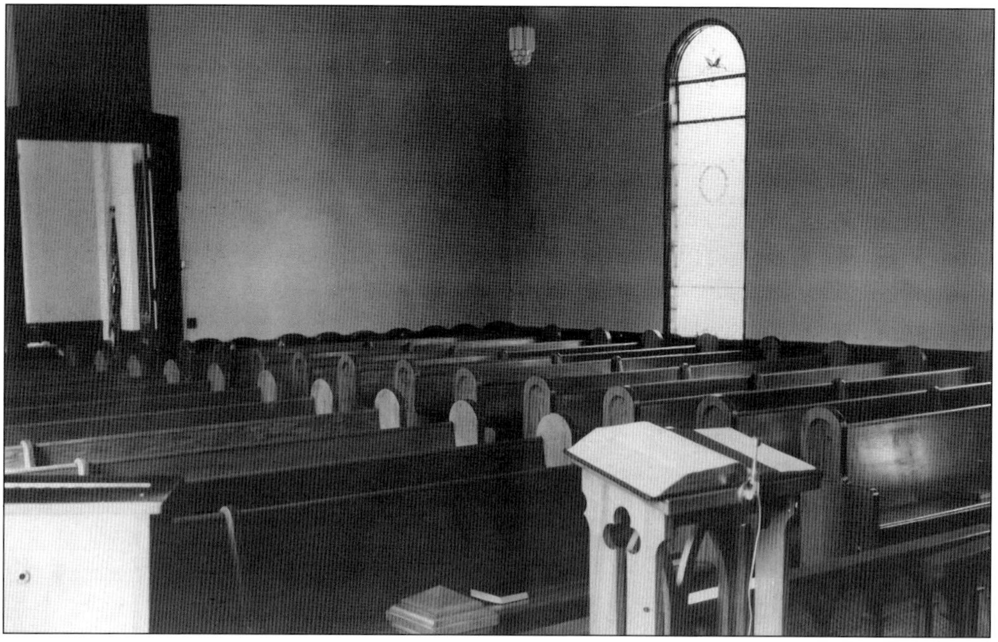

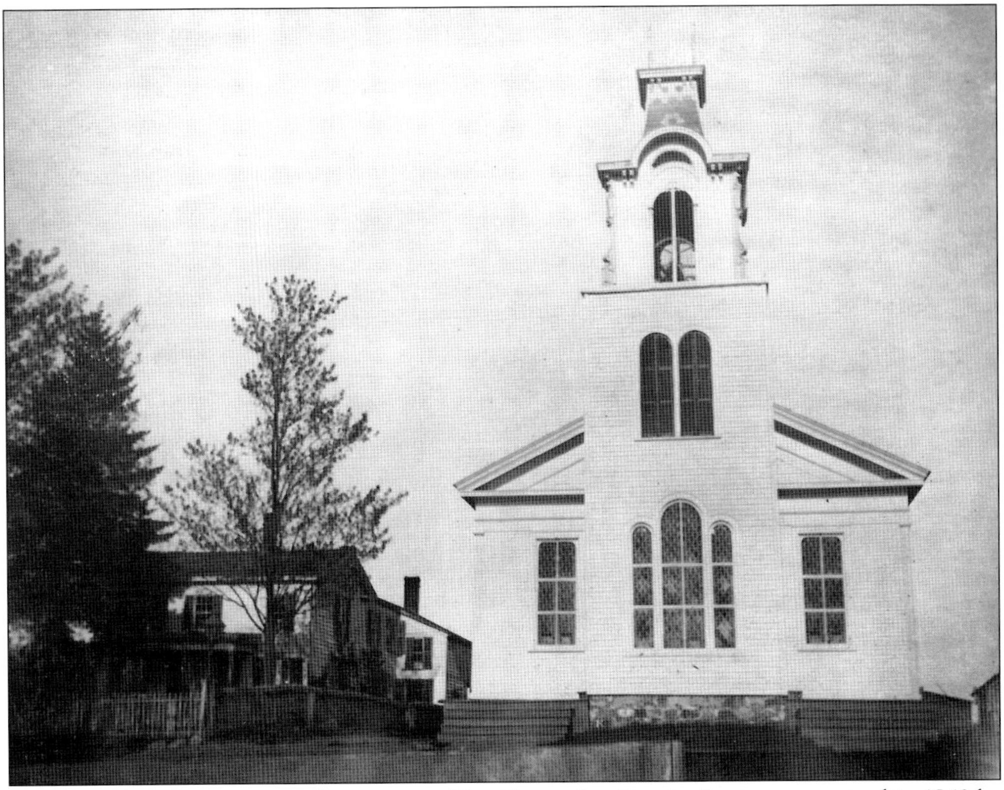

First Baptist Church and Parsonage. The 21-member Baptist Society, organized in 1843 by Rev. Asahel Keith, held its first meetings in the schoolhouse. In 1847, the membership built the 36-by-46-foot Greek Revival–style structure, which cost $3,000. After the Baptists moved to a larger structure outside of the village, other denominations used the space until it was deconsecrated in the early 1990s. During 1994 renovations to convert the building into the Clarkston Union restaurant, owners removed aluminum siding to discover that the clapboard remained underneath. They also renovated the parsonage building next door to use as a business and residence.

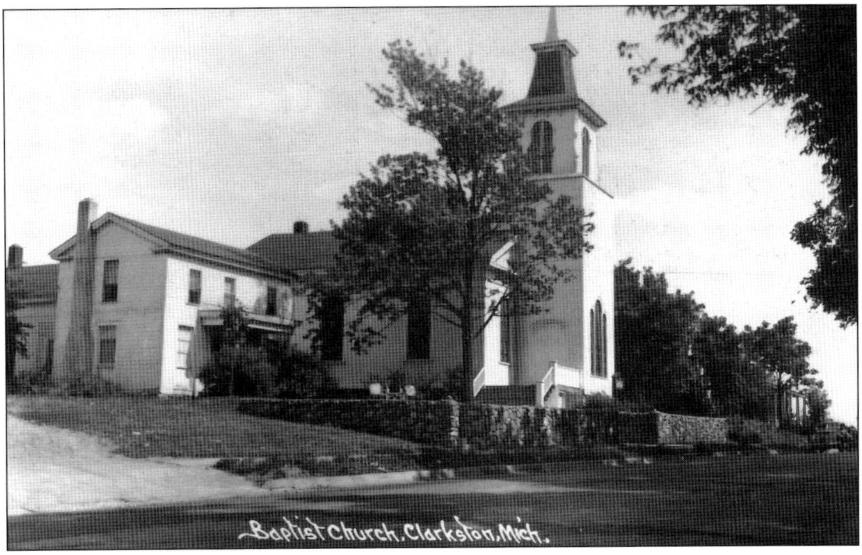

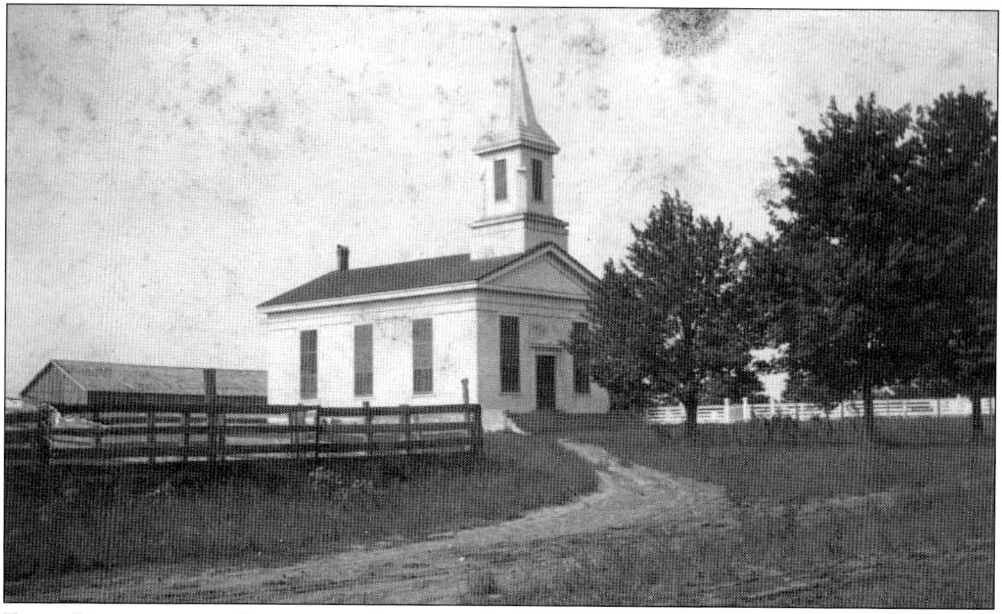

First Presbyterian Church of Independence. Dedicated in 1856, the First Presbyterian Church of Independence is among the oldest of the Detroit Presbytery. Declining membership caused the church to dissolve in 1932. The church structure again welcomed parishioners with the organization of Sashabaw United Presbyterian Church in 1946. Though the parish moved across the street, it maintains ownership of the building, using it on occasion.

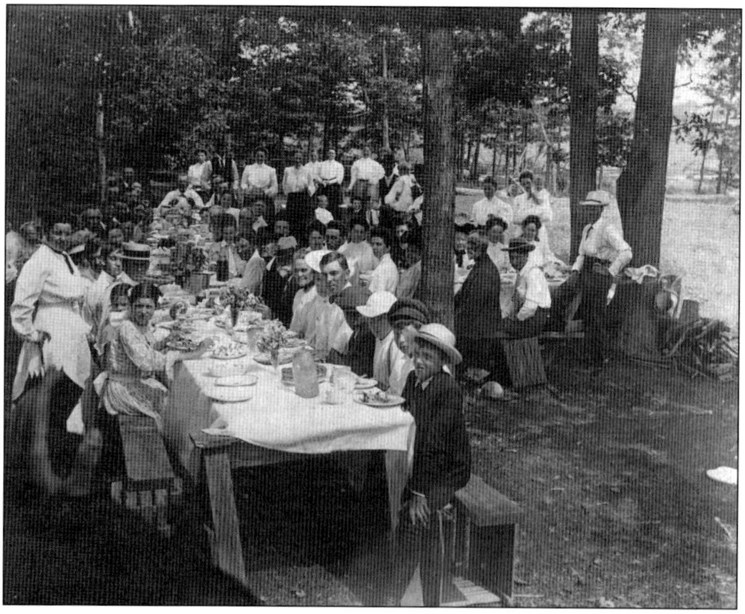

First Presbyterian Sunday School Picnic, c. 1910. A large group gathers in fellowship at a Sunday school picnic at the First Presbyterian Church. The man wearing the banded straw hat, seated at left, is Fred Stewart, longtime janitor at Clarkston High School. Note the photographer's hand and "dark cloth" at lower left.

Nine

Modern Clarkston

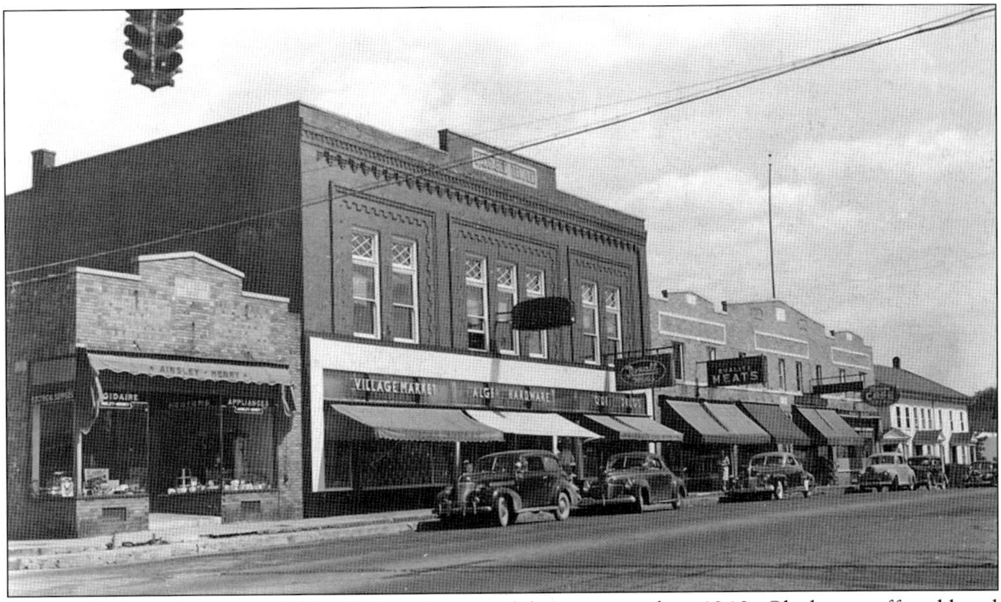

South Main Street, c. 1940s. Before the era of the supermarket, 1940s Clarkston offered local shoppers all they needed to run their households, even within this single image featuring the Village Market, Alger Hardware, O'Dell Drugs, and Terry's Market of Quality Meats.

ALGER HARDWARE. Alger Hardware was a mainstay at 6 South Main Street, just as the Alger family itself was on North Main Street. After Joseph passed away in 1929, his children, including son Roy pictured here with his sister Viola, continued running the family business.

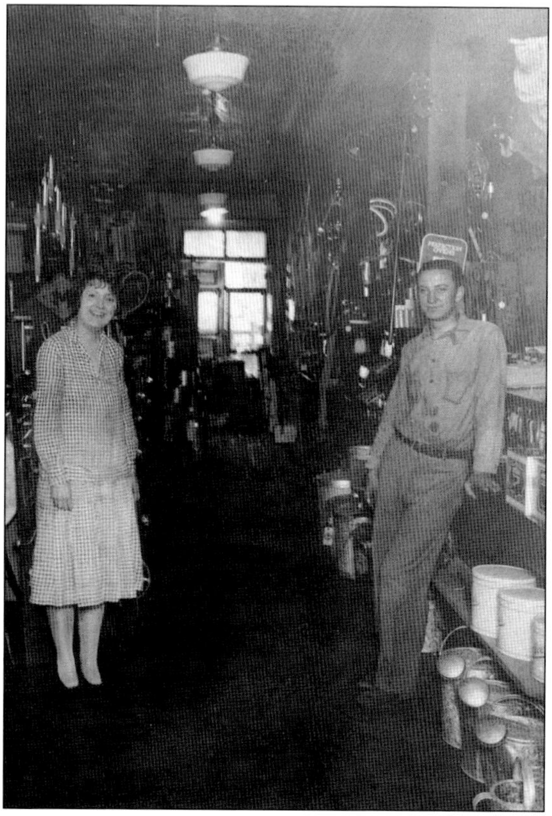

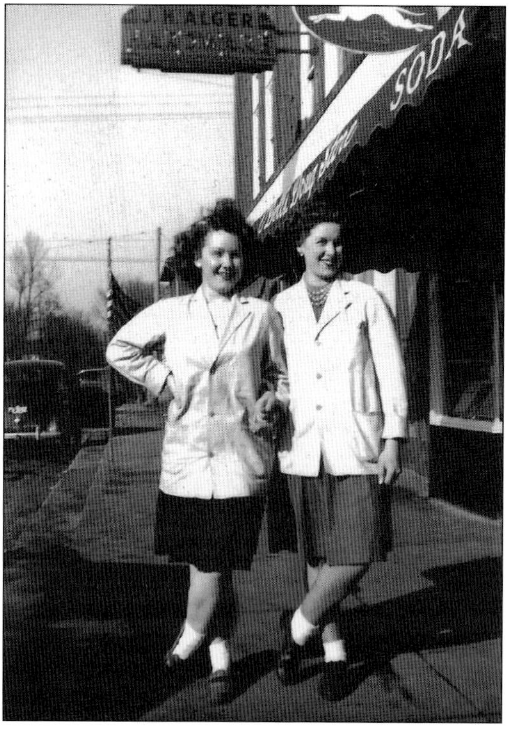

O'DELL DRUGS. Two young women stand outside O'Dell Drugs, probably in the early 1940s. Gerald O'Dell came to Clarkston in 1934 and opened his store in the former location of the post office. It became a favorite after-school stop for children eager to enjoy a chocolate sundae.

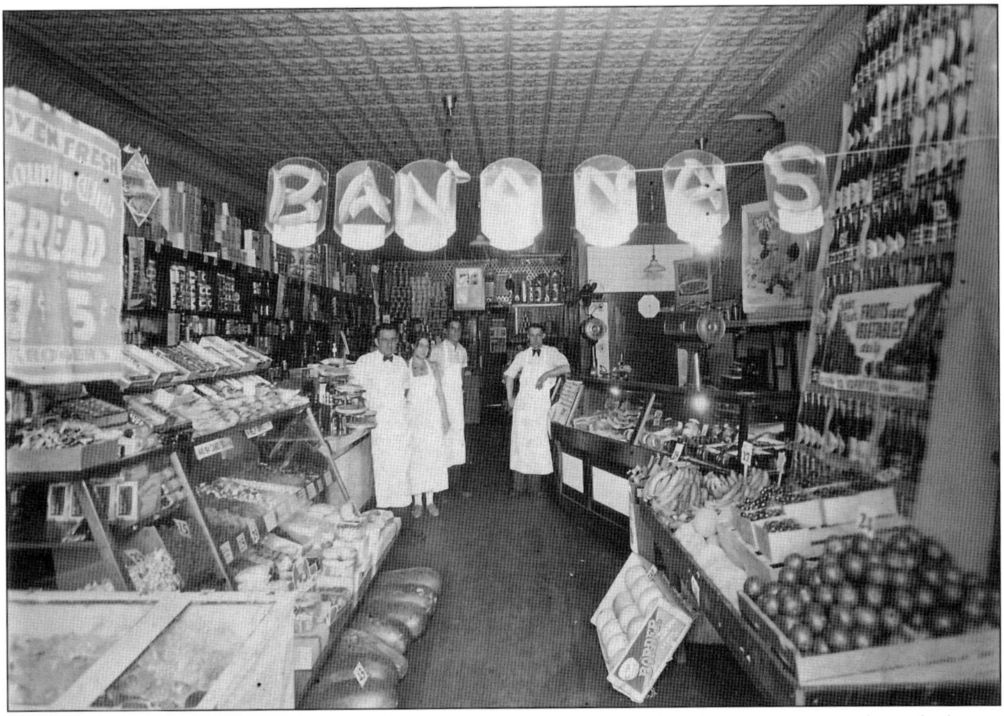

Terry's Market. Earl Terry worked diligently to own a meat market. When he arrived in Clarkston in 1928, he worked at Frank Dunston's meat market at 12 South Main Street, in which J.L. Waterbury bought interest. By 1937, Terry began the process of buying the business, which became Waterbury and Terry Quality Meats and eventually Terry's Market. It closed in 1967. Notice the tin ceiling, which still hangs in the building today, now the Union Woodshop restaurant.

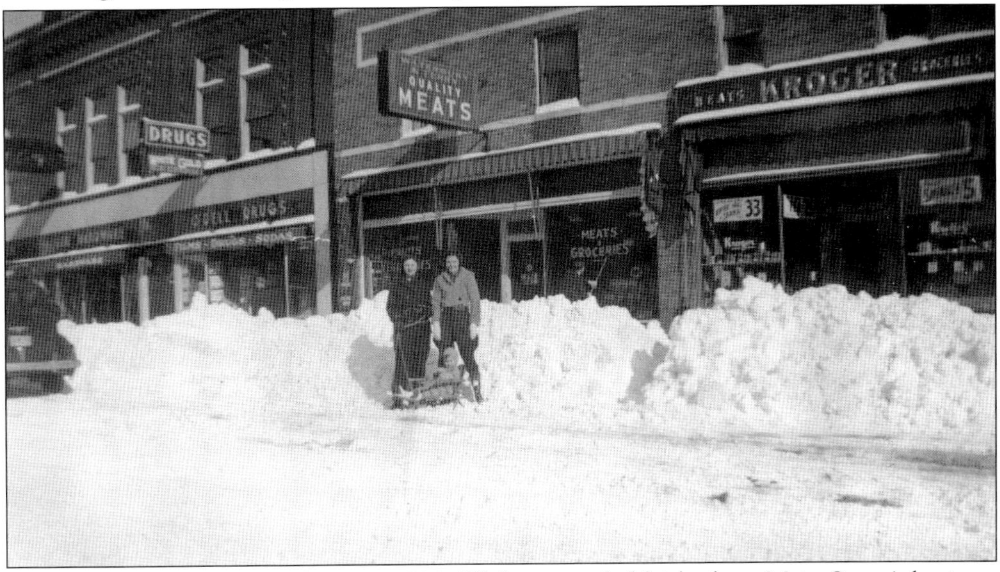

A Snowy Scene on Main Street, 1939. With snow piled high along Main Street's business district, Uldene Jones (right) takes a break from pulling her son Bobby on his sled. (The third person is unidentified.) Notice the early village location of Kroger, which later moved across the street before becoming a supermarket outside of the village.

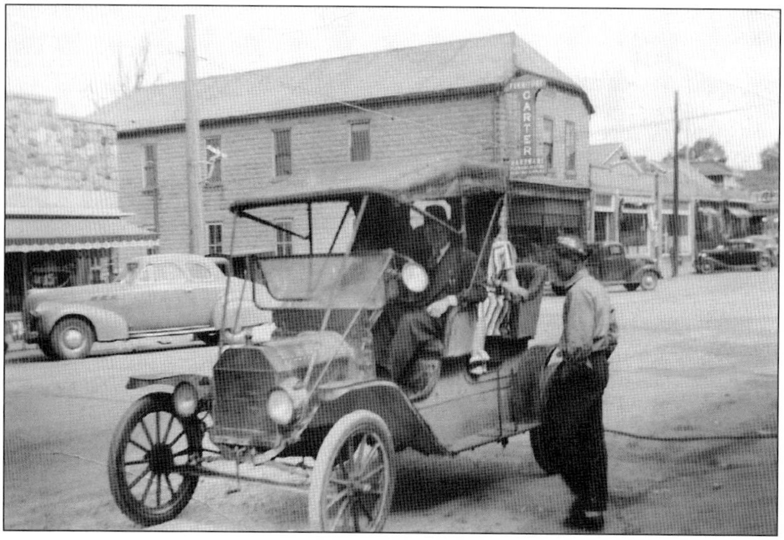

Robert Beattie. Ford dealer Robert Beattie drives a Model A as he speaks with one of his employees in front of Beattie's Garage at 32 South Main Street.

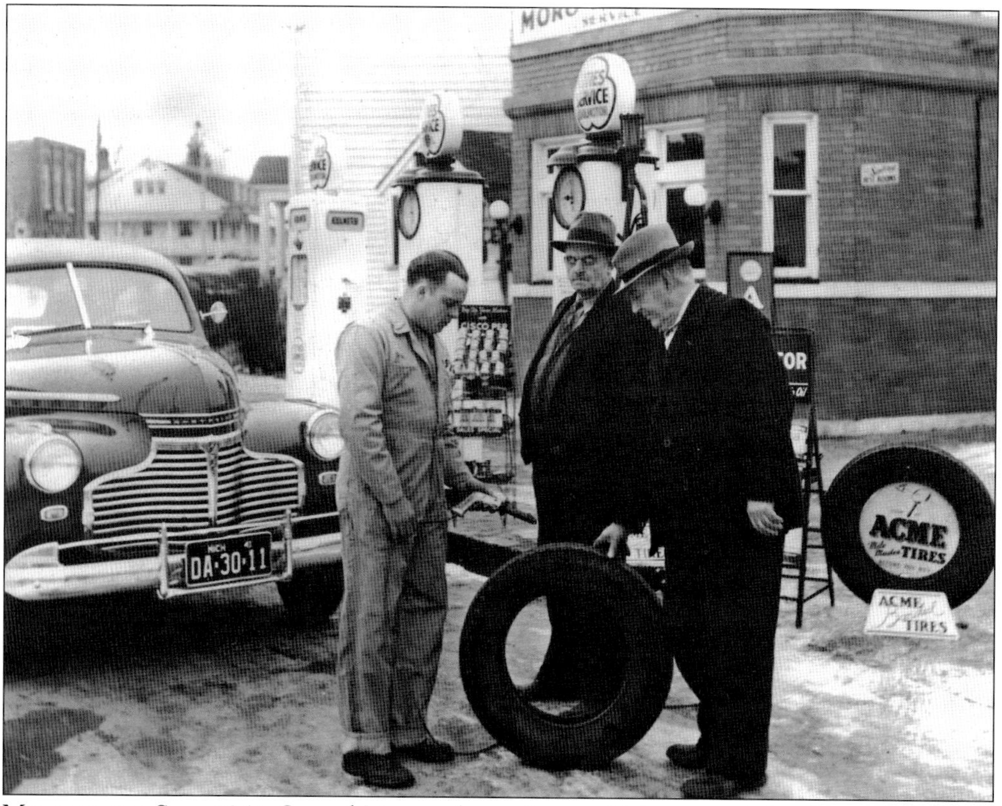

Morgan and Son, 1941. Samuel Morgan (center) started Morgan and Son Cities Service gas and service station at 28 South Main Street in 1932. Morgan's son Richard "Dick" Morgan (left, wearing mechanic's uniform) went on to run Morgan's for almost 50 years before retiring in 1981. Dick Morgan's own son John took the helm until 2010 when he sold it to longtime employee Scott McIntyre, who retained the name Morgan's Auto Service and the hometown spirit. (Courtesy of Scott McIntyre.)

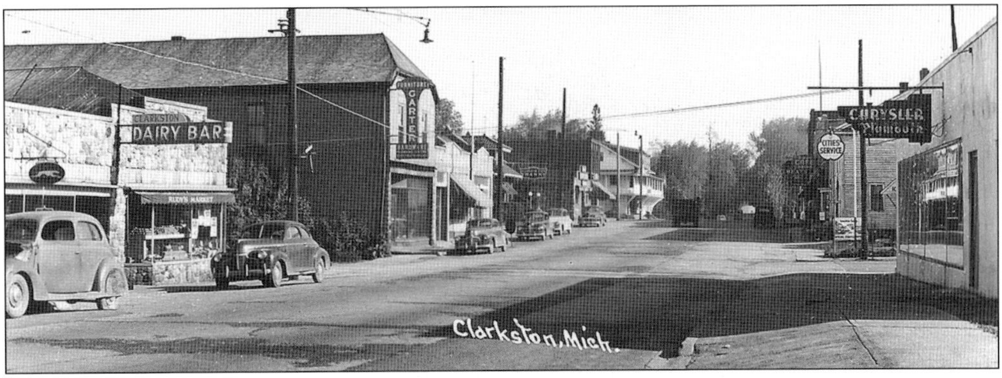

Main Street Looking North, c. 1940s. Main Street flagship store Garter Furniture and Hardware stands tall as it hails customers throughout Clarkston. By this time, nearby Beattie's was a Chrysler Plymouth dealership and George Smith's former carding mill housed the Dairy Bar. Clarkston native and longtime resident Chuck Robertson recalls his days as a *Pontiac Press* newspaper delivery boy and how he and fellow newsboy Ric Huttenlocher would pick up their papers at the Dairy Bar and sometimes manage to play an entire game of eight ball in five minutes flat—at a cost of 1¢ per minute—before delivering their newspapers.

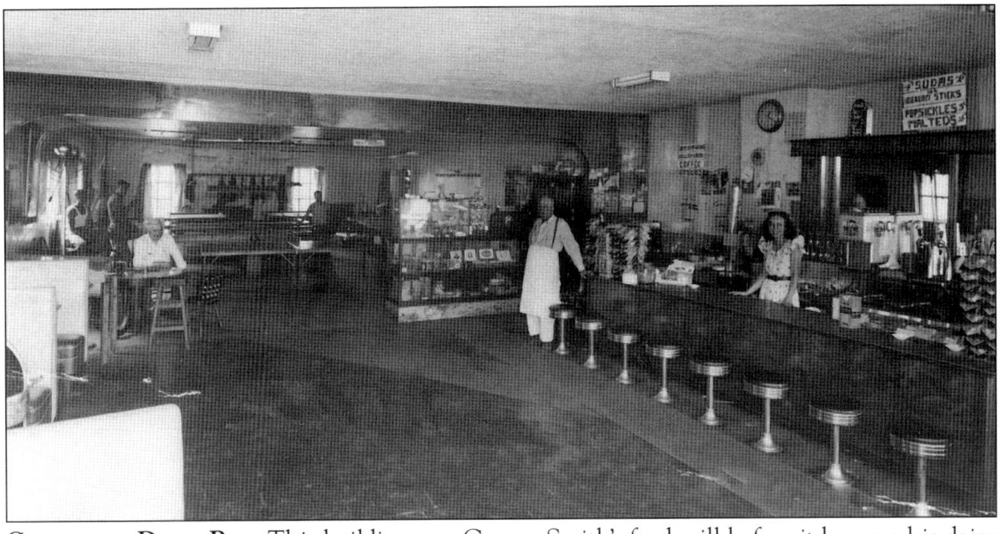

Clarkston Dairy Bar. This building was George Smith's feed mill before it became his dairy bar, where he served ice cream and snacks on the building's south side. The young women who worked behind the counter rushed to work during their lunch break at school to accommodate other students' orders—many of whom flocked there for hamburgers and the jukebox—before everyone rushed back to finish their schoolday. George and Adeline Smith sold the building and business in 1974.

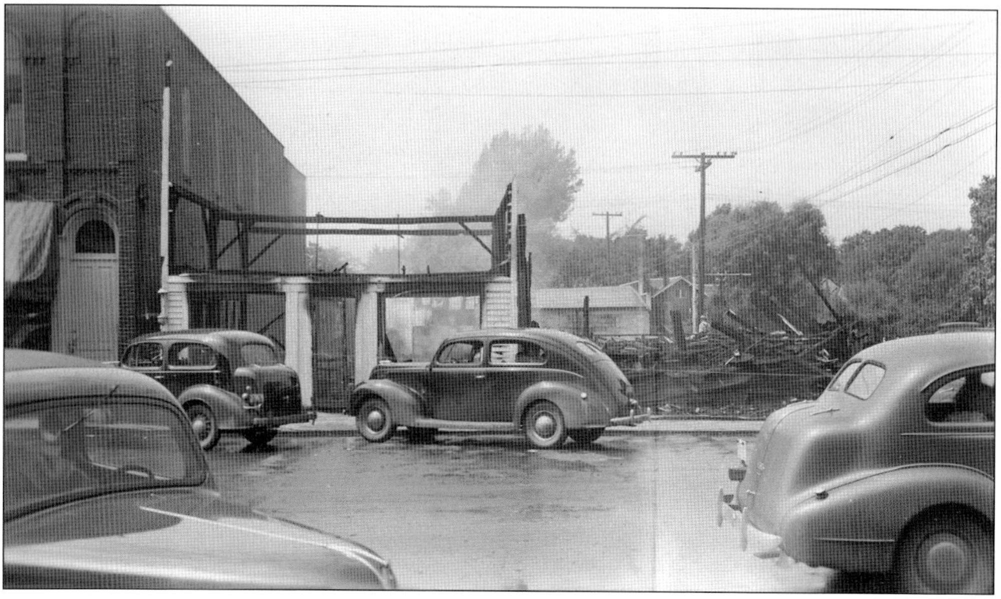

Rudy's Fire and Rudy's at the Mill. Grocer Rudolph "Rudy" Schwarz came to Clarkston in 1933 and started his business on the southwest corner of Washington and Main Streets, which also housed the Clarkston Venetian Blind Company. In 1939, the blinds company caught fire and took out those two buildings in addition to a barbershop next door. Because the company had seven fires in six years, Schwarz was unable to get insurance, but he set up shop temporarily in township hall and eventually became George Smith's tenant on the other side of the Dairy Bar building. After one more move, Rudy's arrived at its final and most-familiar location.

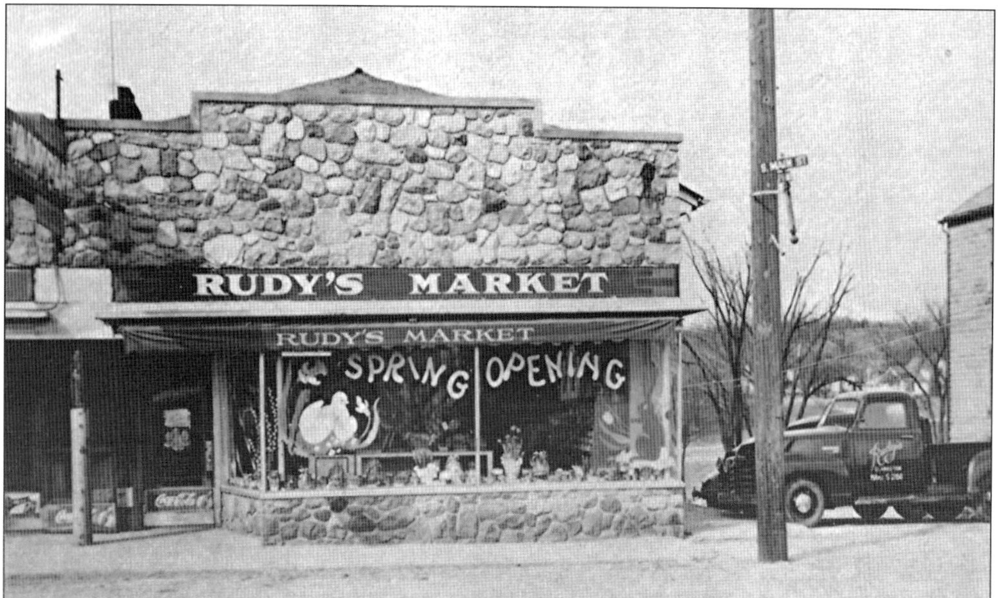

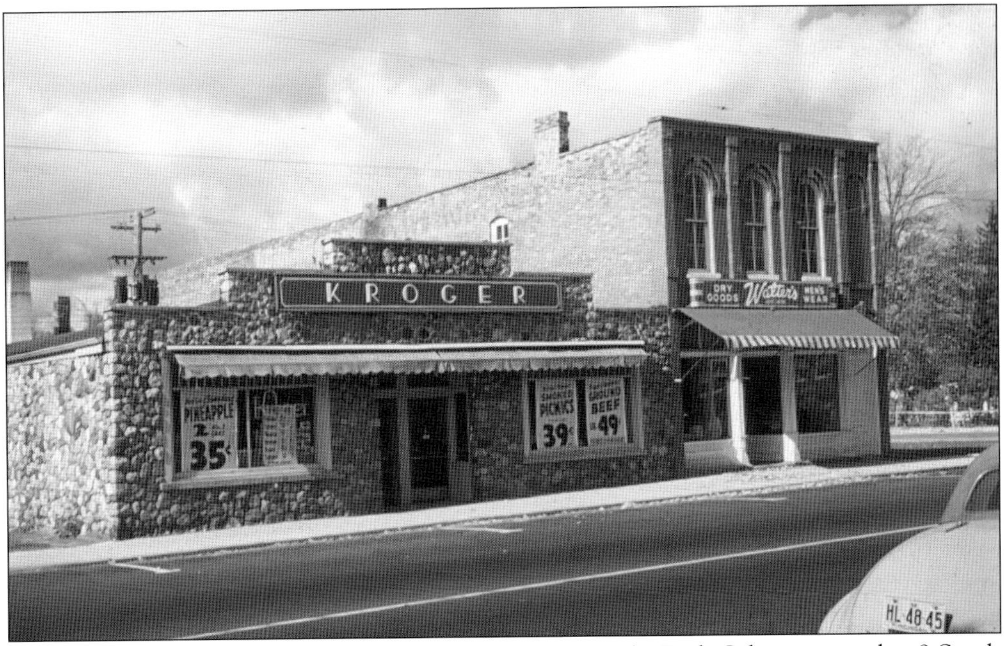

The Clarkston Kroger Becomes Rudy's Market. In 1954, Rudy Schwarz moved to 9 South Main Street, the location most associate as Rudy's. Built in 1915, this native-stone building once housed a Ford dealership and service shop and a Kroger branch in the 1940s. Generations of Clarkston children recall Schwarz kindly sharing pocketfuls of candy while mothers shopped, and how older kids could be sent to Rudy's to purchase a missing ingredient or two, putting it on their family's account. Cashier Helen O'Rourke is pictured below with Schwarz in the 1960s. Schwarz passed away in 1992, and his family sold the business in the late 1990s. The new owners, Robert Esshaki and Christopher Thomas, revamped the grocery store but retained the name—and the charm—of Rudy's Market.

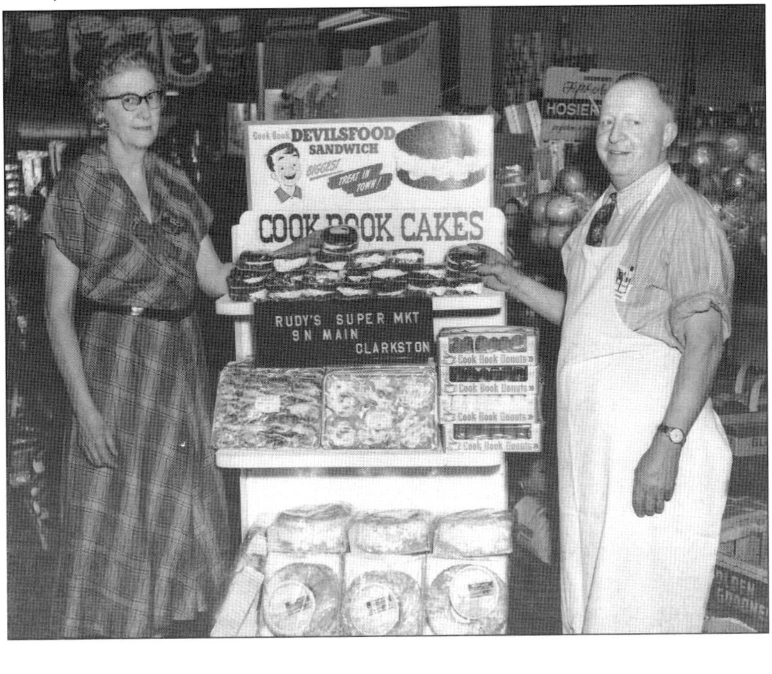

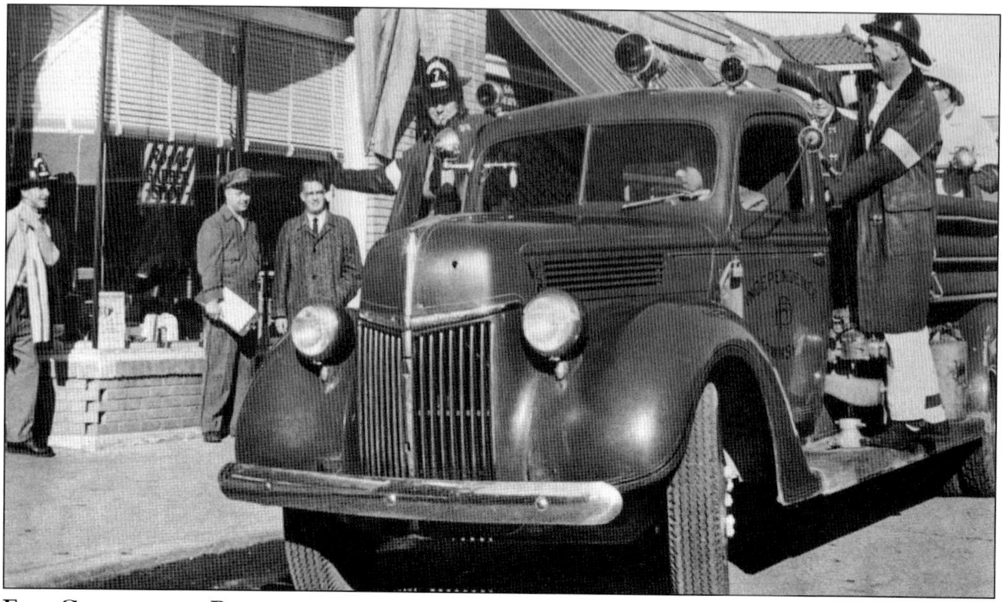

Fire Call at the Barbershop, early 1950s. When people went to Frank "Tink" Ronk's barbershop, they crossed their fingers they would make it out with a finished haircut, knowing full well that at any moment the Independence Township firefighter could be called to action. "You can always finish a haircut," Ronk would reportedly say, "but you can't wait around to put out a fire." Ronk is on the far left, just leaving his barbershop to jump on the Ford V8. Others in the image include Art Kelly, Duane Hurshfall, Rex Fenstemaker, John Ronk, and Bill Wilson. Tink Ronk went on to become Independence Township's fire chief and township supervisor. (Courtesy of the Independence Township Fire Department.)

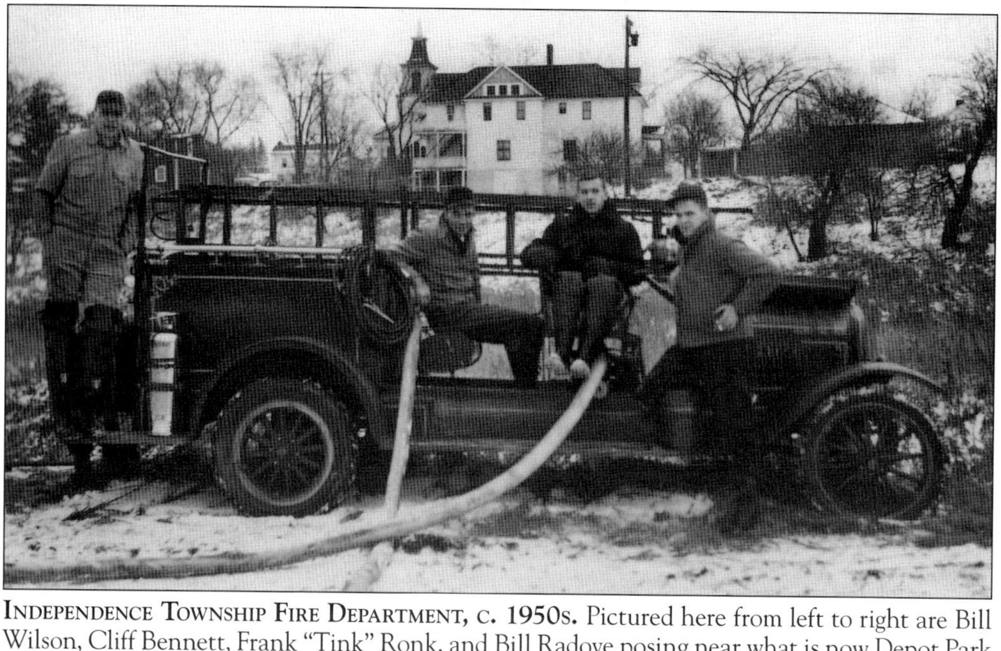

Independence Township Fire Department, c. 1950s. Pictured here from left to right are Bill Wilson, Cliff Bennett, Frank "Tink" Ronk, and Bill Radoye posing near what is now Depot Park with the Independence Township Fire Department's 1925 Model T fire truck. (Courtesy of the Independence Township Fire Department.)

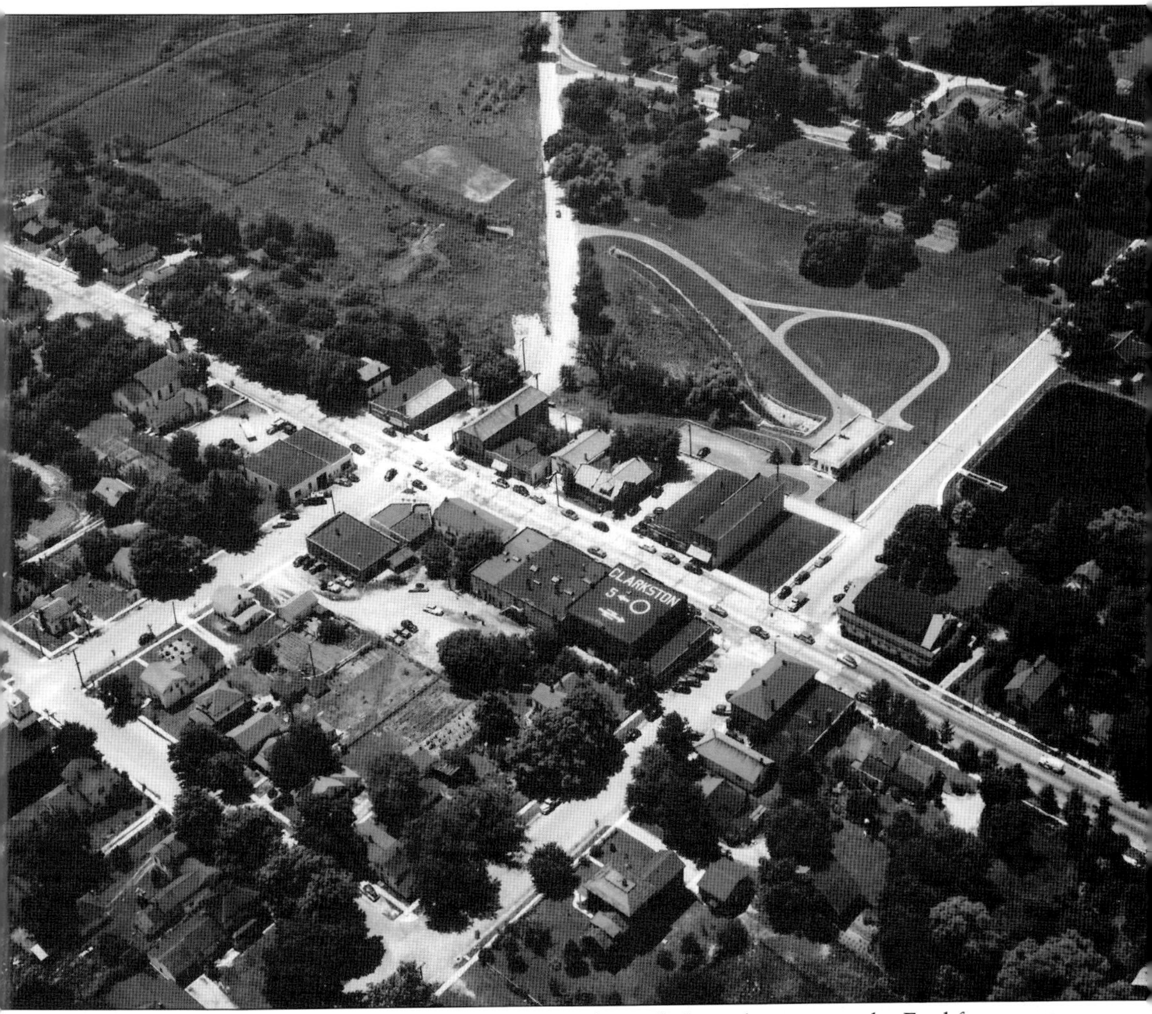

Aerial View of the Village, c. 1940s. Notice the wide loop driveway at the Ford factory on the former mill property and the field that would later become Depot Park. The town name and directional symbols on the roof of the Maccabee Temple at center advised pilots of their location. Locals recall a lookout tower within a mile outside of town where residents stood watch at appointed times during World War II to report suspicious activity overhead.

Discover Thousands of Local History Books Featuring Millions of Vintage Images

Arcadia Publishing, the leading local history publisher in the United States, is committed to making history accessible and meaningful through publishing books that celebrate and preserve the heritage of America's people and places.

Find more books like this at
www.arcadiapublishing.com

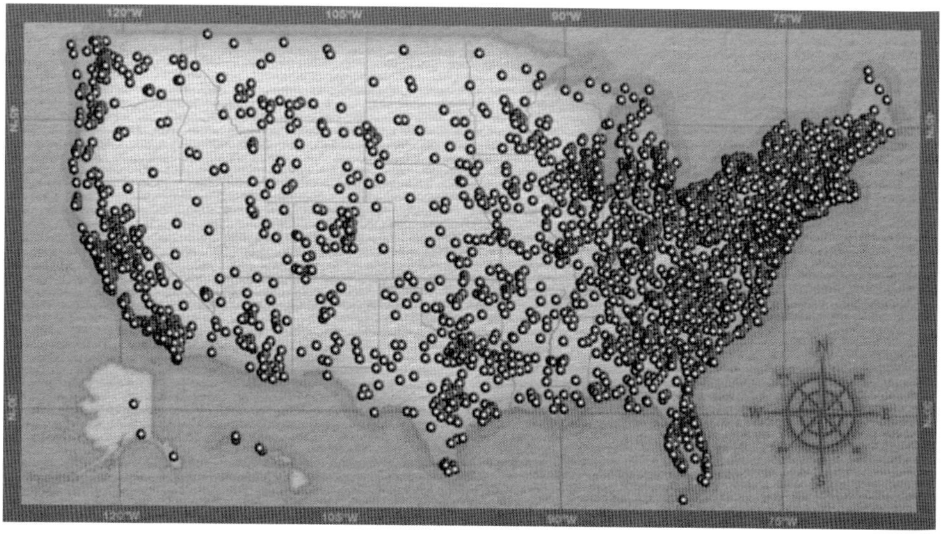

Search for your hometown history, your old stomping grounds, and even your favorite sports team.

Consistent with our mission to preserve history on a local level, this book was printed in South Carolina on American-made paper and manufactured entirely in the United States. Products carrying the accredited Forest Stewardship Council (FSC) label are printed on 100 percent FSC-certified paper.

MADE IN THE USA